On Shifting Ground

Women Writing the Middle East

Baghdad Burning: Girl Blog from Iraq
by Riverbend

Children of the New World
by Assia Djebar

Naphtalene
by Alia Mamdouh

On Shifting Ground

Muslim Women in the Global Era

Edited by Fereshteh Nouraie-Simone

The Feminist Press
at The City University of New York
New York

Published in 2005 by the Feminist Press at the City University of New York
The Graduate Center
365 Fifth Avenue
New York, NY 10016
www.feministpress.org

Library of Congress Cataloging-in-Publication Data
On shifting ground : Muslim women in the global era / edited by Fereshteh Nouraie-Simone.
    p. cm.
Includes bibliographical references.
    1.   Muslim women--Social conditions--21st century. 2.   Muslim women--Arab countries--
Social conditions--21st century. 3.   Feminism--Arab countries. 4.   Women in popular culture--Arab
countries.   I. Nouraie-Simone, Fereshteh.
    HQ1170.O6 2005
    305.48'697'09175927--dc22

                                                              2005020033

This publication was made possible, in part, by public funds from the New York State Council on the
Arts, a state agency, and the National Endowment for the Arts.

Text, composition, and cover design by Lisa Force.
Printed in Canada

12 11 10 09 08 07 06 05   5 4 3 2 1

Contents

Acknowledgments   vii

Foreword   ix

Introduction   xiii

I. Women and the Transformation of Public Space

The Satellite, the Prince, and Shaherazad:
Women as Communicators in Digital Islam   3
Fatema Mernissi

On- and Off-Camera in Egyptian Soap Operas:
Women, Television, and the Public Sphere   17
Lila Abu-Lughod

Singing a New Song: Bonding and Breaking With the Past   36
Sherifa Zuhur

Wings of Freedom: Iranian Women, Identity, and Cyberspace 61
Fereshteh Nouraie-Simone

The Challenge of Globalization in Saudi Arabia   80
Mai Yamani

II. Gender, Communication, and Religion

Globalizing Equality: Muslim Women, Theology, and Feminism 91
Asma Barlas

Feminist Theory, Agency, and the Liberatory Subject   111
Saba Mahmood

The Veil Debate—Again   153
Leila Ahmed

Between Religion and Secularism: Islamist Women of Hamas   172
Islah Jad

III. Women and Citizenship in an Information Society

**The Prospects for Democracy:
Women Reformists in the Iranian Parliament**   203
Elaheh Koolaee

Women and Civil Society in Iran   216
Mehrangiz Kar

Sisters in Islam and the Struggle for Women's Rights   233
Zainah Anwar

Women and the Dynamics of Transnational Networks   248
Meena Sharify-Funk

**Shirin Ebadi: A Perspective on Women's Rights
in the Context of Human Rights**   267
Fereshteh Nouraie-Simone

Acknowledgments

This book is the outcome of the project "Voices of Change: Muslim Women in the Era of Globalization" lecture series, cosponsored by the American University Center for Global Peace and the African and Middle Eastern Division of the Library of Congress. It also includes essays by scholars who were not part of the lecture series, but whose contribution to this volume makes them a member of the project.

The project could not have taken place without the encouragement of Professor Abdul Aziz Said, founder and director of the Center for Global Peace at American University. I am most grateful to him for his extraordinary mentorship and generous support of this project. I also would like to express my gratitude to Mary-Jane Deeb, head of the Near East Section in the African and Middle Eastern Division of the Library of Congress, for cosponsoring the lecture series. My thanks to Betty Sitka and Meena Sharify-Funk for their help in organizing these events. Special thanks to Safoura Nourbakhsh for her translation and helpful suggestions and to Holly Sanders for editing the manuscript, her enthusiasm, and her sense of humor. Many thanks to Barbara Riley and Shelly Ekhtiar for reading and commenting on my work. Special thanks to Florence Howe, executive director of the Feminist Press, for her extraordinary support in bringing this project into the present volume.

I am grateful to Fatema Mernissi for her friendship and the pleasure of her many conversations and encouragement that helped to bring this book into being. It has been a truly collective endeavor and I am grateful to all the contributors for their excellent scholarship and their spirit of cooperation. I express my deepest gratitude and appreciation to all involved.

In the post–September 11 world of Islamophobia, these essays challenge stereotypical views, especially the assumption of a monolithic Islam; static, fixed, traditional, and non-modern, in which women are regarded as effectively voiceless and invisible. The essays also show that tradition need not oppose modernity and, in fact, the examination of tradition may bring to light the rich history of women's activism and resistance to subordination; the modernity of gender politics in contemporary Islamism; local feminism; and the ability to be agent of one's own choice from within a patriarchal context. These essays present women who speak for themselves; women who advocate for change as they incorporate technology from cassette players of the revolution to satellite TV and the Internet of today, in order to affect social and political change in this interlinked global era.

Foreword

Elizabeth Warnock Fernea

The awarding of the 2003 Nobel Peace Prize to Shirin Ebadi marked the beginning of a new relationship between Western women and Muslim women. Ebadi, a long-term activist for human rights, was the first Iranian and the first Iranian woman to win the prize, and her selection forced Western media and Western feminists to acknowledge the attributes of a new and eminent Muslim woman: active, intelligent, and internationally sophisticated. This was a far cry from the stereotypes purveyed by Western travelers and scholars of the past five hundred years, which depicted the Muslim woman as either idle odalisque or slave of the patriarchal family. Over the centuries, there were occasional minority views. Lady Mary Wortley Montagu, wife of the first British ambassador to the Sublime Porte in Istanbul, wrote in 1711 that she believed Turkish women to be the only free citizens of the Ottoman Empire: They had money of their own and could travel about inconspicuously to meet possible lovers, covered as they were by heavy robes and veils.[1]

But the onset of the period of Western colonial rule caused a return to old stereotypes. A frequent justification for colonial invasion of the Middle East was the need to liberate Muslim women from the oppressive forces of Islam and of the family system.

In the twenty-first century, the focus of Western concerns about the positions of Muslim women has shifted again, as this volume testifies. New developments—economic globalization, transnational networks in new information technology, the revival of Islam throughout the Muslim world—have caused a reevaluation of old patterns and an analysis of the effects of globalization on Muslim women's lives as well as their relationship to secular Western feminism.

The Muslim women of today are different from their mothers and grandmothers. To begin with, they are much healthier, thanks to national and international campaigns to eliminate epidemic diseases such as tuberculosis and smallpox. In the late 1950s, after all countries in the area gained independence from Western colonial rule, the new nation-state offered free universal education to their citizens. This was very important to women, who previously had few opportunities for education. Now millions of women in elementary through graduate schools have used their new literacy to learn more about their religion—Islam—and about women's rights in Islam. Volunteer study groups have formed in many countries, where women meet weekly to discuss the implications of Islam in their lives. Educational opportunities, such as the growth of television, radio, and the Internet have opened new doors to knowledge and provided tools for analysis and self-criticism not available fifty years ago. The volume that follows is a cooperative effort to trace the directions of the new cyber-world. Fourteen essays are included, written by Muslim women from Egypt, Pakistan, Saudi Arabia, Iran, Palestine, Malaysia, and the United States.

Taking Marie-Laure Ryan's statement, "The dream of a new identity begins with new forms of expression," Fereshteh Nouraie-Simone sets the tone of the book when she writes, "Cyperspace is a liberating territory of one's own." Certainly, in many countries where women are more or less housebound, where cell phones are banned and unfettered travel is not allowed, the freedom and privacy of the Internet cannot be overemphasized.

Mai Yamani further suggests that the forces of globalization—economic, social, and political—may eventually impact the Saudi royal family, encouraging them to open the nation-state's doors to allow change, municipal elections, women suffrage, and a democratic society with the participation of all citizens. Elements of globalization continue, such as trans-state communication within the Arab world and transnational communication across geographic boundaries. Yamani believes firmly that "Globalization will destroy the old Saudi Arabia, [though what will replace it] remains highly uncertain."

Yamani's vision is supported by activity in other Muslim countries, such as Malaysia, where e-mail communication has helped the grassroots movement for improving women's rights known as Sisters in Islam. Begun in

1988, the group is exploring ways "to push the boundaries of women's rights within Islam, within Malaysia, and within our faith." They have formed discussion groups to read the Qur'an together and to engage progressive Islamic scholars. They also network with other Islamic women's groups struggling toward the same goal. They regularly send memoranda to the Malaysian government, write letters to newspaper editors, and run a weekly legal literacy column in the largest selling daily newspaper in Malaysia. The column, which focuses on Islamic family law, has been so well received that they have opened a legal clinic to handle the hundreds of phone calls and e–mails requesting assistance on Islamic family issues. The author Zainah Anwar, who is executive director of Sisters in Islam, sees the group's activities as challenges to the old order, whereby only men were seen as competent to interpret Qur'anic principles. She concludes by stating, "The fact that Islam is increasingly shaping and redefining our lives means all of us have to engage with the religion if we do not want it to be hijacked by those who preach hatred, intolerance, bigotry, and misogyny."

Some authors advise embracing globalization as a force for the improvement of women's status. The facility and openness of communication in the new technological age may also further more traditional groups' organization: The *ulama*, for example, and Islamist movements, generally.

Those traditional movements tend to support and encourage "the vexed relationship between feminism and religious traditions," according to Saba Mahmood. Women's activism within the Islamist movements, she reports, has been viewed with suspicion by feminist scholars in the West—a suspicion that gained credibility after September 11, 2001—and the eventual association of any Islamic movement with terrorism.

Mahmood reports on her research with the urban women's mosque movement that is part of the larger Islamic revival in Cairo, Egypt. What conceptions of self, discipline, and moral agency animate these groups in Cairo? According to Mahmood, the practices of what she terms a "non–liberal movement" rely heavily on the past, on the virtues associated with approved patterns of behavior of Muslim women throughout history. "*Sabr*" or patience is one, as is "shyness" or modesty, femininity, and piety. Mahmood argues that such practices do not necessarily mark inferiority or submission, but rather "articulate a positive and immanent discourse of being in the world."

Mahmood's work, especially on modesty, ties directly into the contemporary debate about the veil, i.e., Islamic dress, which is discussed by Leila Ahmed. As the process of globalization continues around the world, Asma Barlas poses an interesting possibility of "globalizing equality." Barlas's central argument is "to define Qur'anic hermeneutics of sexual equality that I believe needs to be at the heart of democratic reform in Muslim societies." Therefore, Barlas believes that "theology matters" in any formulation of the effects of globalization and new technology on women.

Of primary concern is the issue of financing technology. In the present Muslim world with unemployment and poverty rampant—especially among women—with the gap between rich and poor growing daily, the percentage of women who will have access to technology is very small indeed.

Still, the capabilities are there in television and radio as well as e-mail, and as a result, change is taking place in every Muslim society. In her essay on soap operas in Egypt, Lila Abu-Lughod points to the "new heroines" as role models for women—literally, the "stars" of these serials, which are aired regularly all over Egypt. This is possible because of the growing number of households in Egypt with their own television sets.

Thus, globalization is clearly an important issue in the Muslim world today. The advantages and disadvantages of the phenomenon, as well as its influence on current struggles for women's rights, human rights, and democracy, are ably presented and analyzed in this groundbreaking volume written by Muslim women themselves.

Note

1. Lady Mary Wortley Montagu, *The Selected Letters of Lady Mary Wortley Montagu* (New York: St. Martins Press, 1971).

In Iran, women are producing blogs, voicing opinions and exchanging ideas in an Islamic republic that still limits freedom of expression. In Egypt and Malaysia, women are joining together to study the Qur'an, challenging repressive interpretations of Islamic theology and religious laws. And throughout the Arabic-speaking world, satellite television stations have spawned "new Shaherazads"—women journalists and hosts whose voices have a powerful impact on the public discourse.

The rise of global communications is one of the many forces of change that are transforming the lives of Muslim women today—and in turn, being transformed by them. Throughout the Muslim world, women are making their voices heard: documenting the realities of their own lives, exploring their changing identities, and insisting upon greater participation in the public sphere.

On Shifting Ground brings together diverse perspectives on the challenges and opportunities, the contradictions and complexities facing Muslim women in the twenty-first century. These essays, by distinguished scholars from a variety of disciplines, address the broad topics of women's participation in the public sphere and the role of the new media in the process of both personal and political empowerment. This exploration, in turn, yields vital new insights into Muslim women's identity formation, their sense of agency in their own communities, and their participation in civil society as a whole.

As the varied interpretations of feminism, identity, and agency discussed in these pages reveal, Muslim women's efforts to shape their public and private spheres is not a new phenomenon. Women have long been active and resilient negotiators within their own cultures. Nor are globalization and technology in opposition to Islam. Rather, access to communications resources, and the opportunity it brings for greater engagement in public discourses on human rights and civil society, only extends the inherently pluralistic nature of Islam that welcomes cultural diversity and multiplicity of interpretations.

In the West, however, these dynamic realities have often been rendered invisible, or obscured by stereotyped representations of Muslim women. Even among Western feminists, Muslim women are too often seen as passive victims, rather than as agents who are actively engaged in efforts to reshape their individual selves, their cultures, and their societies. Islam is generally viewed, through Western eyes, as static, traditional, antimodern, and misogynistic. The contents of this volume, however, demonstrate that tradition need not be fixed and unchanging. These essays present various examples of individuals, organizations, and societies striving toward their own visions of modernity—and of Muslim women demanding full participation in this project.

We, in the twenty-first century, live in a world defined by a fragmented, decentralized, and chaotic current of change that encourages mobility and a multiplicity of ideas, voices, and identities.[1] We live on shifting ground, where the complexities of globalization and the development of new media have inadvertently nurtured transnational networks, connected geographically distant places, "deterritorialized" space.[2] A hallmark of contemporary existence in the global era is the way in which "the intensification of worldwide social relations . . . link distant localities in such a way that local happenings are shaped by events occurring many miles away."[3] This transformative process of globalization creates a "time-space compression," where information and ideas travel halfway around the world in a split second.[4] This, in turn, leads to a "geographical restructuring" of social relations that demonstrates the complexity of the interaction between global forces and local contexts.[5]

The two trends of globalization and localization work both with and against each other. Much has been said about the tendency of mass media and electronic communications to impose dominant cultures on others. But in fact, the "cultural flow" of globalization is from local to global, as well as the reverse.[6] Despite globalization's attempt to homogenize culture, technology has led to a multiplicity of images and experiences which demonstrate that the growing flow of information, labor, and capital is not producing a "global village" of one unified culture but rather "globalized villages," linked by new information technologies in an expanding public sphere.[7]

Globalization and modernity have converged to create a decentralized and ever more portable inventory of mass media products. Broadcast television, satellite television, telephony, audiovisual recordings, the Internet, wireless technologies—these are the contemporary sites of dynamic tensions between the local and the global, the religious and the secular, the public sphere and the private sphere. Technology becomes both a purveyor of change and a means of establishing one's true "local" within the barrage of global images, sounds, and ideas.

These tensions and transformations have had an impact on Muslim women, for whom new technologies are breaking through boundaries set by family, community, culture, religion, nation, and region. As women see their own experiences reflected in those of other women in similar or different situations, they come to new understandings of their own personal and local identity, and at the same time achieve a consciousness of shared identity across locations. Such consciousness-raising can be a source of inspiration as well as affirmation, as local sites of women's activism become points of origin for a wider recognition of the varied ways in which women's quest for equality, freedom, and justice can be defined and expressed.

In this way, the expansion of the public sphere through the use of new technologies makes awareness and interaction possible for women across the Muslim world on a scale never before experienced. It allows women to share ideas on organizing, leadership, and self-determination. This empowerment is occurring from a popular base, from individuals to organizations, giving the periphery increasing influence over the historically dominant center. This is true whether the individual in question is a young university student, writing her "blog" from Iran, or a woman from a traditional family, engaged in the Mosque movement in Egypt on a personal quest of faith, who studies the Qur'an to arrive at her own interpretation of the text. The major impetus for change is coming from individuals, who drive these movements by reinterpreting their religion and reconstructing their societies.

This book challenges the reader to view the transformation taking place in the Muslim world, and especially among women, from within their own context: the personal, individual lives and the societies in which they live. *On Shifting Ground* illuminates the global and local forces in play, asking the reader to relinquish preconceived notions of Western-style feminism as the only goal for all women, and secular, Western-style democracy as the only viable political structure for all societies.

These essays are unified by their exploration of women's varied responses to global influences: their embrace of the technological and cultural changes introduced by globalization and, perhaps more importantly, their reshaping of a local identity along religious, social, and cultural lines. Navigating these contradictions, Muslim women are helping to build their own futures on shifting ground.

The essays in part one of the book directly address the impact of mass media and communication technologies on Muslim women. One vitally important development in the media began in the 1990s with the emergence of hundreds of Arab satellite television stations, broadcasting from London to Qatar to Cairo, providing access to a communication medium that transcends class and literacy as well as national borders. In "The Satellite, the Prince, and Shaherazad: Women as Communicators in Digital Islam," Fatema Mernissi argues that women—in front of the camera, behind the camera, and at home watching the screen—exert considerable influence in this relatively new medium.

First, the owners and creators of programming must listen to their audience, which wields tremendous financial power with the click of a remote control. Women, a vital audience demographic, become players, instead of pawns, in this new media.

The transformation of women on the screen is just as remarkable as the empowerment of those in front of it. The new image of the "Middle Eastern woman," seen anchoring news broadcasts, defies the Western stereotype of the subordinated woman, veiled and mute. Mernissi describes the new "Shaherazad" newscaster as an intelligent, mature, opinionated woman, whose beauty and wit fascinate. She is popular not only with women, but with men, who identify with the female broadcasters over the politicians, military leaders, and power brokers they report on. Mernissi notes that Arab men have always been known to admire the strength of women, while women understand that power is not possessed, but exercised.

Mernissi demonstrates that in a globalized world in the midst of transformation, these new Shaherazads are playing a decisive role in encouraging satellite-connected Muslims to see gender differences as an enriching possibility, while awakening civil societies, stirring voices that were previously ignored. Clearly, the technology is a catalyst for powerful market and cultural shifts, crossing socioeconomic, education, and gender boundaries. ✓

Another form of viewer identification is revealed by Lila Abu-Lughod in her essay "On- and Off-Camera in Egyptian Soap Operas: Women, Television, and the Public Sphere." Abu-Lughod interprets the varied impact of television on the broad, diverse female audience for soap operas, which often have themes tied to political and social issues. Middle-class housewives, rural women, urban domestics—women of all ages and education levels—follow the televised dramas, identifying with the characters. They also pursue the private lives of the actors off-screen. In this way, a "special brand of community," or localization, is established among these women through their common interest in the lives of the television stars.

Much of mass media can be defined in the way Abu-Lughod describes Egyptian television dramas: a pedagogical tool and a space for imaginative life with complex and sometimes contradictory implications for women. The programs themselves are purveyors of values that increasingly represent the consumer-driven, middle-class morality popular with Egypt's secular government. The responses of the audience vary, depending on locale and background, but the tension inherent in global/local, secular/religious, and modern/traditional dichotomies can be identified in this cultural phenomenon.

In "Singing a New Song: Bonding and Breaking with the Past," Sherifa Zuhur writes about women's invasion of the public sphere in the entertainment field as they challenge traditional prohibitions against public performance. She finds that Arab women's faces, voices, images, and words have become thoroughly integrated into public life. Music videos, Internet chat rooms, online and print fan magazines are all media that drive sales for these entertainers, and make them visible and audible in the public space as never before. Zuhur focuses on traditional Middle Eastern music, as opposed to the many hybrid forms now beginning to gain popularity in the West. She comments on a revived interest in the age-old forms, observing a tendency to localization that serves to preserve and repopularize traditional singing styles. Zuhur refers to a new popular sound that interchanges Western and

Eastern musical ideas. The appeal of both traditional and new popular music grows as its reach is extended through technology—portable communication media in the form of audiocassettes, CDs, music videos, and the Internet—sustaining and expanding its viability.

The interaction between the global and the local can be seen at work in the transnational network of local communities that is linked culturally through communication media. A collection of varied music, both in traditional and hybrid forms finds its way across the globe on cassettes and CDs, or is attached to an e-mail sent to a relative in a foreign country. The arts, music, and the entertainment industry provide a unique basis for the "imagined communities" containing individuals in geographically disparate localities, linked through global communication technology, which reinforces close cultural bonds.

Like broadcast media, the Internet provides boundary-free travel, and exposure to information and ideas that can challenge norms. Internet technology affords writer and reader the freedom and safety of anonymity. This anonymity removes from online interactions any predetermined notions based on physical, gendered presence. It also liberates women to freely articulate repressed identity or forbidden subjects. "Wings of Freedom: Iranian Women, Identity, and Cyberspace" shows Iranian women bloggers speaking their minds on the Web with an unaccustomed candor, discussing their fears, concerns, frustrations, and hopes for the future in virtual public space. Freedom of the self in the "cyber-Islam galaxy" (Mernissi's phrase) allows for the possibility of dissent, resistance, and agency to nurture individuality.

The diffusion of diverse images of women in public—on the streets, on the television, on the stage—as well as of the voices of women—singing songs, writing on the Web, making their thoughts and feelings known—has profound cultural implications. These phenomena affect not only the women who are seen and heard but also the women who see and hear them. The public act transfers to the private sphere, imprinting a new image or voice in the minds of those watching or listening, and breaking ground for others to follow. In "The Challenge of Globalization in Saudi Arabia," Mai Yamani argues that even the Saudi ruling family, with its insular and repressive policies, cannot protect itself from "winds of globalization," as the wider worldviews provided through communications technologies expose flaws in their system. The forces of change brought on by globalization are undermining Saudi Arabia's political establishment—while aiding the export of extreme religious ideology.

The shifting ground created by global/local tensions is traversed in several essays in part two of this book that explore the varied meanings and impacts of the veil, religious identity, and feminism. Asma Barlas, in her essay, "Globalizing Equality: Muslim Women, Theology, and Feminism," cautions against the assumption that communication technologies are a panacea for all social problems. Barlas further cautions against generalizations about "Islam," "Muslims," and ideas of a single "global public." The actions of individuals, generalized and overlaid onto a society as a single movement, can impose notions of universality on what is truly a varied, uneven plurality.

When the problem of change in Muslim societies is too closely identified with the binary concept of theology vs. secularism, Barlas argues, issues such as the uneven distribution of power and technology are ignored, and the societies' inherent capacities for change and self-criticism are dismissed and undermined. The richness of Islam lives in its openness and its spanning of cultures, continents, and multiple interpretations. Its success is in part evidenced by the fact that so many diverse peoples are unified under one religion, but they are not by any means unified under a single interpretation of the faith. Barlas encourages us to see the dynamism within individual communities across the globe, and within Islam itself. She reveals the ways in which technology can further women's participation in their faith by facilitating the reappropriation of religious texts, by reading equality in the Qur'an, and opening a dialogue on the role of women in Islam.

In an era when individuals must navigate the shifting global influences transforming their public and private lives, many experience a sense of instability, leading to a yearning for a firm, stabilizing factor. This search can take many forms, as evidenced by the recent groundswell of interest in the preservation of cultural uniqueness, the quest for political authenticity and authority, and a revitalized search for some kind of eternal truth. The religious revival and the renewed interest in institutions such as family, community, and local culture can all be interpreted as the search for secure grounding in the shifting world we inhabit.[8]

In her exploration of the Mosque Movement in Egypt, Saba Mahmood views Egyptian women's study and interpretation of religious texts, in a quest to reappropriate their faith from within paternalistic traditions, as a fundamental piety movement arising out of a personal journey in search of faith. Women teachers defy the practice of male-only interpretations and instruct women on the meaning of the Qur'an, encouraging their followers to reread the sacred text through the prism of their own self-realization and autonomy.

Mahmood sees women's agency not as an act of resistance to domination but as an action developed from within subordination. For Mahmood, choosing religion can be an act of liberation and self-assertion. The reappropriation of the religious texts, which begins as an expression of piety chosen by the individual, can eventually enable change in the public sphere as well as a transformation of personal identity. Viewing the Mosque Movement within the context of a world revival of religion, and the Islamic revival in particular, Mahmood emphasizes the movement's power as a means of personal fulfillment and moral regeneration for the individuals involved and also as a public actualization of agency, created by women's choice to embrace and reinterpret their faith.

No stronger image of the Middle Eastern woman persists in the Western psyche than that of the woman with her head covered. The veil has come to be seen as a sign of oppression, and seldom as an expression of personal choice, piety, or political identification, or as a rejection of the Orientalist mindset. Women who choose to wear it are frequently young, educated, and politically aware. Their choice has many meanings and many origins, but it is often a choice, not an imposed restriction.

To limit the understanding of the veil to one interpretation, or even a handful of interpretations, is to risk the oversimplification and stigmatization of a powerful and complex symbol. Such a limited view also confines the investigation of women's agency itself to a restricted set of political, religious, and personal definitions. Wearing of *the veil* must be viewed with an open eye to the many messages, some intended, others inherited, all within the context of the society and the individual.

Leila Ahmed's "The Veil Debate—Again" takes a historical view of reactions to and meanings of the veil. Veiling has a history of misogynist extremism and abuse by Western colonialism, with different meanings at different times. Ahmed criticizes the early advocacy of abandoning the veil as a symbol of "backward" and "uncivilized" practice as a reflection of colonial attitude. She discusses her own inherent dislike of it as a symbol of submission to patriarchy, but at the same time challenges assumptions about the veil—both her own and the reader's. She examines the intense "localness" of the meanings of the veil within the context of a particular society. In the United States, for example, the veil has been adopted by wearers to make their "Muslimness" visible to the world, and as a statement based on principles of justice. Ahmed challenges the reader to view the fragmented, diverse, and shifting meanings of wearing the veil, with emphasis on whether the wearer does so by choice or by decree.

Islah Jad, in "Between Religion and Secularism: Islamist Women of Hamas," views Islam in the context of the Palestinian national struggle, focusing on the political implications of the Islamic resurgence as a local movement in the context of occupation. Jad shows how the Islamist movement of Hamas has risen in popularity in large part due to its attention to the economic needs of the populace, which fills a void in services and community programs left by the secular, nationalist PLO movement. This economic role, coupled with the search for a stable spiritual framework and the security of a group identity, has fused with "Islamist feminism" in intriguing ways.

Like Ahmed, Jad shows women shaping their own lives, beliefs, and identities on the borderland where secular feminist influences meet debates on gender in the Islamic movement. Women's activism is expressed through the reformation of their individual private space, while at the same time their personal choices contribute to a remaking of the public space.

Muslim women's search for stability on shifting ground, when not directed toward faith or toward culture, often manifests itself in the pursuit of political participation and social justice. The essays in part three of this book address the political and social activism of women in the Muslim world. The vision of a civil society that embraces and upholds principles of human rights is seen by many individuals as the crucial element that will allow Islamic societies to negotiate the upheavals of the global era, with its shifting and conflicting power bases, both internal and international. The full participation of women is, in turn, perhaps the most crucial element in creating such societies. This is true not only because women's equal participation is necessary to democratization, but also because women have proven most adept at finding ways to balance a regard for universal human rights with a respect for tradition. The challenge facing today's Muslim women is to discover ways to develop these vibrant and inclusive civil societies, without alienating cultural and religious identity, and within the context of existing institutions.

In Iran, the Islamic government's reaction to globalization has been a return to local identities, reinforcing traditional values and conservative social norms. Nevertheless, Iranian women have long been active in demanding equitable access to civil resources, while working against the forces of patriarchy and social inequality. In spite of living under a policy of restricted public space and social interaction, they have succeeded in bringing about political change through subtle tactics, negotiations within the accepted frameworks.

Women's power as a voting bloc in Iran was felt in the reform movement of the late 1990s. It was largely because of the mass participation of women in the election of 1997 that Muhammad Khatami, the reformist president, was elected, and that a group of women was subsequently elected to the Parliament. Among these women was Elaheh Koolaee, an outspoken voice in Parliament for women's rights. In "The Prospects for Democracy: Women Reformists in the Iranian Parliament," Koolaee describes how the Women's Faction in Parliament, from 2000 to 2004, demonstrated that women working together could be an effective instrument of change, affecting the nation's laws and institutions. Female reformists in the Iranian Parliament gained influence in government by promoting women's activism, fighting to secure some rights in cases of divorce, child custody, and inheritance.

Koolaee believes that reform is best achieved from within the system, allowing it to proceed organically, if sometimes in a painfully slow manner. "Collective action in politics is a new experience for Iranian women," she writes. Individuals and groups must learn to work together for a common goal. "Given the complex political situation, Iranian women favor slow change that builds on rights already established."

But the mode of change itself is sometimes in dispute. Mehrangiz Kar, a human-rights lawyer and activist, wrestles with a central question facing women in Iran: Is the empowerment women seek attainable from within the institutional structures as they exist—religious, civic, economic, and

——— similar to questions that divide social, liberal,
radical feminists ask in Western feminism

social—or does lasting change require core alterations to the structures themselves? Reformists such as Koolaee seek gradual change through elections, new interpretations of Islam, and reliance on social and economic pressure to bring about the power shifts. The faithful who seek reform claim Islam can and should adapt to address human rights and women's rights, within the Islamic context. But as she discusses in "Women and Civil Society in Iran," Kar believes that the patriarchal bias inherent in the existing institutions of the Islamic Republic can only be changed through a fundamental reordering of the institutions, or their power base.

Kar supported the reform movement in Iran, and hoped that it would succeed; but she believes that problems are endemic to the structure of the Islamic constitution and the legal framework of the Islamic Republic. She notes the veto power of several bodies of the ruling theocracy, which can effectively cancel out reform efforts made by the elected president or Parliament. Kar strongly believes in separation of religion from politics as the first criteria for building a democratic state—and one where women will be full participants and have equal rights.

The transnational experience of women in secular and religious nongovernmental organizations (NGOs) can be linked to the movement of the individual in a pluralistic system, remaking public and private spheres, leading to a new dynamic of identity formation.

Zainah Anwar encountered both struggles and triumphs in creating "Sisters in Islam" as a grassroots organization in Malaysia—a progressive Islamic feminist group and one of the groups most successful in challenging the patriarchy and misogyny of the legal system. Their advocacy finds its voice in widely circulating Qur'anic arguments for gender equality through memoranda or letters to government on law or policy. They are also employing new technologies, with a website that allows their members to effortlessly cross geographic borders within the Muslim world, bringing together those seeking an alternative to the established interpretations of religious texts.

Anwar's essay, "Sisters in Islam and the Struggle for Women's Rights," explores the need to reconcile Islam with one's private life, and she clearly identifies herself as an activist determined to "work from within," embracing Islam while also working to transform its practice.

Sisters in Islam is one of several NGOs considered in Meena Sharify-

Funk's essay, "Women and the Dynamics of Transnational Networks," on the growing influence of women's associations and international networks, which increasingly provide the opportunities for discourse in Muslim societies. Sharify-Funk sees the potential for this growing movement both as a means toward broad social change, and as an agent of individual empowerment, as women discover they are not alone in their struggle. In finding like-minded others, women come to identify themselves as part of a larger group, transcending boundaries and conventional roles imposed upon them by their communities, while exposing themselves to broader horizons of thought and action. This empowerment can have a profound and lasting impact—locally and globally, in the public and private spaces of Muslim societies.

It is appropriate to conclude the essays in this volume with the words of Shirin Ebadi, the first Muslim woman to receive the Nobel Peace Prize. In an interview I conducted in Tehran in 2003, shortly after the announcement of the award, Ebadi affirmed her belief in women's rights as inseparable from the context of universal human rights. As a believing woman, Ebadi looks to the egalitarian aspects of Islam to support her fight for women's rights. As a lawyer, she approaches establishing equality and liberation from oppression through change to the legal system.

Ebadi believes in the social power of the law and the power of reason and justice to influence the law, as the interview and selected readings from her writings included in this volume suggest. Her work is based on the idea that the principle of human rights forms the foundation from which women's rights derive, and that these rights are not in contradiction with fundamental Islamic principles. Receiving the Nobel Peace Prize, Ebadi's life-work writes a new entry in the West's lexicon, redefining Muslim women's agency as visible, powerful, and effective.

The convergence of broad-based education with mass media and mass communications technology in all its forms, combined with the demographic shift toward a younger populace, has empowered individuals and brought pressure on the hierarchical institutional structures at the center of many Islamic societies. These forces have also produced a new public space, in relation to which individuals are redefining their private space and their personal identities.

Much of the hope for the future must arise fᵢ
believe that their agency can make a difference—anc
right to make a difference—in the future of their coɴ
course of their destinies. The internalizing of an awareⁿᵉ
will play a crucial role in the future of women's political parₜ
Muslim world. The use of information and communicatioɪ   ˑgies
for advocacy and democratization can help women who are aₜ the core of
the struggle. In this collection of essays, we discover just a small sample of
the rich multiplicity of women's voices, and an indication of the vital potential for change that women, individually and collectively, possess.

Fereshteh Nouraie-Simone
Washington, D.C.
May 2005

Notes

1. For a further exploration of the ideas discussed in these paragraphs, see Anthony Giddens, *The Consequences of Modernity* (Palo Alto, CA: Stanford University Press, 1990); David Harvey, *The Condition of Postmodernity* (London: Blackwell Publishing, 1990); and Fredric Jameson, *Post Modernism, or, the Cultural Logic of Late Capitalism* (Durham, NC: Duke University Press, 1991).

2. Arjun Appadurai, *Modernity at Large: Cultural Dimensions of Globalization* (Minneapolis: University of Minnesota Press, 1996), p. 4.

3. Giddens, *The Consequences of Modernity*, p. 64.

4. Harvey, *The Condition of Postmodernity*, p. 240.

5. Doreen Massey, *Space, Place and Gender* (Minneapolis: University of Minnesota Press, 1994), p. 68.

6. Janet Abu-Lughod, "Going Beyond Global Babble," in *Culture, Globalization and the World-System*, ed. A. D. King (New York: Macmillan, 1991), p. 132.

7. Jon Anderson, "New Media & Globalization in the Internet Age," keynote speech at the Middle East Virtual Community (MEVIC), August 2000, http://www.mevic.org/keynote.html.

8. Harvey, *The Condition of Postmodernity*, p. 292.

Part One

Women and the Transformation
of Public Space

The Satellite, the Prince, and Shaherazad: Women as Communicators in Digital Islam

Fatema Mernissi

During the Ramadan of 2002, I realized that I was becoming a stranger in my own land. The Arab world I was born in, could decode and understand, had vanished forever. Women managed to shock the digital *umma* (the new satellite-connected Muslim community) not only by belly dancing in the most popular television series but also by appearing as film producers and as talk-show anchors. "In spite of the great variety of their topics, the Ramadan television series have one thing in common, regardless of whether their subject is social, historical, or religious: the unavoidable belly dancer who has become a pivotal creature in the events unfolding in these shows," explained Mohamad Mahmoud, the columnist who reports on talk shows in the prestigious weekly *Al-Ahram Al-Arabi*. What surprised him most about the belly dancer was her versatile dimension: "The belly dancer is the key figure who helps businessmen rise to the top, or pulls them down to the abyss. In one television drama, the belly dancer plays the heroine of the popular struggle for liberation; in another, she backs a Zionist movement supporter. . . . Does this extraordinary presence of the belly dancer in the Ramadan television shows reflect reality, or is it simply a seductive maneuver on the part of the producers to attract audiences?"[1]

One has to sympathize with the *Al-Ahram* columnist, because it was not belly dancing per se that he was complaining about; as everyone knows, unlike some born-again Christians, Arab men in general, and Egyptians in particular, are thrilled by such a sight. What he was worrying about was that the ever-present belly dancer might seriously interfere with the spiritually inclined believer's capacity to transcend the voluptuousness of the senses and concentrate on more esoteric blessings. Helping man reach harmony (*wasat*), which is a balance that allows him to resist temptations without drifting to ascetic extremes, is, after all, the key ideal Islam has been promoting for its fifteen centuries of existence. Arab satellite television somehow seems to capture the intoxicating spell of women and endows it with an alarming glow.

The belly dancers were not the only aggressive women who managed to invade the political space created by satellite television. One of the 2002 Ramadan's most polemical, challenging, and extremely popular television shows was a film by a female movie director, In'am Mohamad Ali, about a highly controversial male Egyptian feminist. Qasim Amin wrote *The Liberation of Women* (Tahrir al-Mara'a), a vitriolic pamphlet on sexual equality that was perceived as scandalous by Arab rulers in the 1930s. What made male viewers very attentive to the program (named *Qasim Amin* for its protagonist) was that its director "showed, through her film, that when a competent artist decides to take us to navigate in the past, it is not so much to seek an escape from reality as to enlighten it."[2] The film's key message was that in 1930s Egypt, like today, liberating women is the best chance to empower the country and release Arabs' energies.

The aggressive invasion of Arab media by women as actresses and producers, as well as directors of television channels, did not start with this Ramadan. In fact, something extraordinary is currently taking place in the Arab world: a sudden emergence of women as powerful communicators in satellite broadcasting. The rising demand for articulate intellectuals who combine writing and television experience in the new communication wars in the Arab world is giving women a golden opportunity to enter the power game in the Middle East.

If we define digital Islam as information products transmitted via satellite and targeting consumers in Muslim countries, starting with the satellite broadcasting industry, then definitely, Arab women seem to maneuver skillfully in this new galaxy. One of the most striking phenomena of the post-September 11 era has been the explosion of serious female show hosts and news anchors of Al-Jazeera television. These women are not gadgets manipulated by the satellite television companies, most of which, by the way, belong to Saudi princes. The Al-Jazeera stars are economically powerful because they bring advertisers to the channel by attracting large audiences. And most of them have that magic "Shaherazad mix" of powerful intellect and sharp communication skills that enchants their viewers.

A survey by the magazine *Rose El Youssef* shows how Shaherazad is now on the wanted list. "The Empire of Women," the magazine cover story of the November 30, 2002, issue, revealed to Egyptian citizens that "of the 80,000 persons working in radio and television, 50,000 are women." The article explained how women have developed successful "strategies to chase after talent [*isti'dad*] for top positions in management hierarchies as well as radio and channel leaderships."[3]

The new information technology is definitely producing cataclysmic psychological changes in Arab self-perception, but what is more astonishing is that the invasion of women as aggressive participants in the new field of satellite TV is only a mirror of what is happening everywhere in a less visible way. For example, women also take part in the more intimate activity of surfing the net in the dark corners of the increasing number of cyber-cafes.

"Is the Internet chat *halal* (licit) during Ramadan?" teenage girls ask an Al-Azhar shaykh. This Ramadan was definitely very different, considering the request for a *fatwa* from Egyptian shaykh on the issue: "Is chatting on the Internet forbidden during Ramadan?" Although extremist violence has transformed it into a frightening word, *fatwa* means simply that "you ask a question," explains Ibn Manzur in his thirteenth-century dictionary *Lisan al-Arab* (The Tongue of the Arabs), which is still used today.[4] If there is to be fear, it should be on the part of the religious authority whose duty it is to put its expertise at your disposal to help you solve your problem. The *fatwa* is a test for the authority, not for the questioner. Thus the Egyptian youths inquiring about chat rooms suppose that the shaykh at Al-Azhar University is digitally competent. Indeed, the Internet is reviving the oral tradition of Islam started by the Prophet Muhammad in Medina. Asking for a fatwa was an important part of the constant interactive dialogue known as *Jadal*, which helped Muhammad build a formidable Muslim community in less than a decade (between 622 and 632).

The challenging Ramadan question about Internet chat was accompanied by a huge picture of two adolescent girls surfing on computers and a discreet caption that illustrates the gravity of the inquiry: "Many youths are forced, because of their jobs, to surf the Internet. . . . How is their fasting affected, for instance, if they happen to encounter, by chance, a pornographic website?"[5] This is one of the delicate questions that Jamal al-Kashki, editor of the Ramadan issue of the widely circulated Egyptian magazine *Al-*

Ahram al-Arabi, identified as significant for the Al-Azhar shaykh to answer, if he wanted to stay credible in the eyes of the blushing teenagers.

Don't make the mistake of thinking that those who claim to speak in the name of Islam are technologically backward or Internet- and satellite-illiterate. Believe it or not, it is the most conservative authority of all, the Iranian ayatollahs of the Center for Islamic Jurisprudence of the city of Qom, one of Shi'a Islam's major capitals, who first rushed to the web with the strategic intention of outdoing their fifteen-century-old Arab Sunni rivals. "Several thousand texts, both Sunni and Shi'a, have been converted to electronic form," explained one of the contributors to a 1999 retrospective on digital Islam. "While Sunni institutions tended to ignore Shi'a texts, the Shi'a centers are digitizing large numbers of Sunni texts in order to produce databases which appeal to the Muslim mainstream, and hence capture a large share of the market for digital Islam."[6]

However, I want to focus on the impact of only one particularly exciting dimension of the new information technologies, satellite broadcasting, because it creates the highly political public space where the entire community gathers to debate vital issues. By contrast, the Internet, which is more of an individual experience, does not have that theatrical public dimension so central to Islam, according to which the sexes are not supposed to have the same access and the same behavior.

Let's not forget that the *umma*, the very concept of community in Islam, means "a group moving toward the same goal."[7] Constant communication within the community is what enhances its dynamism, which is why satellite broadcasting transforms the Muslim dream of a planetary community based on dialogue into reality. But in so doing, satellite broadcasting challenges the behavioral code, which sets different rules not only for the sexes but also for religious and political minorities. This challenge explains both why Muslims have become so intoxicated with the new technologies and why focusing on the satellite's impact is the best angle from which to decode the puzzle of digital Islam.

I want to caution the reader to avoid the stereotype that links Islam with archaism. This is a fatal strategic mistake, not only because the new technologies are being used as instruments by Islam's advocates, but also because competition in the market for digital media products is forcing those who control the media to shift to free speech and interactive dialogue.

Yet, as enigmatic as the future of this digital Islam might look today, one thing is certain: most key players, from orthodox (Sunni) Saudi oil princes to Shi'a Iranian ayatollahs, have grasped that power will belong to satellite-equipped communication wizards. And this explains the discreet but nevertheless ferocious race for digital power among Muslim countries, where even elementary notions such as "center-periphery," which should give a geographical advantage to the Middle East, are challenged. "A country such as Malaysia, usually considered to be on the margins of Islam both in terms of geography and religious influence, has invested heavily in information and networking technologies."[8]

The Iranian ayatollahs rushed to invest in the new technologies in the early 1990s, but Saudi oil princes were more cunning, in that they realized early on that they had a fantastic advantage over Iranians and Indonesians. Since the Arabic language happens to be both the sacred and the common medium, investing in satellite communication was the shortcut to global supremacy.

Saudi Arabian propagandists were the first to create planetary media lobbies; in the 1980s, they armed themselves with digitally printed transnational newspapers and satellites. Then, in 1991, MBC (Middle East Broadcast Center), owned by Walid al-Ibrahim, a brother-in-law of King Fahd Ibn Abdel Aziz al-Saud, went on the air. When it started, MBC had no competitors, but soon its "12.5% religious programs, 75.5% entertainment, and only 9.5% information" got on the Arab viewers' nerves.[9] Consequently, audiences deserted it in 1996, when Al-Jazeera began its 100 percent news channel, giving viewers the opportunity to see uncensored news twenty-four hours a day. But the other reason for the exodus was that MBC's systematic censorship was projected through the superficiality of its entertainment programs, alienating viewers, especially women.

Censorship-muzzled propaganda and entertainment channels such as MBC were losing audiences and advertising because even when they invited intellectuals on talk shows, both the guests and their host failed to communicate in a significant way, caught as they were in "a television terrorized by freedom of thought."[10] Entertainment meant promoting singing and dancing men and women, and it proved to be a fatal business move. Al-Jazeera offered a different image of both informer and informed.

Middle Eastern women were interested in Al-Jazeera's more energetic femininity, displaying in programs such as sports performances. "One of Al-Jazeera's programs, 'Sports News' (Akhbar Riyadiyyah), has devoted several episodes to the role of Arab women in sports and has highlighted the championships that have been won by various female sports figures."[11] But besides sports, the forceful female news anchors fascinated both men and women. A news channel such as Al-Jazeera, which is funded by the emir of Qatar with the objective of strengthening civil society and free speech, offered intelligent, articulate speakers and program hosts of both sexes to the possibility of becoming stars. So it is no wonder that MBC has now shifted assets from its money-losing entertainment channel to a new one devoted to information only, in an attempt to catch up with Al-Jazeera and be "closer to the audience."[12]

The explosion of satellite broadcasting has transformed the passive *umma* everyone was abusing into a precious audience for advertisers—an audience of which 36 percent is illiterate, 64 percent of that percentage are women.[13] The proliferation of satellites launched in the region, by both Arabs and non-Arabs, has heightened the competition for audiences in all sectors, public and private, legitimate and terrorist.[14] This has made it possible for smaller operators to compete with the propaganda-manufacturing oil lobbies, and it has reduced the latter's revenues by fragmenting audiences. Because of the oil reserves, all major players—heads of state, ayatollahs, or private investors, such as Saudi princes—have to listen carefully to what the viewers want, both to gain political power by influencing public opinion and to attract advertisers. "With a population of over 300 million people, all speaking the same language in a highly strategic region of the world," remarks Pierre Daher, the chairman of LBC's (Lebanese Broadcast Center), "we have all the potential we need to compete with the rest of the world, and attract billions of dollars in advertising budgets. If we don't do it, someone else will."[15]

Although women have managed to compete for higher positions in Egypt, which has a powerful movie industry (ranking third after the United States and India), their influence has remained local. With the satellite media industry, Arab women are competing for pan-Arab influence and beyond it, for global sway.

Women are among the winners in this power shift because "the new information technologies are basically anti-hierarchical and detrimental to power concentration," explains Nabil Ali, an Arab linguistics and digital technology expert. "Destroying space and time frontiers . . . these technologies blur the familiar distinctions our civilization has operated on up to now, such as the separation between student and teacher, learning and teaching, production and consumption."[16] It is precisely the collapse of this latter distinction that is radically transforming the Arab world. The irony is that the camp of pluralism and democracy is rapidly winning in the Arab world since September 11, not because the left has won the battle, but because the conservative heads of state and oil princes who have invested their assets in extremist propaganda are now shifting to courting audiences in general and promoting women in particular. In her article, "The New Order of Information in the Arab Broadcasting System," Tourya Guaaybess makes the ironic comment that we are witnessing an unexpected "growing market of political liberalism."[17] In any case, it is startling to realize that the much longed-for democratic revolution is happening in the Arab world not because the left has subverted the system but because authoritarian regimes and oil lobbies are rapidly realizing that in the cyber-Islam galaxy you can only keep power in if you share it with citizens of both sexes.

Media lobbies who once scorned Arab citizens and bombarded them with propaganda are now shifting to interactive programming to please viewers who can surf freely among channels. Satellite broadcasting has destroyed state boundaries and empowered illiterates, because it "bypasses the two most important communication barriers—illiteracy and government control of content," says Hussein Amin in his "Arab Women and Satellite Broadcasting."[18] This revolution is radically changing roles. Citizens have shifted from pawns on the chessboard to becoming major players.

Channel surfing has become an Arab national sport. Empowered by cheap satellite household dishes that allow them to surf more than a hundred Arab satellite channels, previously passive Arab viewers, half of whom are women, have become ferocious "surfers" and choosy difficult-to-please audiences. Consequently, you can no longer have access to Arab oil by manipulating only Arab heads of state, diplomats, and army generals. The new information technology is forcing all Middle East players, local and foreign, including Americans, to create channels in Arabic. The decision of both Iran and the United States to launch Arab satellite channels to communicate with the masses illustrates this digital technology-induced shift of power from the states' bureaucratic elites and private oil lobbies to citizens. Hussein Amin has argued that this new technology "has the potential to empower Arab women in the exercise of their right to seek and receive information and ideas."[19] His prediction seems to be starting to materialize and change reality.

To better understand the empowerment dynamics of satellite broadcasting, one has to keep in mind the intense competition not only among channels but also among satellite operators, which is forcing everyone to switch as quickly as possible from diverting audiences with propaganda and songs, to responding to the citizens' need for up-to-date information provided by credible communicators. The planetary race to create Arab satellite channels has generated a boom in the recruitment of intelligent powerful men and women who have adequate training in written and oral communication. And of course the Shaherazad profile, the brainy, self-confident storyteller, is in big demand.

The competition to recruit successful broadcasters is causing Iranians, Americans, and Saudi emirs to seek a very specific profile of journalist: the intellectual who is trained in writing and has television experience. The ideal woman has the profile of Ghada Fakhri. According to Abdallah Schleifers, "Ghada Fakhri used to work with Al-Sharq al-Awsat, and then she worked for Al-Jazeera as a correspondent in New York, followed by being a correspondent for Abu Dhabi Television and now we have succeeded in tempting her to join our project."[20] The man talking with so much enthusiasm about the talents of Ghada Fakhri is Salamah Nemett, a Jordanian with experience in both printed and visual media. LBC recruited him as managing editor for the newly-created "Super News Center" whose objective is "to train print journalists in TV journalism."

Indeed, Arab audiences are fascinated by strong female hosts, newscasters, and war correspondents. Female stars have proven to be a fantastic asset for the Saudis' most threatening TV rival. Al-Jazeera is winning crowds every night through the eloquence of its female news anchors. While state-owned stations and oil-funded channels traditionally censored their staffs and denied them the right to decide freely about program content and guests, Al-Jazeera's success is due precisely to that freedom its programmers and speakers enjoy and which allows them to become credible communicators. "Channels that want to be viable are required to rely much more heavily on high-impact 'brands' and product lines. Al-Jazeera demonstrated the value of such assets when it developed a range of programs whose titles and presenters have become household names inside and outside the Arab world," explains Naomi Sakhr.[21] The most famous reporters in the Middle East today are probably the Palestine-based Al-Jazeera female reporters Shirin Aub 'Aqla and Jivara al-Badri, who are admired for their courage and professionalism. "History will remember that day when there was no one to speak up in the entire Arab world, from the Atlantic to the Persian Gulf, but women such as Shirin Aub 'Aqla and Jivara al Badri and Leila Aouda," comments Ali Aziz, the columnist of the Egyptian magazine *an-Nuqqad* (Critiques), "while male leaders and ten-gallon-hat-wearing generals have disappeared from our sight and hearing."[22]

How to explain this sudden passion of the supposedly macho Arabs for Al-Jazeera's powerful women? While Amin Hussein, a mass communication's expert, gives a technological answer to the question (the satellites' empowerment of women), the artist Ahmed Ghanem offers a more sophisticated psychoanalytic explanation: the Arab male's identification with the woman as the victim who is taking revenge on her aggressors.

For Amin Hussein, the satellite has empowered women both by giving them access to the broadcasting machine as message makers and communicators and by boosting their self-confidence as audiences and discriminating media consumers. "Arab satellite services have responded to the demand of Arab women to portray their true image and role in society to balance the common stereotype in the West of the downtrodden Arab woman without rights and without a role to play other than daughter, wife and mother." According to his analysis, "Talk shows, news, and programs feature interviews with female leaders in business, government, politics, and diplomacy. . . rather than covering only their role in the household of food preparation and as sex symbols in television commercials and video-clips."[23]

But for Ahmed Ghanem, an artist who is more interested in aesthetics and hidden emotions that program our attraction to what we identify as beauty, technology does not explain it all. Unless you bring in Arab men's psychological complexities as they unfold in their instinctive techniques, Ghanem argues, you grasp only one part of the bewildering communications revolution transforming the Arab world.

Ahmed Ghanem was one of twelve intellectuals whom the Kuwaiti magazine *Al Funun* (The Arts) invited to contribute to their summer 2002 issue on decoding the mystery of the *Fada'iyyat*—Arabic for satellite TV. (*Fada'iyyat* literally means "space ships," or rather, "space-clearing engines.") I was one of many people happy to read of an Arab man who, unlike our much-publicized extremists, declares publicly that he feels empowered by a woman's strength.

Ghanem speaks as both an artist and a designer in his study "The Esthetics of the Private Satellite Channels." He argues: "If we consider the laws and psychological mechanisms that in each satellite channel define for the female speaker the code for dressing and expressing herself, as well as the way she uses the screen's space to unfold her personality, then we cannot escape noticing that the aggressive [*hujumi*] style of the Al-Jazeera female speakers is a very distinctive kind of beauty that is very specific to them and makes them stand out when compared to other channels, especially if we remember that Al-Jazeera is a news (as opposed to entertainment) channel, and that these women's job is to inform the viewer. The fact that the majority of this channel's female speakers are far from being young and insecure and display on the contrary, maturity in both age and emotional equilibrium gives them a cerebral charisma and audacity that exercise a particular enchantment on the viewer. The Al-Jazeera female speakers exude a spellbinding fascination that transcends physical attraction."[24]

Could it be that Al-Jazeera's powerful women have such an attraction for Arab men because they trigger childhood fantasies when they enjoyed their mothers' storytelling and improvisations on the *Thousand and One Nights*? Could it be that the satellite is reviving Arab men's childhood universe, where Shaherazad, the powerful female inventor of adventures, empowered them as children? What is certain, according to Ghanem, is that by contrast the way women's strength reflects the freedom of speech they enjoy as journalists on Al-Jazeera, the superficial beauty of the fragile female speakers on entertainment channels reflects a passivity that does not excite him as a man, if only because, as he says, that passivity "mirrors the rules of the game on those televisions. Rules that reveal that only the masters are players."[25]

What is extraordinary about Ahmed Ghanem's analysis of digital Islam's new game is that, as a male, he does not identify with the masters, the princes or ayatollahs who can afford to buy satellites, but on the contrary, he feels his own fate to be linked to that of the women. In my view, this rejection of the archaic role of the dominant male, whose masculinity increases with women's passivity, is the breaking news in digital Islam.

The novelty in this galaxy is that many Arab men who crave their own emancipation from authoritarian censorship have become alert enough to disconnect power from gender. Many of the male viewers of satellite broadcasting do not seem to think that their masculinity is threatened if women show their power. The problem now is how to interpret this new phenomenon.

Is this only a transient phase, or are we witnessing a civilizational shift in the perception of the difference? Are the satellite-connected Muslims coming to perceive sexual difference as enriching? Are they even preparing themselves to embark on a less threatening global universality? Is the satellite reviving the cosmic vision of the Sufis? For the Sufi, the stranger (the different other), be it a woman or a foreigner, is not a threatening enemy. On the contrary, Sufis celebrate diversity as an enchanting display of human complexity in their concept of the cosmic mirror. "The mirror is like a single eye, while the forms [it reveals] are various in the eye of the observer," is how Ibn al-'Arabi encouraged his contemporaries to enjoy foreigners as fabulous reflections of the same divine being. "The essence of primordial substance is single, but it is multiple in respect to the outer forms it bears with its essence."[26]

Satellite broadcasting has raised not only the challenge of femininity but also the question of religious and ethnic minorities, such as the Kurds and the Berbers. Morocco has declared Berber a national language and established an institute to enhance its role in a dynamic society.[27] The satellite has changed the frame in which the Israeli-Palestinian conflict is addressed, so that it is impossible to exclude either party. "Palestine-Israel: Peace or a Racist System?"[28] is how the influential Palestinian journalist Marwan Bishara frames the question, ruling out any extremist alternative that negates peace. This question is no longer "Does the state of Israel have the right to exist or not?" Now everyone must ask how harmony can be engineered from difference.

As for the Sufis and women, it is no wonder that male Sufis celebrate femininity as energy, an opportunity for men to blossom and thrive. For Ibn al-'Arabi, the female lover is "*tayyar*" or, literally, endowed with wings, an idea that the Muslim miniature painters often tried to capture. Sufi men seem to explore the unconscious of the Muslim psyche, where myths and legends, sacred and profane, endow women with extraordinary powers. From the dazzling Queen of Sheba to the irresistible Zuleikha in the sacred Qu'ran, to horse-riding Shirin in the Persian legends and the subversive Sharazad in Arabic tales, to modern women artists today, the feminine stands as a challenge in Islamic art. This brings us to understand better why intellectually dazzling female Al-Jazeera hosts enchant male viewers.

But I would like to add one final emotional nuance that seems pertinent if we are to grasp the nascent trends of the digital Islam galaxy: Sufis were very popular in a medieval Islam that had to face the constant attacks of Christian crusaders because they addressed the question of fear. Sufis helped medieval Muslims face their fear of the unknown by diving into knowledge. "The human being can master his anxieties by channeling his energies into learning. . . . The issue is confusion. Confusion creates anxiety (*hayra*), and anxiety creates movement and movement is life."[29]

Fear, say the Sufis, triggers the desire to discover its source. In so doing, it produces a positive movement from within. The worst is to be petrified by fear to the point of being paralyzed and forced to shrink inward. And anxiety is indeed the daily share of many of us, Muslims or not, who witness the apocalyptic vanishing of our familiar frontiers.

Fatema Mernissi is a scholar, writer, and sociology professor. She is currently the senior researcher at Muhammad V. University in Rabat, Morocco, where she conducts workshops to strengthen civil society's communication capabilities. The focus of Mernissi's writings as well as her teaching has been to nurture a pluralist Islamic civil society where humanism—not extremism—is the foundation. She is author of several works including *Beyond the Veil: Male-Female Dynamics in Modern Muslim Society* (1975); *The Veil and Male Elite: A Feminist Interpretation of Women's Rights in Islam* (1987); *Dreams of Trespass: Tales of a Harem Girlhood* (1994); *Scheherazade Goes West* (2002). Mernissi's books have been translated into many languages. Her current research interest is pluralism in cyber-Islam and communication as the new frontier. Mernissi has received recognition and many awards, including the 2003 Prince of Austria's Award for Letters and 2004 Erasmus Prize on Religion and Modernity.

Notes

1. Mohamad Mahmoud, "Necessity or Seduction? Ramadan Films" (*Daroura aml-ghra? Drama Ramadan*) television program insert *Al-Ahram Al-Arabi* no. 299, December 2002, p. 18. *Al-Ahram Al-Arabi* is a Cairo-based avant-garde magazine. Its website is www.ahram.org.eg/arabi.

2. Zaynab Muntacir, "*Qasim Amin wa Faris Bila Jawad: Bayna Harim As-Sultan wa Sultan Nafsuh*" (Qasim Amin and Rider Without a Horse: Between the Sultan's Harem and the Sultan Himself) *Rose El Youssef*, (Egypt), no. 3885 (November 23–29, 2002).

3. Husam 'Abd al-Hadi, "The Empire of Women: Of 80,000 Employed in Radio and Television, 50,000 are Women," *Rose El Youssef*, no. 3886 (November 30–December 6, 2002), pp. 43–45. *Rose El Youssef* was one of the first avant-garde magazines to be created by a woman, Fatema El Youssef, who founded it in 1925.

4. *Aftahu fi-l amri, abana lahu . . .* and the verses of the Qur'an "*ystaftunaka qul Allahu yuftikum*" (Spirat 4-An-Nissa, Women, Verse 176) and "*ayyas 'alunaka su'ala ta'alumin*." Ibn Manzhur, "The Tongue of the Arabs" (*Lissan al Arab*) (Cairo: 1979) Dar al-Ma'arif, vol. 5 p. 3348. Ibn Manzur was born in Cairo in 1232 and died in 1311.

5. Jamal al-Kashki, "Fatawi al Halal wa-I-Haram," *Al-Ahram Al-Arabi*, no. 295 (November 16, 2002), 73.

6. Peter Mandaville, "Digital Islam: Changing the Boundaries of Religious Knowledge?" International Institute for the Study of Islam in the Modern World Newsletter, March 1999, pp. 1 and 23.

7. "*maqsiduhum maqsidun wahid*" (Ibn Manzuer, *Lisan al-'Arab*, vol. 1, p. 134).

8. Mandaville, "Digital Islam." For a quick glimpse of the speedy digital Arab galaxy buildup, see René Naba, *Guerre des ondes, Guerre des religions: La bataille hertzienne dans le ciel Méditerrannéen* (Paris: Harmattan 1998); Muhammad El-Nawawy and Adel Iskander *Al-Jazeera: How the Free Arab News Network Scoopdr the World and Changed the Middle East* (Cambridge, MA: Westview 2002).

9. "12, 5% de son programme est des émissions religieuses, contre 75, 5% pour les variétés et 9, 5 pour l'information." Naba, *Guerre des ondes*, p. 85.

10. Walid Najm, "Cultural Programs: The Frequency Is Ridiculously Low and the Content Is Totally Divorced from Reality," *Al-Funun* (Kuwait), no. 6 (June 2001).

11. El-Nawawy and Iskandar, *Al-Jazeera*, p. 59.

12. Abdallah Schleifer, "Super News Center Setting Up in London for Al-Hayat and LBC: An Interview with Jihad Khazen and Salah Nemett," *Transnational Broadcasting Studies* 9 (2002). www.tbsjournal.com.

13. UNESCO Statistical Yearbook for 1999, Table II.5.1.: "Estimated number of adult illiterates and distribution by gender and by region: 1980, 1999 and 2000."

14. "Between 1998 and 2000, several satellites equipped for digital compression were launched to serve areas that included Arab states. Besides Egypt's Nilesat 101 and 102 and the new generation of Arabsat craft, starting with Arabsat 3A, the Hot-Bird satellites of Europe's operator, Eutelsat, also transmit to viewers in the

Mediterranean Basin and parts of the Gulf." Naomi Sakr, "Arab Satellite Channels between State and Private Ownership," *Al-Funun*, no. 6 (June 2001).

15. Chris Forrester, "Middle East TV Continues to Baffle and Bewilder," in *Transnational Broadcasting Studies* (2002).

16. Nabil Ali, "*Tunaiyat al acr: ac-cifr wal-wahid*" (The Century's Duality: The Zero and the One) *Wighaat Nazar* (Egypt) 4, 44, (2002), pp. 34–40.

17. Tourya Guaaybess, "A New Order of Information in the Arab Broadcasting System," in *Transnational Broadcasting Studies* 9 (2002).

18. Hussein Amin, "Arab Women and Satellite Broadcasting," *Transnational Broadcasting Studies* 6 (2001).

19. Ibid.

20. Schleifer, "Super News Center Setting Up in London for Al-Hayat and LBC."

21. Naomi Sakr, "Arab Satellite Channels Between State and Private Ownership."

22. Tariq Ali, "Satellite Dishes" (*Suhun Fadaiya*), *An-Nuqad* (April 2002).

23. Amin, "Arab Women and Satellite Broadcasting."

24. Ahmed Ghanem, "*Shakl al Fada'iyyat al Khassa Yataqqadam*" (The Aesthetics of Private Satellite Channels Are Improving) *Al-Funun*, 6 (June 2001), p. 38, www.kuwaitculture.org.

25. Ibid.

26. Ibn al-'Arabi, *The Bezels of Wisdom* (*Fusus al-Hikam*). Trans. R. W. Austin (New York: Paulist Press, 1980). p. 233. The original text of the first quote reads "*fal-mir'atu 'aynun wahidatun, was-suwaru kathiratun fi 'ayn al-ra'i.*"

27. Since Berber was declared a national language, Berner magazines appear regularly in the newsstands—such as *Le Monde Amazight* and *Tasafut* (Candlelight).

28. Marwan Bishara, *Palestine Israel: Peace or Apartheid: Prospects for Resolving Conflict* (London: Zed Books, 2001).

29. *Fal-Huda huwa an yahtadi al insan ila l-hayrati fa ya'lam. Inna l-amra hayratun wal-hayratu qalaq wa harakah, wal-harakatu hayat. Fala sukuna fala mawt, wa wujud, fala 'adam* (Ibn al-'Arabi, *Fusus al-Hikam*, my translation).

On- and Off-Camera in Egyptian Soap Operas: Women, Television, and the Public Sphere

Lila Abu-Lughod

One morning, I awoke to find white tents pitched on the embankment of the Pharaonic temple that I could see from the house in which I was staying. A chat with my neighbors, all gathered on benches outside their houses, revealed that this was to be the set of a television serial then being filmed in the area. There was an undercurrent of excitement as the women talked about which stars had been spotted, how the noise of the shoot had gone on all night long in the desert, and what they had seen already of camels with litters, horses ridden by turbaned men with swords, and minibuses carrying urban professionals from Cairo. Later in the day, children from all over the village milled about near the tents. They had come walking, barefoot, or riding bikes and donkeys. They pressed in on the director, camera crew, and actors trying to get a scene right. Production assistants with cell phones walked back and forth, shooing the children away, asking trainers to quiet the horses, and generally looking frustrated at these less than ideal filming conditions. Two well-known actors in heavy makeup sat cross-legged in front of a tent, their long flowing dresses (deemed appropriate to the medieval period in which the soap opera was set) making them visibly hot. They repeated the several lines of dialogue until they got them right—without a fly buzzing past, a donkey braying, or a child shouting.

Egypt is famous for such television serials and exports them throughout the Arabic-speaking world. By 2004, when this serial was being filmed, it had become popular to make serials set in the medieval period, often with allegorical significance, even though most dramatic serials are still set in the present and feature pretty actresses wearing makeup, glorious hair, and fashionable clothes. In the 1990s, intrigued by the serials' popularity and their central place in the everyday lives of so many, I began studying in the 1990s the role of Egyptian television dramas in national debates and in the social imagination.[1] I was particularly interested in two groups of marginal women who watch television—poor working women in Cairo and villagers in the disadvantaged southern region of Egypt, known as Upper Egypt—in part because they were rarely the subject of serials. Although I explored the relationship of television drama to national culture, ideologies of develop-ment and uplift, state attempts to manage religion, and the "modernization" of subjectivity, one theme that threaded through everything was the "woman question." Women watch television serials, women act in them, and (some) women write and direct them. What significance could this have? Does this participation in one of the most popular forms of mass media entail or reflect their participation in the wider public sphere from which, according to stereotypes, Middle Eastern women have mostly been excluded? Does women's involvement in media, in fact, open up emancipa-tory possibilities?

The answers to these questions, the case of television drama reveals, are ambiguous. First, it is dangerous to generalize about women. It would be hard to say anything sensible about the female half of Egypt's population of 69 million people, and even harder to characterize the huge group falling under the label of Muslim women. More specifically, women participate in the media in multiple ways. We must first disaggregate viewers from pro-ducers of television drama. Writers and directors, thoughtful and usually politically progressive, tend to be a very small part of an educated cultural elite. They seek to affect the public. Actors, by occupation and income, can find themselves more cosmopolitan than many Egyptians aspire to belong to a more international and glamorous world. They are perfectly happy with publicity, much of it manufactured, despite the ambivalence toward them this produces—challenging as it does moral values about the appropriate behavior of women in the public sphere.[2] And although one cannot treat viewers as passive participants in the media, they are nevertheless more var-ied and far more numerous than those who work in the television industry. They range from professional architects schooled in the United States to middle-class housewives managing family life in provincial towns, from the mothers, wives, and daughters of rural farmers to urban domestics working for others. Enormous differences in political engagement, influence, and identification exist between rich and poor, urban and rural, young and old, interested and uninterested in television. As my experience of watching the filming of a soap opera in Upper Egypt showed, although there were women in front of the camera, none of the local village women were willing to come out and watch the filming. They kept an eye on things from afar and they discussed the movements of actors, whom they knew a good deal about. They kept out of public view since women in the community only went out when they had something to do—visiting a sick person, going to borrow something or going to the market, seeing a doctor, or attending a wedding or funeral.

All this suggests that we can read little directly from the existence of this form of national, regional, and even global communication. As Raymond Williams has noted,

> It is often said that [media have] altered our world. In the same way, people often speak of a new world, a new society, a new phase of history, being created—"brought about"—by this or that new technology: the steam engine, the automobile, the atomic bomb. Most of us know what is generally implied when such things are said. But this may be the central difficulty: that we have got so used to statements of this general kind, in our most ordinary discussions, that we fail to realise their specific meanings.[3]

To assess its social impact or potential, we need to look closely at the social relations embedded in and embedding a media form as they work themselves out within particular social and historical circumstances. Television in Egypt at the turn of the twenty-first century is a pedagogical tool and a space for imaginative life with complex and sometimes contradictory implications for women.

To begin to tease out these complexities, I will first discuss the work of some prominent women involved in television drama production. This will reveal the developmentalist ideologies they promote, ideologies that are meant to advance women but ironically end up devaluing large numbers of uneducated women. Then I will discuss the stars of the serials, because they are a key element both in attaching viewers to the serials and in taking them beyond the shows' pedagogical messages, sometimes in disruptive ways.

Although the actors are concerned with their careers and brood in their international affiliations, they are also very much a part of society. In the 1990s in Egypt, this meant that some of them actually gave up their careers to embrace Islamic piety. Finally, I will turn briefly to some viewers of television in the small hamlet in Upper Egypt where the historical drama was filmed. The involvement of young women in television-watching and their entry into the world of public, paid work coincided in the late 1990s. But as I will show, it is not at all the case that what they learned from television would serve them well, given the conditions of poverty in the region and the way their television-inspired consumer dreams affected their marriage prospects.

Producers' Pedagogical Projects

Egypt has a large TV industry and produces high-quality television drama. Women writers and directors are a minority in television but have been involved since the late 1960s, the early days of dramatic serials that grew out of radio soap operas. Like some other important writers and directors in Egyptian television, many prominent women consider themselves progressive, or at least liberal, and are politically engaged. They also have feminist concerns—that is, concerns about women's status and rights and the dynamics of gender oppression. They are the type of professionals or intellectuals from whom one would expect change to come. The problem I encountered when I watched their television dramas, and especially when I watched them with poor and uneducated women, whether urban or rural, was that I felt uncomfortable with the exclusions their values entailed.

I will try to explain why these Cairo progressives, whom I will call developmental feminists, cannot be seen as using television to emancipate women, even though they themselves find in this medium a means of self-expression and have enormously positive intentions. I will do so by analyzing closely a TV film that many progressive intellectuals in Cairo in the mid-1990s told me I just had to see, as well as some related programs in other genres that women viewers found compelling.

Nuna al-Sha`nuna was a television film based on a short story by the Egyptian feminist writer Salwá Bakr, about a rural girl sent by her father to Cairo to work as a maid. Translatable as *Nutty Nuna*, the title refers to the girl Nuna's odd behavior (jumping around the kitchen doing exercises, repeating phrases of classical Arabic poetry that she does not understand, letting the water in the sink overflow, or looking intently at onions as she cooks). We discover that her odd behavior comes out of her obsession with the school next door. Through the kitchen window, she can overhear the lessons and see the activities of a girls' school. She is entranced and confused by this magical world and spends whatever time she can listening and learning. In the story, Nuna runs away the day after her father comes to Cairo to take her back to the village, to be married. Her father and employers don't know why she does this, but the readers of the short story are privy to her dream on the night before her disappearance. After lying awake for hours, thinking about how she does not want to return to the village "to live in filth and fleas" or to marry and "end up like her sisters, sunk neck deep in hardship and misery," she "dreamt of the school, the girls, the officer's son. She also saw Aytalah [one of the mysterious words in the line of poetry] and he turned out to be a beautiful being. She was not sure whether he was human or *jinn* [a spirit]: he was white, as white as cotton flowers; he had two wings, beautiful with the colours of the rainbow." She clung to them and Aytalah flew with her "far away until she reached the sky and saw the golden stars."[4]

The short story addresses, with brilliant economy and simplicity, a formidable range of issues, from the exploitation of rural girls to the cruelty of class relations in Egypt. Most striking, it manages to create at its center a humane image of the innocent openness of a deprived young girl, and of the cycle of backwardness, as Bakr puts it, that keeps girls in such situations. In the short story, Bakr seems to go beyond the usual liberal and progressive discourses about education in Egypt, painting education not just as a means of social mobility or as something necessary to national development and progress but also as personally emancipatory in that it expands the mind.

This feminist approach to education that sees in it the means for individual growth and personal emancipation, as well as financial independence or social mobility, can be found in other works by women television producers. But let's look at this expression closely. A story that humanizes a servant girl by showing that she wants to know the life of the mind implies an unstated corollary: that the underprivileged, the downtrodden, and the marginal would not in the course of their ordinary lives have rich experiences, mental or emotional. The problem here is that the secular intellectual speaks, at least in this short story, for the subaltern in a voice that is ultimately middle class and wedded to a modernist set of values such as education, science, and knowledge. Nuna is redeemed by her brightness, curiosity, and desire for education. Were she uninterested in this, desiring instead, for example, to go back to the village to marry and have a family, to help a husband work the land to feed their children, to live among her loved ones, family, and neighbors in "the filth and the fleas," or to restrict herself to local knowledges, including popular Islam, she would not have been a heroine.

And this attitude—which one might call developmentalist—may explain why this short story was taken up by television. The story was not just about the feminist and leftist topics of gender and class exploitation, which had gone out of favor by the 1990s and may have been behind the initial opposition to producing the television film, but also about education and that noble goal, enlightenment. The condition of a poor servant girl's becoming a subject and citizen is that she renounce her family, her roots, and if not the idiocy, as Marx would have it, of rural life, then its ignorance.

The major differences between the short story and the film lead one to appreciate that it was probably this familiar and well-meaning nationalist message about education and development that enabled the director to produce and show the film. Unlike the short story, the television production was didactic, moralistic, and hopeful for the future. The theme of education was expanded and modified to remove any ambiguities. And although the progressive messages about class exploitation and even gender remained, they were muted and ultimately undermined by the validation of an educated, enlightened middle class.

The most significant transformation of the short story came in the exoneration of this portion of the bourgeoisie. The unambiguous condemnation of the elite, represented by Nuna's employers, in the story was undermined in the TV film by the creation of a key character: the sister of the materialistic mistress of the house. She is a woman educated in the United States who has just come back to Egypt. She is patriotic and healthy, and she argued for the rights of workers and servants to decent treatment and conditions. She is kind toward Nuna, discovers her secret, then nourishes her desire for education by teaching her to read. This leads her into conflict with her sister, who does not want her to interfere. When Nuna runs away at the end of the film, she eventually appears at this woman's door. The woman nurses her back to health and finds her a job in a school. The enlightened middle-class woman thus rescues Nuna and helps her achieve her dream of education.

The introduction of this new character changes the whole story by framing it as one of morality and paternalism. This character is not only moralistic in the way she lectures her sister and brother-in-law about their materialism, lack of social conscience, and exploitation of inferiors, by her very existence, she proves that social injustice is a moral, not a class, problem. Not all members of the bourgeoisie are to be blamed, this character demonstrates. In fact, the educated and enlightened members of this class will expose the mistreatment of the downtrodden and help uplift them. In this alteration of the short story, a powerful and longstanding narrative convention intervenes—one that runs through numerous films and television serials, associating the Europeanized upper class with immorality and the educated middle class (and those from the upper classes redeemed by education) with patriotism and social concern for inferiors.

Both the paternalism (or should we call it maternalism) and the construction of morality that infuse so many of the highest-quality television serials, feminist and not, are also at work in subtle ways in a kind of television program that rivaled the serials in popularity with the kind of women Nuna is supposed to represent: poor women working in domestic service. In 1997, the program that seemed to have most captured their imaginations and feelings was a (short-lived) unscripted show called *Who Is to Blame?* hosted by a young television personality.[5] The program focused on real individuals with terrible problems. These individuals described their plights, usually the result of mistreatment by parents, spouses, children, bureaucratic institutions, or commercial firms. Relevant others, from relatives to authorities or experts, were questioned about the situation. The goal was to expose the problem, assign blame, and find a solution. Along the way, as I will suggest, viewers were given moral lessons.

These "melodramas of the real" reaffirmed the value of a strong morality, backed by the authority of the educated. For example, in one memorable program about the son of divorced parents who was being mistreated by his father, women viewers kept coming back, in their retellings, to the authorities seated in the studio who asked questions and made judgments about the father's behavior. Furthermore, since this was a charity program, help other than advice was also given. In a program about a fatherless family threatened with eviction, the minister of housing offered the family an apartment. Authority figures, in other words, step in not just to judge but also to lend a helping hand.

This association of moral judgment with educated and enlightened figures of authority establishes dependence as the proper mode of relations between the disempowered and the state or the educated classes. Instead of learning a language of criticism of those in power, or even a language of rights, marginal women who watch these programs are led to fall back on the language of complaint about those who do not help them. This discourse of complaint is the flip side of paternalism/maternalism. It does not threaten, or question, the basic inequalities or structures of political power and class.

Marginal women are asked to imbibe a faith in the goodness of the enlightened middle-class authorities who voice the judgments they would want to make themselves. One important corollary of this faith, which brings us back to the film *Nuna al-Sha`nuna*, is that education is a virtue that justifies hierarchy. Everyone believes that education is necessary, despite plenty of evidence that these days, for any but the elites, with civil service shrinking and being very poorly paid, education rarely guarantees anything. Television films such as *Nuna al-Sha`nuna* that celebrate education, even as they specifically encourage the education of girls contribute to such continuing beliefs in education in the face of dwindling opportunities.

What is the impact of such media-supported notions on urban domestics who, for the most part, buy into but find themselves unable to realize the ideals that education is meant to deliver? A problem with faith in education as central to progress, individual advancement, and the nation arises from the everyday experiences of the kinds of women viewers of television I have worked with in Cairo. For all the older, poor working women I knew, raising and educating their children was their primary concern, and they had vague feelings of betrayal. Most were heartbroken because their sons, and sometimes their daughters, found it very difficult to find jobs despite their qualifications. The women did not know whom to blame nor did they have much sense of the policies and economic transformations that were causing the education dream to go wrong. They felt about this, as they did about many of their problems, that since they worked so hard, they deserved better. The government, or someone, should help. Television drama, as well as the developmentalist rhetoric elsewhere in their world has led them, I would argue, to expect that a helping hand should be forthcoming. However, with globalization, including the economic liberalization policies of the state and the imperatives of structural adjustment and privatization, the government and the elite are no longer sure that they should bother to justify themselves by providing this local helping hand.

In Egypt, religious discourse has appropriated the language of morality that the state is ceding as it pushes for privatization and other capitalist projects that do not find their justification in the language of morality. The domestics I've worked with find sense in the mosque lessons they now attend. For these women, the ideals of religious piety seem more vibrant than others. These ideals promise community and demand only self-discipline not consumption. Moreover, those who promote this path will always have the moral high ground in a nation that has never doubted religion, either officially or in the lives of ordinary people, even if it went through a period, under Nasser, that pushed secular ideals. When one domestic watched the scene in *Nuna al-Sha`nuna* in which the enlightened middle-class woman told Nuna not to call her by the honorific she had been taught by her mistress (*ya sitt*, or *hadritik*) but to use instead more neutral terms like *abla* (referring to her status as teacher), she commented: "Now the Muslims [the more pious] say you should not say *sitt*. Religious people say they'll have to pay for the sin of being called this. They say you should say *hagga* (the term for someone who has been on the pilgrimage) or something else. There is no *sitt* or *sidi* (the masculine equivalent) in Islam. Everyone is equal."

This kind of rhetoric of Muslim equality, even though it is produced in the context of a hierarchy with religious authorities and men at the top and sometimes pushed in authoritarian ways, offers something beyond the rhetoric of development and the increasingly absent helping hand in national projects of uplift. As the anthropologist Saba Mahmood argues, the goals of the piety movement are to encourage people to cultivate virtuous selves, and beyond that to create a virtuous Islamic society.[6] Those who are in the position of teachers use the language of sisterhood and brotherhood. For example, a prominent religious authority responsible for many of the "conversions" of born-again actresses and dancers in the late 1980s and early

1990s (which I will discuss below) talked about them as his "sisters."⁷ Given the structures of power, families' continuing control over the lives and reputations of women, and the very real social and economic inequalities in Egypt, their messages may resonate with many more women than those of feminist developmentalism, with its calls to empowerment through individual advancement and an unattainable or disappointing education and its maternalistic reinforcement of the authority of the educated middle class. Moreover, the language of piety may seem more familiar than the secular language of rights and choice used by feminist developmentalists like the writers and directors of television productions like *Nuna al-Sha`nuna.*

How off-putting the developmentalist language can be is clear from a well meaning but patronizing study of women and television in two Cairo neighborhoods that appeared in 1990s. The book, by Nadya Radwan, is titled, tellingly, *The Role of Television Drama in Building Women's Awareness.* Like so many of her peers, Radwan views illiteracy as one of the most important problems facing Egyptian women and society. Education, she argues, allows individuals to be productive and develops the human resources on which the county's high standard of living and strong economy depend. She justifies education for women not just so that they can be the equals of men but also so the national economy can advance. She blames illiteracy for all sorts of negative practices in Egypt, among them cousin marriage, ignorance about family planning and health care, obsession with honor and revenge in the countryside, drug addiction, polygamy, backward customs such as female circumcision, and male dominance. Although she sensibly calls for more education, she also argues that television drama must play a role in changing values, given the high dependence of illiterate women on it. She argues, for example, that television drama has a responsibility to shed light on the following issues: family issues such as marital choice, marital age, equality, bride price, equal value of boys and girls, importance of family planning, nutrition, vaccinating children, polygamy, divorce, women's rights to be educated and to work, insurance, pensions, and inheritance; issues related to health awareness; and issues of social upbringing, including inculcation of the values of honesty, beauty, love for others, civic consciousness, environmental protection, respect for elders, generosity to the poor, patience, and democracy. Furthermore, she charges television with reducing overpopulation, closing the gap between leaders and ordinary individuals in society, wiping out superstition, and combating antisocial behaviors including noise pollution, bribery, and wasting time at work.[8]

Her staggering list reveals clearly the urban middle-class values that she has no doubt are right for all Egyptian women. As it happens, Egyptian television already treats many of these themes through the developmentalist voices of its progressive writers and directors, especially its feminist women. What I have just been trying to show, however, is how such projects of consciousness-raising are, first of all, usually patronizing, reaffirming the superiority of the middle classes; second, mostly misleading because of the current political-economic circumstances of life in Egypt; and third, often received ambivalently, especially because the alternatives emerging from the Islamic piety movement promise more. The way feminist developmentalism has positioned poor and uneducated women as in need of uplift is problematic; thus what television serials offer them by way of models and ideals is also not transparently emancipatory.

In the Public Eye

If women media professionals make messages for a female public, the women who act in television serials and film use media to make themselves public. These stars are critical for creating a sense of national affiliation among viewers, and they participate willingly in the pedagogy of the television serials, often defending their work as a social service. But at the same time, because of their lifestyle and self-presentation as stars, they offer women other alternatives to the developmentalist messages of the programs in which they act. Yet these alternatives are contradictory and morally charged.

In Egypt, as elsewhere, a special brand of community is fostered through common and mediated knowledge about the nation's television stars. The actors' national fame can be put to use for various purposes. Celebrities in Egypt market goods on television, and although there is less crossover between media and politics than in Bombay or Tamil Nadu, and no actor has become president or governor, as in the United States, some of those involved in television have also tried to work in politics, making use of their connections to the world of film and television. For example, the progressive feminist writer Fathiyya al-'Assal ran in the 1995 elections for parliament as a candidate of the leftist party. Her platform was secular nationalist and anti-terrorist and supported the rights of women and the downtrodden, especially workers and artisans. In an interesting analysis of her campaign in Imbaba, a poor neighborhood where some of the domestic servants I have worked with live, she denied exploiting her connections to the world of television, saying that all the artists who supported her publicly were members of her party and did so in that capacity. And yet a distinctive aspect of her campaign was that she was accompanied in the neighborhood by famous television actors, and her posters and newspaper ads highlighted the support of other actors and writers. Among the ways she was described in the newspaper that supported her was "Fathiyya al-`Assal, a Fighter who Conquered the Impossible," a reference to her award-winning television serial about literacy and independence, *She and the Impossible*.

Mostly what is interesting about so many stars is the way they talk about their work as socially and politically responsible—as an aspect of their patriotism. Like everywhere, stars and characters intermingle in Egypt, with the help of fan magazines, newspapers, and television itself. The actors are asked to comment on the roles they play and the serials in which they act. They talk regularly, in seminars and interviews about the importance of the serials' treatment of national issues. They often justify their work in terms of social and national responsibility, as did Layla `Ilwi when she explained her acceptance of the role of a lost soul who joins a militant Islamist group and donning the face veil (*niqab*) in a serial called *The Family* (1994). She said, "My feelings as an artist and a citizen are inseparable, and naturally I'm repulsed by what is happening around me in my own society as a result of terrorism and corruption. Working in television is extremely difficult, but it is worth it if our message reaches people."[9] This is a film star who has played racy and glamorous roles.

And yet, if you look at some very popular women stars of the last decade, you see how they undermine the developmentalist message. The following two examples illustrate the opposite ways stars do so. On the one hand, they violate codes of propriety and incite viewers' ambivalence; on the other hand, they question their own lifestyles as stars and participate in the trend toward greater religious piety.

When I talked with people about a fabulous serial called *Hilmiyya Nights* that aired in the late 1980s and early 1990s and was rerun often throughout the 1990s, and asked what they liked about it, several of the poor working women I knew in Cairo spoke not of the serious political or social messages but of the main female character, Nazik Hanim, an aristocratic, conniving, blond, magnificently dressed femme fatale played by Safiyya al-`Umari. One young woman whose husband had abandoned her, leaving her with two children to raise on her own, suggested, "Nazik is the reason everyone watches *Hilmiyya Nights*. She's tough; she married four men. She wouldn't let anyone tell her what to do." An older woman who was working because her husband was disabled explained why Nazik was so great: "She's fickle, not satisfied with one type. She married many times. She represents what? What's it called? The aristocracy? She was strong-willed. And stubborn. Because of her desires she lost her fortune." After a short silence she added, "And Hamdiyya, the dancer, did you see her?" She laughed as she imitated a characteristic arrogant gesture of this belly dancer turned nightclub owner, played by Lucy, a gorgeous real-life belly dancer and actress.

These were the two glamorous women characters, played by equally glamorous stars, who had little nationalist sympathy, who wrapped men around their fingers and refused to act like respectable ladies, despite the pleas of their children, their ex-husbands, and their other relatives. The women I spoke with seemed to take vicarious pleasure in these women's defiance of the moral system that keeps good women quiet. These domestic workers were women whose respectability was threatened by their need to work outside the home and as servants. They struggled daily to claim and proclaim their respectability. They hid from their neighbors and sometimes even their relatives the actual sort of work they did, and they had all adopted the *hijab*, the headcovering of the new modest Islamic dress that in Egypt has come to be a sign of Islamic piety and middle-class respectability.

Although fascination with stars, their lives and loves, their clothing and travel, their failures and successes, is just as lively and widespread in Egypt as elsewhere, these most public of women also inspire mixed feelings for their very publicness. Women and girls across the country do not necessarily want to follow in their footsteps, because their lifestyles do not, by and large, conform to the social and moral ideals of propriety that are still quite strong among a range of viewers, even if these women's defiance is intriguing.

The moral questioning of the publicity of acting has even been voiced by actors themselves, some of whom began, in the late 1980s and early

1990s, to offer their public a different sort of nondevelopmentalist message than that of defiant glamour. They did this through their changing relationship to religious piety. The reactions I witnessed to one film and television star, Huda Sultan, tell an important story about the intersection of discourses in Egypt in the 1990s and the confusing role the media play in women's lives, at least in this important Muslim.

The most dramatic phenomenon in the world of stars in the early 1990s was a number of artists' highly publicized retirement from acting, and in the case of women, the adoption of the *hijab*, of a number of "artists." These acts stirred controversy, including accusations of taking money from Saudi Arabian sources for doing this. The religious authorities associated with these stars' "repentance" were very visible figures, well known through television appearances and sermons on audiocassette. Books with titles such as *Repentant Artists and the Sex Stars and Artists Behind the Veil*, and dedications such as "To every retired artist who had faith that what is of God is better and more lasting," carried glowing interviews with these stars and the religious figures who mentored them.[10]

At least one of these stars eventually took off the veil again and went back to acting, but the most interesting case is Huda Sultan. She is an older star who was an extremely successful singer and film star even in the 1950s. She now says she prefers to work in television. She wears the *hijab*, on screen and off. So, unlike her younger "born-again" colleagues, she has not given up acting. She explained in an interview in 1994, "I respect my audience very much and am quite careful to appear respectable in front of them. . . . Hijab is a duty that is not inimical to artistic performance. I am veiled, and therefore I choose roles that are suitably modest, like the role of the mother."[11]

Taking the middle road of wearing the veil but continuing to act seems to have made her universally admired. Directors and screenwriters who have worked with her praise her talent. When she was given a prize at the Forty-Fifth Annual Catholic Center Film Festival (a film festival dedicated to moral values), the announcer said she was being rewarded for her integrity, honesty, and love of people. She thanked the festival organizers graciously for the honor, letting it be known that she had just returned from the `umra (the "lesser" pilgrimage to Mecca, undertaken at a different time of year than the annual pilgrimage).

I witnessed the extraordinary respect and affection directed at her by her colleagues in 1997 when I sat in on the final script reading for a production called *Zizinya*, by Egypt's most popular serial writer. She arrived late. There was shuffling and interest, and immediately a senior male actor got up from the head of the table to give her his seat. Everyone else greeted her warmly. When the reading was over, a large cake from a good patisserie was brought in, to celebrate the end of this stage and the commencement of shooting in a few weeks. Deferentially, all the actors present asked her to cut the cake.

I suspect that only a small elite that is not that fond of Egyptian serials in any case might be offended by the appearance of Huda Sultan in *hijab*. For the rest of the public, including a large middle and lower middle class, the majority of whom now accept veiling, and rural communities, in which women never went without some sort of head covering, she represents the perfect compromise. They can identify with, or at least respect, her moderate piety. Yet because her piety, unlike that of the younger born-again stars, does not seem to entail the condemnation of the popular entertainment of television drama, she gives people license to continue to be captivated by the magic of stars and to partake in the nationwide affective community of those drawn to television drama.

The significance of the enormous affection for Huda Sultan for this essay's argument about the complex implications of women's participation in the media in the Middle East is that media stars do not, ultimately, offer radical alternatives for women in imagining their lives. They are seen by many women viewers as part of a fascinating but problematic enclave that cannot offer models for others except when they participate in wider trends. In Egypt, this has been the case, insofar as they participate, like so many other women, in the piety movement that, since the 1970s, has been offering women the opportunity to enter new public spheres (not just in the mosque but in the professions) and to gain rights, defined within a particular moral and religious framework that is not global, if by global we mean a Western-dominated ideology that includes liberal secular feminism.

The Economies of Television

As I noted above, it is impossible to generalize about the largest group of participants in television: the viewers. But a few glimpses into the lives of my village neighbors in Upper Egypt who watched the filming of that tele-

vision serial can suggest some of the ways television, while opening up multiple imaginative worlds that take viewers far beyond village life in this disadvantaged region and encouraging, through serials that share the messages
of the television film *Nuna al-Sha`nuna* discussed earlier, the education
their daughters and nieces are already getting, also contributes to insoluble
dilemmas and unexpected restrictions on their lives. By way of conclusion,
therefore, I want to discuss a key dogma of liberal feminism: work as an
important element of women's independence and self-expression.

Since 2000, a new phenomenon has been making itself felt in the
Upper Egyptian village where I have done research. Suddenly, what had
seemed unimaginable ten years earlier was occurring: girls who had finished
high school were beginning to take jobs. They begged their fathers to let
them work in government offices or in small shops; some even managed to
get, through family connections, jobs in the Antiquities Service. They
helped in their family households before leaving for work, sometimes even
preparing at dawn the dough for baking bread. But then they went off in
clean long skirts and blouses, always with their hair covered in a proper
hijab, to catch rides to their jobs. Their younger sisters would have to take
over some of their chores, including some cooking.

Given how things work in villages, and the strength of social ties, their
jobs usually came through family connections, and their fathers would be
eventually persuaded to accept the change because they were reassured that
their daughters would be protected "like family" in the workplace, super-
vised and often confined in their movements. But the girls had gained skills
in school; they had also got used to going off into the wider world every day
and were bored and isolated at home.

Perhaps television, with all its role models of working women, had
some part in the increasing acceptance of village girls' working outside the
home. However, economic pressure was the main force behind this new
public role for village girls. In the 1990s, with underemployment endemic,
agricultural land increasingly reverting to large landowners, staple expenses
rising so much that families often used their small amounts of land to grow
wheat for household consumption, and the majority only barely getting by,
people were grateful for any cash income. Young men, whether graduates of
high school or even college, sat mostly unemployed, helping on family
farms if they had any, otherwise finding what they could but not contribut-

ing as much as their parents would wish. And yet expenses have risen, the most critical and difficult of which are marriage expenses. So it has fallen to the girls to work, so they can at least help with their own marriage expenses.

And here is where television may have the most to answer for, not because it encourages girls to go out into the public sphere or work but because it forces them to take jobs that pay pittances, wages that young men couldn't accept, just to contribute to the expenses their families will incur when (and if) they marry. The high expenses of marriage must be blamed in part on television, because the serials, with their fancy sets showing modern kitchens, swimming pools, and other luxuries, and the advertisements that frame them, pushing everything from gleaming ceramic bathrooms to electric dishwashers, normalize consumer worlds far different from the everyday one of the village of two decades ago. Every bride is expected to contribute to the new marital household the kitchen appliances now considered essential: a stove and refrigerator, along with Teflon or stainless steel pots and pans, brand-new dishes, and even household goods like blankets. For most families, vast expenses like these require loans, sales of livestock, and other hardships, and any contributions by daughters help alleviate the financial burden on the fathers.

Perhaps the worst consequence of the combination of the enormous demand for modern consumer items that television has encouraged and the unemployment and general poverty that characterize much of the countryside is that it is actually difficult to pull off a marriage. The burdens on the groom's family are even heavier than those on the bride's, since the groom is now expected to provide an apartment or house, as well as the living room furniture, a gift of gold jewelry, and at least a token marriage payment. Having imposed on themselves this high material standard, not surprisingly, many find it difficult to marry. Men can usually only marry quite late, and often after a period of migration for work. When they finally return or manage to get what they need for the event, they look for young women as brides. This has been leaving many of the young men's peers, girls now in their twenties and thirties, unmarried. So even though they go out to work to earn money to buy what they need as brides, these television watchers with aspirations for modern lives may never enjoy the status and independence that marriage ultimately provides in this community. Eventually, even after a period of schooling and work, both of which take them into more public spheres, their lives will be far more restricted than their dreams, since unmarried women in rural areas, as in most cities, are still expected to live with their natal families and to guard their reputations—forever.

Although this small example of the way television enters the lives of women in one community in one region of Egypt cannot tell us what media in a global society can, in general, do for Middle Eastern or Muslim women, it does suggest that any pronouncements about media's contribution to progressive change for women need to be questioned carefully. Women's access to media, including television, is of multiple sorts. Whether they produce, act in, or watch it makes an enormous difference. But even more complex are the dynamics of the interaction between television and their values, class positions, social standing, and economic circumstances. I have tried to offer some insight into those in the hope of making our thinking about global communication and Middle Eastern women both more concrete and more subtle.

Lila Abu-Lughod is professor of Anthropology and director of the Institute for Research on Women and Gender at Columbia University. She has written widely on gender issues in the Middle East, based on many years of anthropological fieldwork in Egypt as well as comparative thinking about postcolonialism. Her books include *Veiled Sentiments: Honor and Poetry in a Bedouin Society* (1986/2000), *Writing Women's Worlds: Bedouin Stories* (1993), and the edited volumes *Remaking Women: Feminism and Modernity in the Middle East* (1998) and *Media Worlds: Anthropology on New Terrain* (2002). Her most recent book is *Dramas of Nationhood: The Politics of Television in Egypt* (2005) from which the material in this chapter was drawn. Her current research interests are in two distinct areas: Palestinian memory and transnational liberal feminism.

Notes

1. For more on this research, see Lila Abu-Lughod, *Dramas of Nationhood: The Politics of Television in Egypt* (Chicago: University of Chicago Press, 2005).
2. A good deal of literature discusses the moral ambiguities of public performance. For Egypt, see Karin van Nieuwkerk, *A Trade Like Any Other: Female Singer and*

Dancers in Egypt (Austin: University of Texas Press, 1995); Katherine E. Zirbel, "Playing It Both Ways: Local Egyptian Performers Between Regional Identity and International Markets," in *Mass Mediations: New Approaches to Popular Culture in the Middle East and Beyond*, ed. Walter Armbrust (Berkeley: University of California Press, 2000); Sherifa Zuhur, *Asmahan's Secrets: Woman, War, and Song* (Austin: University of Texas Press, 2000); Zuhur (ed.) *Images of Enchantment: Visual and Performing Arts of the Middle East* (Cairo: American University in Cairo Press, 1998).

3.   Raymond Williams and Ederyn Williams (ed.), *Television: Technology and Cultural Form* (London: Routledge Classics, 1990), p. 1.

4.   The story has been translated into English in two collections of Salwá Bakr's short stories: *The Wiles of Men and Other Stories*, trans. Denys Johnson-Davies (Cairo: American University in Cairo Press, 1997); and *Such a Beautiful Voice*, trans. Hoda el Sadda. (Cairo: General Egyptian Book Organization, 1992). I have taken the translations from the latter.

5.   For more on this program, see Joel Gordon, "Golden Boy Turns Bête Noire: Crossing Boundaries of Unscripted Television in Egypt," *Journal of Middle Eastern and North African Intellectual and Cultural Studies* 1 (2001), pp. 1–18.

6.   Saba Mahmood, *Politics of Piety: The Islamic Revival and the Feminist Subject* (Princeton, NJ: Princeton University Press, 2005).

7.   Majdi Kamil, *Fannanat wara al-hijab* (Artists behind the Veil) (Cairo: Markaz al-Rayah, 1993). Mahmud Fawzi, `Umar `Abd al-Kafi—wa fatawá sakhina—fi al-din wa-al-siyasah wa-al-fann!* (`Umar `Abd Al-Kafi and Hot Fatwas on Religion, Politics, and Art!) (Cairo: al-Jiddawi li al-Nashr, 1993), p. 57. I want to thank Farha Ghannam for bringing the latter text to my attention.

8.   Nadiyah Radwan, *Dawr al-drama al-tilifizyuniyah fi tashkil wa`y al-mar'ah: dirasa ijtima`iyah maydaniyah* (The Role of Television Drama in Forming Women's Consciousness/Awareness: A Field-based Social Study) (Cairo: al-Hay'ah al-Misriyah al-`Ammah lil-Kitab, 1997), pp. 241,163, 253–256, 322–327.

9.   Ra'uf Tawfiq, "al-Kalima hiyya al-batal" (The Word Is the Hero), *Sabah al-Khayr*, March 10, 1994, pp. 40–43.

10. For more on this, see Lila Abu-Lughod, "Movie Stars and Islamic Moralism in Egypt," *Social Text* 42 (1995), pp. 53–67.

11. "al-Sitt Huda Sultan ba`d  an ta`atiqat wa ihlawwit" (The Lady Huda Sultan after She Matured and Got More Beautiful), *Nusf al-Dunya*, March 20, 1994, p. 64–5. For more on Huda Sultan, see Walter Armbrust, "Manly Men on a National Stage (and the Women Who Make Them Stars)," in Israel Gershoni, Hakan Erdem, and Ursula Woköck (eds.) *Histories of the Modern Middle East: New Directions* (Boulder: Lynne Rienner Publishers, 2002), pp. 247–275.

Singing a New Song: Bonding and Breaking With the Past

Sherifa Zuhur

An Orientalist painting of a nineteenth-century Arab woman depicts her entertaining in private. Her audience was probably made up of other women in an urban harem, or else the portrait was completely fictitious, for she is unchaperoned and lacks proper outer modesty garb. Certainly, such an upper-class lady did not sing or give speeches in public, though some women began to publish using their own names from the 1870s onward. An edict issued under Muhammad `Ali Pasha forbade women to perform in the streets just like other restrictions in other lands under Ottoman control. Amazing, then, that in the twentieth century, Arab[1] women's faces, voices, images, words, and deeds have become thoroughly integrated into public life and space. In no field is this more apparent than entertainment.[1]

It might appear that female Muslim entertainers are merely a natural outcome of modernization and Westernization. Nevertheless, while modernization and Westernization certainly affect the region, they are insufficient to explain the specificity of women's experiences. And these experiences may help us understand the multidirectional operations of globalization and nuance facile references to social transformation. Women now boldly imprint their moods, their demeanor, sexy or respectable (and more often the former), and their messages on the public consciousness. A kind of schizophrenia emerges when digesting the latest statements from religious clerics concerned with public morality compared with these seemingly carefree and inviting female voices and images.

Certain women's voices clearly invoke intraregional influences; and a few have influenced "world music," or the latest popular music trends in Europe. Still, if we examine Arab women singers and their vocal contributions to the musical canon, we can't help but notice constant references to a value or aesthetic that Arabs call "authenticity." This quality or set of musical rules and expression has synthesized with Western genres from the 1920s to the most recent music videos, and it remains a dominant feature. For that reason, we can say that popular music expresses women's cultural identity. Further, a sharp eye will discern that this process is not being enacted upon women but that they are active agents in it. Women have shaped the modern Arabic music industry and its consumers almost to the same degree that the music industry has molded or influenced them.

The presence of Arab women in entertainment has had disparate and contradictory effects—it has both deconstructed the historic view of women and their sexual allure, and, conversely, reinforced it. Some scholars of Middle Eastern women's studies believe this to be a healthy sign: that women's talent, visual and emotional—and yes, even their sexual appeal—should be accepted, even expected, by most people today in the region.[2] In this respect, women serve as a counterweight to religious messages urging modesty and condemning deviance. The public listens with one ear to the popular preachers and with the other to women's strong voices singing of passion and romance. Apparently, this dichotomy is not exclusive to our contemporary era. Ibn al-Hajj gave examples of female impropriety in the streets of Mamluk Cairo to justify his calls for stricter observance of rules of modesty and decorum.[3] The struggle between religious elements determined to constrain women's behavior and prevent the mixing of the sexes, and indigenous traditions of carnivalesque festivity involving music and dance has gone on for centuries but has clearly intensified since the region's Islamic "awakening," or revival, which began in the 1970s. Now, with myriad Western images that associate women with sex appeal and power, the struggle over women's image, as well as their role in society, has intensified.

We see and hear women's impact on theater, music, dance, radio and television broadcasting, cinema, and video all over the Middle East. In the media, cinema, and theater, women's participation has sparked new perceptions of women through scripts built around female protagonists. Every so often, these fields provide necessary coverage of issues that affect women, such as when Nagla al-Emari, in her show *Kalam fi-l-Mamnu`a* (Talk about the Forbidden), on the BBC, dealt with female genital mutilation. Shows dealing with women's emancipation or restriction practices are not aired as often in other outlets for communicative counterculture. At present, Luna al-Shibl and her show *Lil-Nisa' Faqat* (For Women Only) on Al-Jazeera, may be the most influential host and "women's program," but they do not brave such topics. Television primarily illustrates the entry of women in the public sphere; it spends little time commenting about that process. On the other hand, Arab theater has taken up the issue of conflict between the sexes, in the plays of authors such as Yusuf Idris and Sa`dallah Wannus.

Music has expressed the full spectrum of gendered emotions, along with social commentary about relations between the sexes, be they harmonious or discordant. Direct allusions to women's status are not usually found in the field of music, and some impediments exist to any analysis of a "feminist impact" in this métier. This is so, first because the prejudices against the arts and women are both quite pronounced—hence women's being limited to merely appearing onstage earlier in the century—and elevation in a star system constituted and remains a challenge to the culturally conservative regional discourse. Second, the Arabic songs' ultraromantic lyrics, typically dealing with the suffering and inevitability of love, do not and are not intended to reframe relations between the sexes. They are reflective, not transformative. Unlike the Western singer Alanis Morissette, with her challenging and somewhat disturbing edginess, Arab women do not often push the envelope of gender distress and alienation with their songs.[4] Rather, the very presence of women singing openly about their emotion in itself attests to a universal discourse of passion, and one with which the public strongly identifies, no matter how young and innocent or old and jaded the listener.

Arab women, contrary to popular opinion, play musical instruments. Solo virtuosic instrumental performances, like those of artists such as the late Iraqi `ud (lute) player Munir Bashir, are a fairly recent phenomenon. Women did not typically perform as instrumentalists in early ensembles from the teens to the 1940s although many could play instruments and did so at private parties. The singer Asmahan and her mother, `Alia al-Atrash, played the `ud, and the singer Umm Kulthum could play the *qanun*. In fact, there was a special, smaller-sized instrument crafted for ladies, the `ud *hanim*. Most women were excluded from composition, an exception being Bahija Hafiz. Even today, women rarely play in the orchestras accompanying Arab singers or dancers because the performing environment and late hours are not thought to be suitable for women. They do hold chairs in national symphonies and national ensembles for Arabic music, and there are a number of women soloists, on the piano, violin, and `ud. However, in the Arab world, vocalists take pride of place and remain the most important women in the music industry. The traditional explanation for this preference was that Arabic culture is oral and that the beauty of the language expressed in metered lyrics is the best way to appreciate it. Even those who are fairly ignorant of musical aesthetics can enjoy the textual references in a song. But another explanation is possible. A vocalist projects her or his own personality and emotion in lyrical expression. The public is often able to sense a performer's identification with words more than with musical notes. Here, singers, like actors, are thought to express "real" emotions that they themselves experience. The public identifies with these emotions, either thinking of similar experiences or by understanding—through words—the reasons for sorrow, joy, or rapture. True, a musician must also transmit emotions; this capacity is called *tarab* (literally, both ecstasy [experienced] and enchantment [transmitted]). Not everyone is equally capable of discerning or responding to that *tarab*, but even those without any musical knowledge can relate to powerful lyrics.

As contemporary lyrics have become less poetically inspired, even banal, women singers—especially some of those mentioned below, such as Ruby or Diana Haddad—are nonetheless popular. This mystery can only be explained by the fact that they symbolize other qualities to their public—freedom, sexual allure, youth, or simply the value of seeing the world through an individual lens, a highly polished and esteemed one. Second, earlier generations of female performers established the concept of stardom; indeed, in the first half of the twentieth century, women singers attracted more attention than male singers, as their public performances were still somewhat of a novelty.

Women's actual contributions to vocal music have attracted far less attention than their social history through music.[5] We have been preoccupied with the sociological question of women's licit participation as performers and what that implies for women's images, or women in general.[6]

Female performers were well aware of the social stigma associated with musical performance. Rulers and members of the elite were expected to be musically literate and were often gifted musicians, composers, and singers. The social stigma was carried by entertainers who performed in public, not those who restricted themselves to home performances. Performers such as the male Syrian immigrant to Egypt Farid al-Atrash responded by emphasizing symbols of the professionalization of music—the concert hall, the tuxedoed musicians, the uniform bowing of string sections under a conductor (all contrary to the anarchic, improvisatory and emotionally interactive practices of the Arabic musical ensemble, the *takht*).[7] That stigma is no simple matter of religious aversion to music; women participate in many genres of religious music in the Muslim world.[8] Nor is it simply a matter of social class; today, many performers are college educated, whereas in the past, a wide array of proverbs referred to street musicians' lower-class connections (they might be gypsies) or lack of money.[9]

Nonetheless, past restrictions on women's movements and public appearance carried weight. State officials outlawed or censored public performances by women in the Ottoman lands; this had particular consequences in Anatolia, the Balkans, and in Egypt, among them the tradition of men appearing in women's stead, or dressed as women. During and after the years of the ban, the most sought-after artists sang in private homes segregated by gender. Sometimes, as in the nineteenth century, entertainers merely moved from one location to another—from Cairo, when they were banned, to upper Egypt and the northern Sudan.[10] In the latter half of the twentieth century, new patterns of entertainment tourism emerged, for instance, the Gulf Arab audiences who attend performances in Cairo, not least because women perform onstage.

With these social attitudes in mind, female singers and their audiences maintained certain fictions that, to some degree, rationalized their participation in the profession. Many performers claimed that they had entered the field of music out of financial need. Others claimed that they had always felt destined to sing, or their talents were recognized when they were children, and once their careers were set into motion, it made little sense to abandon this "trade" or "fortune."[11] Quite a few ran away or otherwise eluded disapproving families, and most dropped or changed their family name; Nuhad Haddad became Feiruz, Amal al-Atrash became Asmahan. Others emphasized their respectability by appearing onstage with a family member, or by generating public interest in their marriage, motherhood, charitable acts, and patriotism.

Today's singers reflect some of these themes in their biographies. Invariably they claim descent from musical families (often fathers) and see music as their destiny. Sana Suoissi, a Tunisian diva posts this biography on her website:

> Born in Bab Saadoun (Tunis) to an artistic family, she was influenced, from her earliest years, by her musician father (an `udist) who communicated his passion and innate rhythmical sense to her. This musical childhood caused her, early on, to discover the world of song. At just ten years old, she participated in concerts with such great singers as Adrien El Chaaouchi and Oulava. Little by little, as she grew up, her love for music was proven. At thirteen years old, she enrolled in the conservatory in Tunis. This academic approach was very useful and complemented her study of the `ud, which she pursued for two more years. . . . Music and song aren't just her passion, her talent . . . They are her life.[12]

In addition to these themes, the younger singers claim to represent earlier singers:

> Karima Skalli is the latest golden voice of the Moroccan stage. Nurtured since her childhood on the love of singing, at the age of nine, she sang a whole song by Oum Khaltoum (elsewhere detailed as Aghadan Alqâk) in front of her family. Karima Skalli grew up in this permanent immersion of the great voices of the Egyptian classical repertoire: Oum Khaltoum, of course, but also Souad Muhammad, Leïla Morad, Mohamed Abdelwahab and above all Asmahane. Gifted with a truly virtuoso voice in this classical register, which she perfectly mastered, Karima Skalli was soon surrounded by firstrate composers and poets. In the first place, the great Moroccan lutanist and composer Saïd Chaïbri, who discovered her so to speak, and the distinguished poet Abderrafie Jwahri.[13]

The Egyptian superstar Umm Kulthum began performing as a child. In her early concerts in Cairo, her male Bedouin Arab headgarb was simultaneously a gimmick and an acknowledgment of her family's need to protect her honor. She appeared with her own relatives in her chorus, but art won out over tradition when she replaced them with a professional musical ensemble in 1926 after reviewers complained of their "ugly voices roaring like . . . a camel."[14] The contemporary Arab world remembers Umm Kulthum in her later years, when she was matronly, with dark glasses, elegant and powerful but not threateningly sexy. Nevertheless, she had a series of romantic affairs that her various biographers and biographical media programs did not highlight.[15] One could argue that her longevity and her firm control over the industry, as the head of the musicians' syndicate, allowed her to transcend her earlier femme fatale image in a way that Asmahan, her rival in the late 1930s, who died in her youth, never could.[16]

Both singers were financially dependent upon their income from singing, but Umm Kulthum did not retire when she became a very wealthy woman. So, this plump, distinguished middle-aged woman proclaimed with every note she sang that it was respectable to be a singer, that one need not give up religion if one loved music, and further, that women did not need men to direct them professionally.

Asmahan at first appeared onstage as a soloist, with her brother Farid in her orchestra and her eldest brother Fu'ad as her chaperone at private parties. Her publicly honorable image was maintained by her marriage to a cousin, a Syrian Druze named Hasan al-Atrash, who was a political figure rather than an entertainer, and who twice interrupted her singing career. Behind the scenes, she made an *intifadha* against family supervision, moving into her own apartment in the fashionable Immobilia building in downtown Cairo, and drank, gambled, and partied like other women of her set—and more importantly, for our feminist analysis, like men.[17]

Asmahan occasionally struggled with the press and inherently sexist attitudes, as did other female entertainers. There were no female journalists. Male journalists showed their biases in their coverage of the stars. Her primary public relations voice, Muhammad al-Taba`i was in love with her but was quite concerned about propriety and her lack of it, although he found her bundle of emotional contradictions compellingly charming. The media began an ugly rumor of espionage, one that was repeated about other entertainers. Her purported love affairs were a favorite topic, as was the "unnatural" disposition of artists, who must, journalists felt, long for a normal domestic environment.

Some entertainers responded by emphasizing their respectability at all costs. Najah Salam sang with her husband, Muhammad Salman. Feiruz, the consummate Lebanese singer, performed for many years with the composition team of `Asi and Mansur Rahbani, her husband and his brother, and later on with her son, Ziad. Also, singers protective of their honor were concerned about appearing in public concerts or on film. Asmahan's appearance in her first film caused young Syrian Druze men to shoot at the screen, even though her brother was her costar. Twenty years later, an album jacket proclaimed about the young Feiruz, "She has refused to appear on the screen or on the stage in spite of the huge sums of money offered."[18] A similarly demure tone is taken in describing Samira Tawfiq: "Film producers are still asking her to be the leading lady in their films but she does not yet think the time is ripe for this."[19] Samira and Feiruz overcame this reluctance, but Feiruz, unlike many of her peers, did not emigrate to Cairo. Similarly, many contemporary singers are married and therefore expected to have children, although they are now less bound by the earlier discourse of honor.

Women who became famous in music have other commonalities: they were "discovered" or mentored by a successful musician or composer; they chose innovative, excellently composed, or very well-arranged compositions; and they competed fiercely with other performers. The most significant of these common factors for female singing stars is the second, and this rendering of top-quality compositions is a combination of taste, swift adaptation to new trends, successful networking and public relations, and audience appeal.

Relatively few women achieved stardom; the vast majority perform at weddings and private parties or in small clubs. The number of clubs, once counted in the hundreds, has greatly declined in Cairo due to Islamist pressures, and those remaining may no longer hire singers but make do with a disc jockey, a band, and one or more belly dancers.

Nevertheless, a certain echelon of women struggled with their families, society, and peers, and climbed the ladder of the entertainment industry. It is clear today that their efforts benefited younger contemporary performers. The star system had two layers, music and cinema. As in Hollywood, film producers realized substantial box-office returns if they featured musical celebrities. Certain singers were not exceedingly talented actresses; Umm

Kulthum, for instance was quite stiff onstage, and the usually historical plots of her films were equally graceless. Those who could effectively perform in both genres found that the distribution of films beyond the local audience enhanced their careers. Otherwise, the recording industry was essential to their success. The recording companies typically published small booklets with short blurbs about two or three featured performers, along with lyrics to their songs, to generate sales. Magazines and newspapers also offered entertainment gossip and promotion.

The creation of female stars and the publicity and gossip attached to them also had a mixed effect on the progress of women's image in the region. Such larger-than-life figures, belonged to their public, which felt entitled to comment on their private lives, their graciousness or *gaffes*, and their spending habits. The early stars filled a gap in the lives of other women, particularly those confined by marriage, who could vicariously identify with their adventures. They demonstrated a large degree of female agency, for they selected their own programs, costumes, and career directions. "Managers" did not play the same role as do Western entertainment agents today. These women hired and fired orchestras, engaged composers, and built their own patronage system.

Today, the top female singing stars possess this same degree of agency. Indeed, they are like CEOs. And they have a similar psychological attraction for their audiences, who have few role models. Young Arabs may dress just like their Western counterparts, but they encounter far more social pressure to marry than do American youth. Many are engaged or already married in college. The veneer or illusion of eternal freedom conveyed by the singing stars is as appealing to some young people as the allure of 1950s and 1960s vocal stars for their parents.

Virginia Danielson has stressed the fact that Umm Kulthum obtained legitimacy through her ability to sing in a neoclassical style.[20] But we should never forget that Umm Kulthum was a consummate innovator whose songs and musical settings featured *le dernier mot* (the latest trend), whether in the drama and power of her initial vocal phrases in "Faat al-Mi'ad," or in the darbukka and saxophone solos in the introduction to "Fakkaruni." Classical (meaning neoclassical) ability was also attributed to Asmahan, the Lebanese singer Nur al-Huda, despite or alongside her comedic talents, and Mary Gibran, who was, like Asmahan, an immigrant from Syria, and who could render the earlier, "classical" songs of `Abd al-Humuli and others associated with the origins of the modern Arab tradition.[21] These abilities were not enough in themselves. To appeal to a modern public, these women had to innovate.

From the 1950s on, people periodically complained that popular musical hits were solely "for dancing," reflecting a perceived difference between serious and frivolous music. Actually, this distinction was never rigidly enforced, but a parallel convention was broken when Souhair Zaki, one of the best-known belly dancers, incorporated an Umm Kulthum song into her nightclub routine. One also heard from conservatives and proponents of the "class war" or Arab socialism that stars and their audiences behaved or dressed in a frivolous way. This critique, along with the popularity of social realism in other artistic fields, and in tandem with the Arab tradition of politicized and panegyric verse and song, encouraged singers to take up political themes. For instance, a variety of singers, from Asmahan to Sabah to Feiruz, performed lyrics that invoked Arab unity or brotherhood. But in general, no women made this an exclusive trademark as the male Lebanese performer, Marcel Khliefa has done. One cannot imagine that this would have been commercially viable, since the public expected and enjoyed romantic lyrics.

Sabah and Feiruz had lengthy careers, though Sabah, a blond bombshell, was perennially criticized for her glamour, cosmetic surgeries and relationships. She was certainly not the only star to appear in films that were merely vehicles for musical performances.

In comparison, audiences idolized Feiruz, seeing in her, rightly or wrongly, a purer role model. Feiruz sang a number of political songs and recorded an album dedicated to Palestine, which is nearly forgotten today. She is instead most frequently associated with Lebanon, her homeland, to which she dedicated various popular and patriotic songs, although her career suffered from the lengthy civil war in that country.

Feiruz, like Asmahan, affected the musical field by actually altering the aural expectations of a female singer. Her great musicality and bell-like soprano voice had not been the aesthetic ideal and could not be replicated by all the other female singers. This is actually part of a long and complex process of changing audience aesthetic expectations that began with Umm Kulthum and others in her day and continues up to the present. Umm

Kulthum, with her powerful *fallaha* sound, provided a contrast with the Arabo-Turkic styling of her popular rivals such as Munira Mahdiyya. Umm Kulthum's innovations, in tandem with compositional changes and new orchestral arrangements, caused the early Arabo-Turkic repertoire and delivery to go out of vogue by the 1950s. Feiruz's composers first featured her in "folkloric" settings, which were highly innovative in their glorification of Lebanese characteristics of sound and popular culture. She also made popular a more modern ballad form, as in her song "Habbaytak bi Sayf," and can be heard singing an Arabo-pop-jazz style in her more recent recordings. This in no way detracted from her vocal command in such neoclassical formats as her Andalusiyyat album, and in her settings of medieval poetry such as "Hamil Hawwa Ta'ibu."

The singer Leila Murad, expanded her popularity via a series of five films directed by Togo Mizrahi. Although she was of Moroccan Jewish origin, Murad performed songs inspired by Egyptian folklore; she converted to Islam when she married Anwar Wagdi and starred in twenty-one more films that proclaimed her a modern woman beset with contemporary dilemmas. Her retirement at thirty-eight years old was probably hastened by the Suez War, after which minorities left Egypt and their properties were sequestered.

Many female singers migrated from other Arab states to Cairo as there simply was no other recording or performing scene of its size anywhere else. The wonderfully expressive singer Faiza Ahmad emigrated from Syria and never attempted repatriation. This meant that, in contrast with the contemporary male singer Sabah Fakhry who performs in the Aleppine vocal tradition and primarily in the Arab East, she recorded and performed primarily in an Egyptian style. Women singers have not typically resisted this Nile-centered hegemony and it continues, although some singers today spend more time performing in the Gulf and recording there.

Other performers are now in danger of being forgotten. There was the actress and singer Shadia, who was also noted for her sex appeal and who came close to marrying Farid al-Atrash. Farid just could not make up his mind to take the plunge, and when he finally did, Shadia had wed another man. Also, Su'ad Hosni, more actress than singer, recorded songs following her success as Zouzou, a cheerleader-like belly dancer/university student who gives up her "backwardness" (that is a dance) for her future in the film *Khalli Baalak Min Zouzou* (Pay Attention to Zouzou).[22] Actually, the embarrassing social status of Egypt's favorite dance form was unresolved, although dancing was clearly more objectionable than singing. Under the influence of socialist realism and the glorification of peasant culture, folkloric dance was created in the Middle East, and the first and most influential troupe, the Mahmoud Reda Ensemble, memorialized itself in a film called *Gharam fi Karnak* featuring the upper-class performer Farida Fahmy.[23] Hosni, on the other hand, was redeemable, as she was not a "real" dancer but merely an actress, performing in a demonically cute feminine style, which contemporary singer Natacha Atlas wickedly mimicked on her *Gedida* CD of 1999.

Since the 1970s, a lively interchange of Western and Eastern musical ideas has taken place and altered both the sound and the reception of many contemporary female singers. This new sound is referred to generically as *al-gadid*. While it properly dates back to the 1930s, its development in the last thirty years absolutely deserves additional serious scholarly study.[24] The rhythmic and danceable component of songs is paramount in *al-gadid*; the electronic keyboard and guitar have to some degree usurped the position of the classical instruments like the `ud, although the better singers retain a few traditional instrumentalists, who are featured in solos. Various thematic inspirations from Gulf music, upper Egypt, flamenco, rap, rock, and *rai* may be heard. Singing ensembles are not the norm; rather, solo performers and their ensembles predominate. Today's most popular singing stars perform *al-gadid*, and not a classical sound. There are many reasons for this shift, which has, in a way, made these singers more accessible to their public.

Umm Kulthum's dominance, as head of the music syndicate as well as diva, made it quite difficult for other female singers to rise to her stature, even after her death. And, although she was able to maintain her audience as she aged, many singers, like actresses, were expected to retire earlier than their male colleagues. Among those who might have risen higher but for these constraints, the truly talented singer Najat al-Saghira stands out. Called "al-saghira" the "young" or "small" to differentiate her from a different female singer Najat `Ali, Najat attracted fans after the release of her hit song "Irja` Ilayya" (Return to Me), based on the lyrics of Syrian poet Nazir al-Qabbani. Al-Qabbani, whose sister had committed suicide rather than enter an arranged marriage, wrote often about women and the political need to confront tyranny, sometimes using a woman's voice. The lyrics of Najat's "Irja'" are feminist in that the singer announces her own needs and desires, but simultaneously "unfeminist" in that they express a woman's need for a relationship. Najat added her own very emotional, even hypnotic rendition of certain lines in her concerts in the 1970s, leaning therefore toward inspired interpretation rather than slick polish.

The singer Sharifa Fadil blossomed briefly with her hit "Fallah Kaan Fayyit Biyghanni" (A Peasant Man Was Passing and Singing). She wielded more influence in the industry though her nightclub, al-Layl, than through her songs. Al-Layl became a hotspot, catered to large crowds of Gulf Arabs, and featured wildly popular performers such as the singer Ahmad al-'Adawiyya and the belly dancer Fifi Abduh. Another singer Warda al-Jaza-'iriyya, enjoyed quite a lengthy career, although she never acquired the label of "Umm Kulthum's successor" that some felt she deserved. Warda constantly updated and transformed her musical style, moving from "'Ayun al-Sud" (Black Eyes) a full-length song à la Kulthum, to songs incorporating musical themes of the Gulf countries and the shorter, but irresistible, "Ana 'Arfa, Kull Shi 'Annak" (I Know Everything About You), a nationally indeterminate song, equally a hit in Damascus, Amman, and Cairo. Warda, like the mid-century singers who made references to Arab nationalism and pride in their songs, establishes a sense of community for her listeners by bridging borders, sectarian boundaries, and class distinctions.

There are exceptions who specialize in classical or political genres such as the Palestinian musical ensemble Sabrin, which features the voice of Kamilia Jubran, who also plays the *qanun*.[25] Jubran is, however, very much a part of the ensemble, not a soloist. And while Sabrin's lyrics ignite their audiences, their musical style is somewhat eclectic, appealing neither to the young with their ear for *al-gadid*, nor to families nostalgic for the "classics." Whether one is referring to the West Bank or Gaza or to the territory inside the Green Line, one cannot speak of a Palestinian female singing star—a sad situation due to the lack of recording, film, and club venues, difficulties in travel, and other economic issues.

A similar exception, a large ensemble with male and female choruses from the village of Tarshiha, in Galilee, perform an older repertoire, illustrating the importance of their musical heritage and their ability to maintain it despite the years of Israeli authority. Nearly all the ensemble members have other professions, meaning that music is not their livelihood but, as in the past, a significant part of their life. This group would never have arisen without the efforts of a local music educator, the late Hikmat Shaheen, and sadly, elsewhere in the region such legacies are being lost.

Some music is preserved in exile—for instance, Farida `Ali, an Iraqi exile, performs Iraqi *maqam* with a Europe-based ensemble.[26] Other performers, such as Syrian Suzanne Haddad, sings both operatic and Arabic music, have crossed genres. Haddad possesses a clear, powerful contralto and plays well to the audience of the Sacred Music Festival, held in Fez, Morocco. This particular audience is, as Umm Kulthum once said, "in a Sufi state," receptive to music and styles that would not necessarily attract the "Arab street." None of the aforementioned modernist or neoclassical singers obtains the recognition or the name-power of the pop stars.

Alternative images of women singers more in tune with freedom fighters and martyrs than sex symbols are projected by the media. Palestinian television broadcast an old clip of an unidentified singer who sings the following lyrics while the camera presents updated images of a suicide bombing:

Shake the earth
Raise the stones
Allahu Akbar, Oh the young ones.
You will not be saved, oh Zionist . . .
I will willingly fall as a *shahid* [martyr].

In folk genres, women have tended to play a strong role in the initial and local performing scene. Arab women were famous for battle songs like the modern-day martyr's verse above, as well as lullabies, and wedding and mourning songs. As folk genres have been introduced to world music, an important contemporary means of broadening audiences, women singers' prominence has decreased. It is difficult to say why this is so: perhaps the traditional background of these female singers constricts their appeal, or perhaps the marketing strategy of Western companies focused first on men, as in the case of *rai* singers. In the early *rai* phenomenon in Algeria, Cheba Fadela initially appeared alongside Cheb Sahraoui and, like Rimitti, Zahwaniyya, Djiniya al-Kabira, and Habiba al-Kabira, was a "mother" of the genre. Yet these particular singers are known in Algeria but relatively

unknown in Europe or to other Western audiences, compared to Cheb
Khalid or Cheb Faudel.[27] As *rai* conveys both transgressive and traditional
discourses of lament and passion, women's roles are particularly interesting.
These women sing raunchy, if not bawdy, lyrics, as is actually quite common in other folk genres. The music, however, is a mixture of Algerian
vocal melodies and Mediterranean-influenced simple accordion and guitar
accompaniment—not "true" Arabic music. The phenomenon of women's
lesser fame is also evident in cases such as Umm Dalaila, of the Western
Sahara, among Moroccan singers, and in Saudi Arabia, where women's traditional singing is distinct from that of regionally known, commercially
popular male singers, such as Muhammad `Abduh. In the Gulf, women
singers perform at gender-segregated parties.[28] Their lack of influence
beyond local audiences increases the influence of pop singers from Egypt,
Lebanon, and Tunisia, particularly on the younger generation.

Few venues aim to educate Arab music audiences about other regional
talents and styles or try to bridge the neoclassical and pop genres as does the
Arab Music Festival and Conference to some degree. It is held annually in
Cairo. As with visual art, it seems, knowledge of local and Western artists
trumps knowledge of others in the region; so while a Turkish folkloric
group was invited to the festival, only a very small number of listeners in the
Arab world are familiar with, or are aficionados of Turkish or Iranian performers. Unfortunately, the festival's funding is insufficient to cover artists'
travel expenses or the hefty prices many performers demand. Many Egyptians have heard the Syrian singer Mayada al-Hinawi's recordings and hoped
that she would attend the festival, bridging national boundaries, and coun-
teracting a bombardment of Western music. But because of the festival's fiscal policy, the well-established Mayada canceled, as did her rival, another
Syrian singer, `Asala Nasri.

Women singers' jealousies and rivalries are a favorite theme of the
media, and have been for decades. This theme applies to other visible or
powerful female figures, and most probably expresses society's continuing
distrust of influential women. When Umm Kulthum's key composer and
accompanist, Muhammad al-Qasabji, featured Asmahan in a composition
instead of Umm Kulthum, a rivalry, real or invented, was born. Umm
Kulthum was rumored to have had a hand in Asmahan's death. Now that
new interview formats exist, contemporary stars' spats become known to a

larger audience. Mayada and `Asala's rivalry, mentioned above, went on for some time. After `Asala claimed in a public interview that Mayada was an "old woman" and was too outdated, their verbal warfare increased. Finally, they made up on television on Maestr, a show hosted by the Lebanese television personality Nishian. This provided a new gimmick for celebrity-oriented television, and a show on the Lebanese channel LBC featured call-ins from `Asala and Lebanese singer Nawal al-Zughby, also former rivals, to say they are now getting along. Eschewing competitiveness is an approved theme, but at the same time, the industry encourages that competition.

Instead of depending on live performances, which may be attended by only a select group, most regional fans now get to know their favorite entertainers through the media, for instance, through video clips. Stars like Diana Haddad impress their fans with their busy schedules, which are posted on the Internet as news items. For example, one brief announces that Diana visited Lebanon briefly to attend her younger sister's engagement party, then she was off to perform live in Kuwait and Algeria, and next she will somehow produce a new album in Egypt while also touring in the United States.[29] Now that stars are more active and mobile than ever before, their shopping sprees, marriages, engagements, breakups, salaries, and legal imbroglios are all considered news.

A slightly different objection to the younger singers' sexual allure is that they are importing the Western adoration of youthful beauty into an industry that had until fairly recently venerated its older performers. There is no question that Western stars who fail to whiten their teeth, submit to numerous cosmetic surgeries, and sport clothing perhaps inappropriate to their age or station in life lose in the battle for concerts and recording contracts. Singers were a little more immune to this image mania than actors in the pretelevision and video era when they were primarily heard and not so often seen.

Despite the buzz generated by new types of media, male and female Arab singers have not had a very large influence on Western music. Few Washington-based "Middle East experts" know anything about popular culture of the region; rather they dismiss it because it is politically insignificant. In fact, they would be hard-pressed to name the top three singers, soccer teams, or favorite dishes of their contacts in various Arab countries. The media, outside of PBS, virtually never broadcasts Arabic music, which is more often heard in France than in the United States. A few Arab singers participate in world music, or other forms of fusion. Singers in exile have taken the lead, so they occupy a very different type of niche than their regional counterparts. Singers perform at both ends of the spectrum— Arabic pop with many world elements, or world music, such as Sting's incorporation of a few Arabic elements that are nonetheless limited to his background singers, percussionist, and collaborating guest artists.

Natacha Atlas, half English and half Middle Eastern, is a versatile performer. Her 1999 CD *Gedida* includes wildly echoing *mawwawil* (vocal improvisation), various Arabic styles, as well as a stinging rap cut preceded by the grainy sounds of Arabic radio. From her ballad "La Rose" (in French), that earned her the Victoire de la Musique 2000 award, to her more recent rendition of James Brown's "It's a Man's World," Atlas offers the kind of edgy comment characterized above as unusual for female Arab singers. Others are exploring the possibilities of Arabic sound, as does the Canadian guitarist Jesse Cooke on one cut of his CD *Nomad*, for which Maryam Tollar and Roula Said sing the traditional lyrics to "Qadduka l-Mayas." This type of mixed-genre (flamenco-rumba, rock, folk, and Arabic) performance mediates and modifies the "Arab sound"; it is compelling with its driving percussion and strong female voices, but not threatening.

Back in the Arab world, genre, and subgenre matter. Singers with a "Western sound" attempt to bridge the gap by reissuing "oldies." Annoushka, the college-educated winner of the gold medal at the 1994 Francophone Song Festival for the song "Mon Amour," muses on the question of musical identity. She was frustrated by the Egyptian media's complaints that she is not an "Arabic singer" and should not attempt the "classics."[30] This older repertoire, heard frequently alongside newer compositions in various televised or staged musical competitions along the lines of *American Idol*, establishes nostalgia as a key mood for Arab music listeners but may also alienate younger audiences, who say, for instance, that they cannot understand their parents' worship of Umm Kulthum.

Television has become ubiquitous in the region, and the music and dance shows are consumed as family entertainment. Friends drop in and out, children sing along with the sexy stars and everyone awaits the scores. Saudi-owned MBC2 TV, a twenty-four-hour station as popular as al-Jazeera, runs music videos, American sitcoms, talk shows such as Oprah

Winfrey, and movies. Music tracks are also played o
feature on mobile telephones. In Iraq, al-Sharqiyy
ment gap, and while one critic calls music videos a
brain candy,"[31] Iraqis seem to take the show as evid
the Arab world and that a "normal" life includes l

Music videos have had a huge impact, but on a narrow
here singing stars and their directors and producers clearly take cues from
their Western counterparts. Top male performers, such as `Amr Diab are sur-
rounded by beautiful women (he is rumored to have been involved with the
actress Salma Hayek), and female soloists flanked by handsome men exude
sexual tension. Previously, singers at private parties used a vaudeville-like format, sandwiching special songs between segments of their previously recorded hits. These videos market each song or hit separately. Would-be stars
invest in their own audition videos gambling with all their savings in some
cases. They have been heralded as "manifestations of an Arab female culture
that is more affirmative and open to the West," one in which visual images
suggest a "more open and sexually promiscuous culture" which shows that
the culture is changing.[32]

The Internet plays a role in the careers of the new singers, and so such
current favorites as Nancy Agram (incidentally, the new face of Coca-Cola
at a reported $1.5 to $2 million fee), Haifa Wehbeh, Diana Haddad, and
Ruby post biographies and photographs along with links to fan-club chat
lines. The chat lines buzzed in late 2003 with the news of the grisly murder
of the Tunisian singer Zikra and two others at the hands of her businessman
husband who then committed suicide. Zikra left her homeland and, like the
male Iraqi superstar Kadhim al-Sahir, built her career in the Gulf, subsequently moving to Cairo. The fan chatter mostly personalized the matter to
the husband, describing him as "insane," rather than perceiving any problem with male control and abuse of women in a patriarchal society. What is
certain is that the memory of Zikra's presence onstage in her lifetime defies
her murderer's act in silencing her.

Criticism of contemporary singers' provocative appearances or onstage
behavior and lectures about their negative effect on Muslim "values" are constantly in the news. In an echo from the Arab socialist era, an Egyptian
Member of Parliament protested that Nancy Agram detracted from more
important matters, such as Iraq. Agram's supposed bad influence on youth

...ined an issue. Given the history of the region, and current and past ...s to confine women to women-only settings, it is significant that audi-...ces reject the message that moral damage is caused by their favorite singers, or that their frivolity is dangerous. Some complain that video clips normalize erotic messages that with all subtlety give way to the physical.[33]

Ruby stands in a long line of singers and dancers accused of being too suggestive in their performances. The powerful Egyptian music syndicate labels her performances pornographic and has refused to let her register. She attempted to register under another name and recorded outside of Egypt, in Dubai, to elude their strictures, so they are now suing her for recording and performing without membership.

On some level, this reflects the industry's concern with the Islamists' twenty-year campaign against female entertainers. Singers are not the only targets, and Islamists are not the only ones imposing restrictions. There were complaints when the Egyptian Minister of Information prevented the television series *Bint min Shubra* (A Girl from the Shubra District), starring Laila Elwi, from being aired on the grounds that it would affect the "religious and social harmony" that had existed. Video clips are now withdrawn with some regularity for being too risqué, and some performers encounter travel bans. Earlier, the public witnessed scores of dancers, singers, and actresses "reverting" to Islam and adopting modest dress, then the government, at least in Egypt, appeared to label this as extremism. Was it? Or wasn't it? Should female entertainers be allowed to feed the masses at Ramadan and go on *hajj*? Or should they do penance, branded with scarlet letters?

The public is of two minds—some parrot the idea that women should not show their bodies or sing; others find all of this moralizing tiresome. Islamist claims to represent the masses have merely taken up the previous claims of Arab socialists. It seems to me that these younger singers are often concerned by perceived limitations on their media images and by this current battle over Arab and Muslim culture. They are, however, more free from the heavy weight of social disapproval experienced by singers earlier in the century. For these younger stars, as in the West, any publicity, even negative publicity, usually boosts sales. There have been some uncomfortable brushes with Islamist authorities, as when Zikra was censured for saying that she had suffered as much in her life as the Prophet Muhammad. Her recording sales did not suffer.

The Islamist movement arose in the region in the 1970s, the boom years for the entertainment scene in Cairo. The civil war in Lebanon forced the closure of nightclubs there, and customers flocked to Egypt. One very negative outcome of the Islamist onslaught on entertainment has been the removal of live dancing from Egyptian television programming. While some artists "repented" and dutifully donned the *hijab*, most did not, if only because the vast majority are not superstars and rely on their performing income.[24] Today, popular Egyptian televangelist `Amr Khalid criticizes the entertainment industry more mildly than others do; he speaks, rather, of the inauthenticity of its artistic level and its replication of Western values:

> In our last episode, a young man suggested an idea to show how we lack innovation in art: he suggested that each of us write the lyrics of a song we like and then read them. You will laugh at the naivety of the words. You will find either useless, unlinked words, or vague words as the singer sang this song according to the composer's tips. A pretty lady would dance beside the singer to cover his bad voice. Where is the innovation? Where is the beauty of words? Is this not the state of our art now?[35]

Khalid supports the *hijab* for women, but not their "oppression." Women appeared on his show *Words from the Heart* from its opening clips, featuring a "reverted" star, Sohair al-Balbali now clad in *hijab* to its action-oriented, modern lesson format. Will young women identify with earnest do-good/feel-good religiously sanctioned messages? Or with the provocative singers?

Outside Egypt, the struggle between Islamists and entertainers varies by country. In Algeria, performers were actually murdered by Islamist extremists. In Lebanon, where many performers are non-Muslims, the mixed composition of society constrains Islamists to some degree. Among Palestinians, Islamists have also called for sobriety and containment of public festivities such as weddings since the al-Aqsa *intifadha*. This has not dampened the spirits or musical celebrations of many, but in the Negev, someone burned the home of some Bedouin musicians, after warning them to stop performing. Despite constraining certain individuals or groups in particular areas, the Islamists have failed to dampen the public's perennial love for music and dance. What fun is a *mulid* (celebrations in honor of holy men and women) without music or dance? What better way is there to mock the crowded ferry boat ride across the Nile, or a traffic jam, than to dance and sing?

Other attempted compromises made by Islamists and entertainers can be seen. For instance, some private Islamic schools include music in their daily program, primarily songs accompanied by piano and featuring "Islamic" lyrics. Certain popular restaurants no longer feature belly dancers but show instead the more covered-up "dervish" dance, the *khil* (in which dancers imitate horses, sometimes individually, but in one version under a cloth cover with one dancer each for the front and hind legs), or a belly dance performed by a fully covered dancer to the song of a fully covered singer. These compromises satisfy neither the preachers nor the members of the public who remember entertainment as it was before.

Entertainment has always played an important role during Ramadan. Actors and singers are featured in the Ramadan television special series. These series take up religious themes, and the performers appear in modest, usually historic dress. Some performers feel that the themes of the series are hackneyed and repetitive,[36] but these occasions show, as do the Sufi ceremonies that feature singing (in Egypt, these are male singers[37]) that musical or theatrical expression is not incompatible with religion.

Women entertainers, then, are poised to become a new symbol in the fight against Islamist extremism. According to some, they are more progressive than "political men," and since Islamists use the media quite well, the race is on with the entertainers.[38]

Arab women's ability to musically innovate and control their careers, their visibility, and the overtly feminine or sexualized aspect of their presence in public has ensured the continuity of their musical roles. Arab states that segregate their performers or audiences, as in the Gulf, are not immune to the singing stars, as their own new televison stations demonstrate.

Consequently, Arab entertainment news sites sympathetically present information about the oppression of women singers and women's music in Iran, such as that of the mysterious but popular singer known as DJ Maryam. One such site claimed women's struggle against Islamist oppression is directly linked to their music: "It is obvious that her existence, whoever she may be, and her growing popularity among young Iranians symbolize a yearning for change and reform in Iran," and the footer quote reads: DJ Maryam symbolizes the notion of freedom.[39]

While these Arab observers may make more of DJ Maryam's significance than she does, they are referring to seemingly endless public debate about "virtue," women, and song that is being waged in the Muslim world they are part of. Given the recent history of Arab women singers, the current divas may represent a certain degree of artifice along with that sexuality deemed so dangerous that we cannot even discuss it. One suspects, however, that silencing women's voices will produce nothing but pious hypocrisy and music behind closed doors.

Sherifa Zuhur is a distinguished visiting research professor of National Security Affairs at the Strategic Studies Institute (SSI), U.S. Army War College. Her research includes Islamic movements and insurgencies, modern Middle Eastern politics, war and peace in the Middle East, and social/cultural developments in the region. She has published seven books including *Revealing Reveiling: Islamic Gender Ideology in Contemporary Egypt* (1992), *Images of Enchantment: Visual and Performing Arts of the Middle East* (edited, 1998), *Asmaha's Secrets: Woman, War, and Song* (2000), and more than twenty-seven monographs, articles, and chapters in edited books. Her most recent book is *The Middle East: Politics, History, and Neonationalism* (Institute of Middle Eastern, Islamic, and Diasporic Studies, 2004). She coauthored *Islamic Rulings on Warfare*, an SSI monograph with Youssef El-Enein.

Notes

1. Since my expertise is in Arabic rather than Persian or Turkish musical forms, I am writing about Arab women who experience many of the same influences in the Muslim environment, including the insistence on sexual honor, be they Christian, Muslim, or Jewish. Arab identity is more of a musical unifier than Muslim identity since the musics of Iran, Turkey, South Asia, and Muslim Africa reflect local traditions and features.
2. Personal communications with Afsaneh Najmabadi on this point.

3. Huda Lutfi, "Manners and Customs of Fourteenth-Century Cairene Women: Female Anarchy versus Male Shar'i Order in Muslim Prescriptive Treatises," in Nikki R. Keddie and Beth Baron (eds.), *Women in Middle Eastern History: Shifting Boundaries in Sex and Gender* (New Haven: Yale University Press, 1991).

4. Robert Walser, "An Unfortunate Slight: Gender, Schizophrenia, and Alanis Morissette," paper presented at "Skip a Beat: Rewriting the Story of Popular Music," 2003 Pop Conference, April 11, 2003.

5. As in Virginia Danielson, *The Voice of Egypt Umm Kulthum, Arabic Song, and Egyptian Society in the Twentieth Century* (Cairo: American University in Cairo Press, 1997); Ni`mat Ahmad Fu'ad, *Umm Kulthum wa-`asr min al-fann* (Umm Kulthum and a Period of Art) (Cairo: al-Hay'a'h al-Misriya'h al-`Amma lil-Kitab, 1976); other sources in Arabic, and see Sarah Graham-Brown, *Images of Women: The Portrayal of Women in Photography of the Middle East 1860–1950*, (New York: Columbia University Press, 1988) for an example of women in the public eye.

6. Karin van Nieuwkerk, *A Trade Like Any Other: Female Singers and Dancers in Egypt* (Austin: University of Texas Press, 1995). Naturally, the status of the musician in society is of interest, and in this study, singers are secondary to dancers.

7. Sherifa Zuhur, "Building a Man on-Stage: Masculinity, Romance, and Performance according to Farid al-Atrash," *Men and Masculinities*, no. 3 (2003), pp. 275–293.

8. Jihad Racy, "Musical Attitudes and Spoken Language in pre-Civil War Beirut," in Sherifa Zuhur, ed. *Colors of Enchantment: Theater, Dance, Music, and the Visual Arts of the Middle East* (Cairo and New York: American University in Cairo Press, 2001).

9. Ibid.

10. Well described in Antonia Fraser, "Not Chaste but by No Means Common: Female Dancers and Singers in Egypt, 1790–1870," unpublished book manuscript.

11. Sherifa Zuhur, *Asmahan's Secrets: Woman, War, and Song* (Austin: Texas Center for Middle Eastern Studies; University of Texas Press, 2000), p. 45.

12. http://www.sanasouissi.com (accessed December 27, 2004).

13. http://www.fezfestival or see Rabah Mezouane, "Karima Skalli rend homage à Asmahane à l'IMA," ad copy http://www.marrakesh.com (translated by S. Zuhur).

14. Editor of *al-Masrah*, cited in Virginia Danielson, *Voice of Egypt: Umm Kulthum, Arabic Song, and Egyptian Society in the Twentieth Century* (Cairo: American University in Cairo Press, 1997), p. 60.

15. Personal interviews with the late `Adil Sabit, Cairo, 1993 and 1996.

16. Zuhur, *Asmahan's Secrets*.

17. Ibid.

18. *Ghanni ma`a al-nujum, Parlophone*/EMI/LPVDX 104, 1967.

19. Ibid.

20. Danielson, *Voice of Egypt*.

21. Samim al-Sharif, *Al-Musiqa fi Suriyyah: A`lam wa-tarikh* (Music in Syria: Stars and History) (Damascus: Wizarat al-Thaqafa, fi al-Jumhiriyah al-'Arabiyyah al-

Suriyyah, 1997), pp. 178–181; Said Okasa, "The Lady and the Leader: When it Comes to the History of Revolution, Don't Believe Everything You See on TV," *Al-Ahram Weekly*, Vol. 3 Issue 27, 2000), p. 3–9.

22. Walter Armbrust, *Mass Culture and Modernism in Egypt* (Cambridge: Cambridge University Press, 1996), pp. 117–123.

23. Marjorie A. Franken, *Daughter of Egypt: Farida Fahmy and the Reda Troupe* (Glendale, CA: Vassiliansdepot.com/Armenian Reference Books Company, 2001), p. 61.

24. Salwa El-Shawan Castelo-Branco, "Performance of Arab Music in Twentieth-Century Egypt: Reconciling Authenticity and Contemporaneity," In Virginia Danielson, Scott Marcus, and Dwight Reynolds (ccord. eds.), *The Garland Encyclopedia of World Music*, vol. 6, (New York: Garland, 2002), pp. 557–561. Ethnomusicology has incorporated anthropology's totalizing emphasis on authenticity versus modernity and the need for cultural preservation. It is more common to find studies of rural, folk, and supposedly "classical" traditions, than studies of urban, popular forms.

25. Joseph Massad, "Liberating Songs: Palestine Put to Music," *Journal of Palestine Studies*, Issue 227 (Spring 2003), accessed at http://palestine-studies.org/data .abstract-5585.html.

26. About this genre, and for a few examples of female performers of *maqam* and other Iraqi song forms see Neil van der Linden, "The Classical Iraqi *Maqam* and Its Survival," In Zuhur, *Colors of Enchantment*.

27. Marie Virolle, "Representations and Female Roles in the Rai Song," Tullia Magrini (ed.), *In Music and Gender: Perspectives from the Mediterranean* (Chicago: University of Chicago Press, 2003). Also see Marie Virolle-Souibès, *La chanson rai: De l'Algérie profonde à la scène internationale* (Paris: Karthala, 1995).

28. Kay Hardy Campbell, "Folk Music and Dance in the Arabian Gulf and Saudi Arabia," in Sherifa Zuhur, *Images of Enchantment: Visual and Performing Arts of the Middle East* (Cairo: American University in Cairo Press, 1998), and *Samra: Songs from Saudi Arabia*, original audiorecordings by Kay Hardy Campbell.

29. http://www.albawaba.com.

30. Richard Woffenden. "Resume: Pop Star Anoushka Is Participating," *al-Ahram Weekly*, Vol. 7, Issue 38, 4–10 December 4–10, 2003.

31. Bourzou Daragahi, "From Soap Operas to Bottle-Blonde Newscasters to Music Videos, Al-Sharqiya brings Iraqis Entertainment TV," *Daily Star*, July 27, 2004.

32. Jihad N. Fakhreddine, "Between Veils and Videos, Change and Arab Women," *Daily Star*, September 9, 2004; http://www.dailystar.com.

33. Abdel-Wahab M. Elmessiri, "Ruby and the Chequered Heart," *Al-Ahram Weekly* Iss. 734, 17–23 (2005), http://weekly.ahram.org.eg/print/2005/734/feature.htm.

34. For a discussion of this issue, see Karin van Niuewkerk, "On Religion, Gender, and Performing: Female Performers and Repentance in Egypt." In Magrini (ed.) *Music and Gender: Perspectives from the Mediterranean* (Chicago: University of Chicago Press, 2003), and Lila Abu-Lughod, "Movie Stars and Islamic Moralism in Egypt,"

Social Text 42 (1995), pp. 53–67.

35. http://www.amrkhaled.net.

36. Sarah Gauche, "Prime-Time Ramadan," *Aramco World* 54, no. 6 (2003).

37. Michael Frishkopf, "Tarab ('Enchantment') in the Mystic Sufi Chant of Egypt," in Zuhur (ed.) *Colors of Enchantment.*

38. Fakhredinne, "Between Veils and Videos."

39. "Iran's Forbidden Voice," *al-Bawaba*, November 24, 2004.

Wings of Freedom: Iranian Women, Identity, and Cyberspace

Fereshteh Nouraie-Simone

The dream of a new identity begins with new forms of expression.
—*Marie-Laure Ryan*

For several years I have been paying a heavy price for being myself. Every step I take, every word I utter, and every breath I inhale, makes me more aware of the "I" and how much I want to keep this "I" as independent and free as possible. This is my choice to be an individual and not an object of submission to traditional views or unjust social laws. I could have taken the sweets my suitor offered and smiled, I could have kept myself pretty and attractive to please men like an object of desire, I could have tolerated all the rotten patriarchal ideas and considered them part of the blind love that turns into a confined golden cage and cuts down the wings of freedom. Instead, I bit the hand pushing honey down my throat, because it was choking me, this hand full of honey.[1]

This is from Golnaz, a twenty-two-year-old woman living in Tehran.

For educated young Iranian women, cyberspace is a liberating territory of one's own—a place to resist a traditionally imposed subordinate identity while providing a break from pervasive Islamic restrictions in public physical space. The virtual nature of the Internet—the structure of interconnection in cyberspace that draws participants into ongoing discourses on issues of feminism, patriarchy, and gender politics, and the textual process of self-expression without the prohibition or limitation of physical space—offers new possibilities for women's agency and empowerment. The absence of the physical body in electronic space and the anonymity this offers have a liberating effect on repressed social identity, as "electronic technology" becomes "a tool for the design of freely chosen identities."[2]

The popularity of weblogs (frequently updated online journals), or blogs, among Iranian youth in recent years is a radical phenomenon. Young women, many in their twenties, have embraced the new technology with enthusiasm. They write freely and intimately about a disparate range of topics, from diary entries to discussions of feminism and gender politics. Iranian female bloggers share personal experiences, discuss issues, express feelings of outrage and frustration, and reflect on what is not allowed or tolerated in controlled Islamic physical space. They have claimed cyberspace for their expressions of individuality and desire for freedom.

> I want an embrace that would take me to a place where there are no questions and answers, no talk of the first time, when, and where. I want a lover's embrace, a warm tangible embrace to hold me tight with lips that kiss, to close my eyes and let go, to be completely free in an unadulterated moment that will never repeat itself. I want warmth that dispels the darkness of that apartment on the sixth floor and makes it vanish. I want an embrace that would make my soul dance, whirling around like dervishes, to free it, to empty it, to give it peace. I want moments that can not be repeated, a kind of drunkenness with the familiar drowsiness after lovemaking. An embrace that dissolves me in itself.[3]

In a controlled society under theocratic rule, self-expression is a rare privilege. Cyberspace provides a public social space that allows free expression of self outside the confines of the politically manipulated physical space. Here a young, independent woman can have mastery over her environment and can assert her agency—with a voice that, with some exceptions, has rarely been heard before. For the generation of Iranians born after the revolution of 1979, and particularly for women, the Internet provides an unfettered, direct connection to the outside world, opening a new horizon for dialogue, self-expression, and dissident voices. The Internet is a medium of empowerment that bypasses traditionally imposed gender identity, and roles and images of subordination. Scott Bukatman sees electronic identity, which he calls "terminal identity," as a radical threat to a traditional concept of fixed identity. He says, "we find both the end of the subject and a new subjectivity constructed at the computer station."[4] This "terminal identity" is complementary to Sherry Turkle's sense of the emergence of a new concept of identity, self-presentation, and the changing notion of self-hood, she redefines "identity as multiplicity."[5]

More important when considering the effect of access to cyberspace is the liberating potential of online representation through text for uncensored articulation of repressed or forbidden subjects. No tale is unworthy of nar-ration, and no other medium can carry the stories of everyday life as easily, quickly, and widely as the blogs. Furthermore, cyberspace provides a new extended, safe public space for the active agency of the narrator, as well as a created identity. The dissemination of delight, frustration, and inspiration can then be read in many places at once with the click of a mouse. Identity, audience, and content—suddenly fluid—pour into an expanded public space, both virtual and vital.

Barbara Page writes:

The conscious feminism of the writer animates her determination not simply to write but *to intervene* in the structure of discourse, *to interrupt* reiterations of what has been written, *to redirect* the streams of narrative and *to clear space* for the construction of new textual forms congenial to women's subjectivity."[6]

Parastoo, one young journalist-blogger, echoes her:

The Internet is a new space for us that provides new sphere of pos-sibilities. Space and possibility to obtain what is missing in public space: connection and communication. To build up a connection with physically removed persons without knowing their outward personal or social identity. To create text and context without knowing the readers.[7]

The proliferation of blogs in Farsi since 2001 is the direct result of the work of Hossein Derakhshan, a young Iranian tech-journalist living in Canada, who introduced a user-friendly "How-to Blog" manual in Persian and made it freely available online. Shortly after that, a twenty-four-year-old educated Iranian woman started her first blog with the online identity *Khorshidkhanoom* (Lady Sun) in November 2001. Her blog began: "For the voice of women to be heard and to write about whatever comes to mind, of things I like or dislike."[8]

Her blog soon became one of the most popular, measured by an increased number of hits and links to other blogs. Soon many young, educated women started their own blogs, greatly increasing the Iranian blog community—known as Weblogestan.

> It is a very good feeling to know one is not alone in this new world of wires, chips, keyboards and numbers. So, I am happy to be an electronic Lady Sun. We are like scattered bits and pieces coming together in cyberspace to make a whole complete picture to show the world our true selves. These weblogs are the real mirror representing us and Iranian society. The more participants there are, the more mirrors there are to reflect our situation . . . this space is our sanctuary. Cyberspace is the place of our becoming. In every single blog there is part of Iran. Cyberspace is our social space of freedom. Here is a free city, where we can express ourselves freely, and we can write whatever we like.[9]

Women bloggers are young professionals: university students, journalists, NGO activists, and literary and social critics—mostly residing in Tehran, where technical resources are most likely to be easily available. Women use the Internet as individuals for personal use in chat rooms and for e-mail; as journalists, writers, website designers and graphic artists for professional resources, and as a wide cross section of bloggers who, through journal writing, daily updates, and intimate self-expression, articulate their own values forcefully—discussing feminism and social equality—free to reveal their inner feelings and ideas.

> I have not been born as a subordinate sex, or as biologically inferior. I have been brought up as one with allocation of roles and expectations. I am a product of cultural biases of a patriarchal order that talks about an inherently womanly nature, so that when a girl

climbs trees or jumps up and down, she is warned or bullied—told that a girl is not supposed to jump from heights—to safeguard a little piece of skin (hymen) as proof of her honor. At 16, I wanted to become a guerilla fighter, instead I became a woman warrior fighting with my pen—a powerful instrument that can not be silenced.[10]

With seventy million inhabitants and two-thirds of the population under thirty years of age, Iran has a vibrant, youth-oriented society that seeks to make a connection to the outside world through the Internet and the rapidly growing blogosphere. The popularity of weblogs with Iranian youth cannot be overestimated. More than sixty-five thousand different blogs in Farsi allow young Iranians to write, interact, and voice opinions on everything from politics to daily activities, while making Farsi the fourth most popular language on the Internet after English, French, and Portuguese.[11] An estimated four to seven million Iranians use the Internet, and although the number of Internet users, even at the highest estimate, is small relative to the total population of Iran, the Internet attracts the brightest and best-educated young people, offering them immediate access to an authentic voice, an independent forum for opinions and a swift exchange of information.[12] Since 2000, the Internet has grown more rapidly in Iran than in any other Middle Eastern country, creating a new communication environment for independent news and political discussions based on an invaluable medium.[13] In the absence of a vibrant public space or "street corner" of an agora, cyberspace offers a viable alternative to the silenced public forum.[14]

Such intense use of the new technology of the Internet, with its proliferation of blogs and electronic journals—some of which substitute for banned reformist newspapers—has alarmed the authorities and has posed another challenge to the regime. So far, government efforts to block weblogs or servers have not been very successful. However, the government has started a campaign of intimidation, including the arrests of some bloggers and online journalists on unsubstantiated charges of "undermining national security through cultural activity."[15]

Fereshteh Ghazi, a young online journalist, was arrested in fall 2004. Held for over forty days in solitary confinement, she later wrote in her blog, "Our first sin was to open the window, the other to destroy the wall." To which another blogger, Hanif, who had also been subjected to intimidation and arrest, added his voice: "One other sin is our youth, because we do not accept at face value every nonsensical, irrational word."[16]

After Ghazi's release from prison, she posted this message on her weblog:

> It is exactly forty days since my release from that damning hell, but I have not been able to overcome the horrible nightmarish hell of solitary confinement, feeling brutally naked and losing all sense of values one keeps dear. It is in those frightening moments of the dark cell in the mysterious silence that one hears the inner voice of God that gives one strength to go on, to realize the power of the pen, to see the pointless interrogations, insults, injuries, threats, beatings and all that as trivial—and to become more determined not to be silenced. To write and write: in newspapers, on the weblogs, on sites, on doors, on walls and on any space one can find—no matter how difficult the situation.[17]

The paradoxical juxtaposition of mass education with prohibited public space, enforced regulations, and new autonomous communication media has triggered a proliferation of weblogs and online journals, making the Internet a new medium of accessibility for discourse, opportunity for dialogue, and possibility for transgressing borders without crossing them.

The revolution of 1979, which was based on popular support, led to the theocracy of modern Iran and profoundly altered Iranian society. It dismantled the historical institution of monarchy and reshaped the relationship of state and society into a complex political system. The concept of popular sovereignty paralleled the concept of clerical leadership, legalizing enforced policies of Islamic restrictions, most notably those regarding gender segregation. At the same time, rapid population growth until the mid-1980s doubled the country's population. The policy of general access to education initiated by the Islamic regime radically increased the number of educated young Iranians by allowing large numbers of young men and women from traditional families to obtain a higher education. Political activism, mass education, and rapid urbanization resulted in a politically aware, socially active, and technically savvy generation that has found its voice in the blogosphere.

Women are a primary source of this exciting dynamic energy. They are visible everywhere—in cyberspace and, despite restrictions, increasingly in public spaces: on the streets, in shops, restaurants, concert halls, and movie theaters, in the workplace, and at universities—segregated but not limited. These are educated, committed women: activists, intellectuals, journalists, writers, filmmakers, television camerawomen, teachers, lawyers, nurses, doctors, workers, and now—bloggers.

The daily, active presence of women in various committees, neighborhood mosques, and Islamic associations of different governmental and semi-governmental agencies or foundations has increased traditional women's public participation and visibility in the workplace, but at the same time, it has revealed the limitation of their civil rights. Female activists, both religious and secular, are questioning male-dominated interpretations of religious texts, demanding legal rights and social equality.

It is an ongoing paradox that the Islamic regime encourages the education of women and public participation but limits women's legal rights—a confusing message that women are liberated but legally inferior. A young woman in Iran, where daily life is regulated by tradition and ideology, will find herself segregated but not prohibited from public activity; educated but legally subordinated; finally prepared to pursue a career but expected to submit to traditional gender roles. Islamic public policy includes rules and regulations regarding dress codes and morality codes, an arbitrary polarization of right and wrong that has led to an identity crisis in the young generation.

It is one year since I started my weblog and I wonder have I been truthful to myself. Have I dared to reveal my inner thoughts in cyberspace outside the confinement of the shaped identity, to take off the mask that has silently registered centuries of male assault and denigration? What is the use of these writings if not to defend the rights of women, to cry out? To shout about the violation of the most essential rights of human beings and how those rights have been auctioned off arbitrarily for a black veil, a dress, a bottle of hair color, or a crystal vase.[18]

Young women are stifled in a system that controls the definitions of faith, morality, and truth. By connecting local conditions to global forces, these women are ready to challenge the validity and universality of religious decisions that limit individual rights and civil liberties—questioning the very integrity and legitimacy of those in power.

> The weblogs can differ in style, content, patterns and text, but they all cry out the same thing: we are tired of all this monkey-business—enough of hypocrisy, deceit! You have made a mockery of everything. Iranians are not stupid; we know and do not want guardians or wardens. The more there are of us bloggers, the more they have to hear us say: this generation will not be fooled. We are not stupid, we can think, we can write, and we know the harm being done to our society. They should be accountable.[19]

Clearly this generation is not afraid of questioning authority, including parental authority, and women are especially concerned about a future without hope or freedom to choose. A 2003 survey of young Iranian women commissioned by Center for Promoting Women's Participation of the President's Office, revealed that the primary concern of women was unemployment and the lack of job opportunity. Secondary concerns reported were the absence of security, the lack of recreational facilities, and their inability to compete in sports. The astonishing finding was that marriage ranked the lowest as a priority or preference to advance women's social position—only 7 percent ranked marriage as a path to improvement of their social lives. The questionnaire was sent nationwide—to 120,000 women—ages fifteen to sixty, in ten urban and rural clusters. It polled individuals about the needs, priorities, and preferences of Iranian women as a whole. The results, categorized by age, education, income, marital status, and place of residence, showed that the highest number of responses (23 percent) came from participants ages twenty to twenty-four. The young female population was most worried about low income (34 percent), economic problems (18 percent), sociocultural problems (11 percent), and job insecurity (9 percent).[20]

Economic concerns and identity issues for women became even more complex as female enrollment in educational institutions increased significantly at all levels. More than 63 percent of new university students are women. More than 61 percent of medical students are women. Health ministry officials were so alarmed by this that they recommended a gender quota system to mandate a 50 percent ratio of men to women, in order to "balance" enrollment.

Despite educational advances, women still lack job opportunities. Economic crises due to decades of fiscal mismanagement, corruption, flight of capital, and eight long years of war and destruction severely reduced the economic base for these newly graduating students. Although women's advances are offset by threats, paradoxes, and complications, women continue to confront the government, pressuring the Islamic regime to relax on social control. The invasion of the Internet by the Iranian youth could not have come at a more vital moment for women in Iran.

> Sitting in front of the window, with wind blowing from behind to carry me from place to place—from here to there, from there to here—in a safe place to put down my load, I am free to realize my worth: to love, to hope, to recognize my capacity for resistance and to continue the struggle.[21]

Lack of privacy in public space and constant surveillance to ensure correct moral behavior foster an atmosphere of fear and paranoia, reinforcing the need to create separate public and private existences. As they grew up surrounded by theocratic rules and regulations defining legal, moral, and proper behavior, young people had to find ways around these restrictions in the public sphere.

Intimidation by regulation of the public space is intimately tied to social control of identity. Women's mobility in terms of identity and "their place" in the public space are closely connected.[22] Oppressive restriction of women's dress, behavior, movement, and speech has made the female body an object of male obsession in Iran. Public spaces are an arena for suggestive remarks and jokes at the expense of female *clothed* body. As one blogger wryly writes in "memoirs of a crowded city":

> My body topography is a source of arousing the repressed, neurotic, deprived male sexual instinct. It is fascinating to observe how this veiled clothed body, wrapped in yards and yards of fabric in a loose undefined shape, becomes the source of attraction to the

deprived male desire and the target of so many prurient remarks. In the crowded city, my big nose and big breasts are subject of demeaning remarks. At Revolution Square, it is my hips they like; further downtown in Darvazeh Dowlat, the talk is about my chassis; at Vanak square, the favorite target is my breasts, and for the truck drivers of Ekbatan, the object of obsession is my vagina, calling it out loud by name as they pass by. So I learned to deal with the verbal assaults by spending half my salary reserving the front seat of taxis for a little ride to work in peace.[23]

Women's experience with social limitations is shaped by their experience of public space in relation to the power in which the repressed social attitude and belief system are embedded. "Moreover, in certain cultural quarters, the mobility of women does indeed seem to pose a threat to a settled patriarchal order."[24] The obsession with the woman's body, dress, and woman's social interaction is part of an endless discourse on gender that has turned into a metaphor for sexual domination and exclusion.

As the capital and the center of political activity, Tehran exemplifies all of the physical and social constraints. It is a crowded, chaotic city with an atmosphere of depressed stagnation. Most of the streets are named after martyrs. The cult of martyrdom is embedded in public images displayed in the city's murals and in Zahra's Paradise—a vast cemetery in south Tehran—with rows and rows of gravestones marked by photographs of young men, the casualties of the Iran-Iraq war. In the past two decades, Tehran has undergone a radical transformation, stretching horizontally and growing into a huge metropolis without a center, a rambling, fragmented sprawl, haphazardly assembled. Highways crisscross each other, filled with noisy, chaotic, restless traffic.

The once familiar world of walled gardens, old trees, and shaded lanes has disappeared. The trees that lined the streets and filled family compounds are gone. Gardens that once absorbed the polluted air and helped the city breathe are missing. Hidden under smog is snow-capped Mount Damavand, where the legendary Iranian hero Rostam was victorious over demons and the tyrant leader Zahak was left to die. Literally and symbolically, the Alborz mountain range, a reminder of Iran's heroic past, is no longer visible. But it is not the images long submerged in memory that define a city; rather, the city is a construct of "social relations, meeting and weaving together," shaped by its political character and local culture.[25]

When the younger generation became old enough to assert its identity, the politics and social spaces of the city had undergone dramatic changes. Hundreds of new mosques, slogan-covered walls, and billboards displaying images of martyrs and leading clerics define the character of Tehran—its identity and social structure transformed into an Islamic landscape. The replacement of secular authority by the Islamic ideology changed the face of the city. Lines of social division in pre-revolutionary Iran were distinct, and "spatial differentiation" was determined by wealth—the rich in the Westernized north and the poor relegated to the traditional south.[26] After the revolution, with the breakdown of social barriers, some inhabitants of south Tehran who were affiliated with the new authority moved uptown to confiscated homes and villas, effectively reshaping the neighborhood, social divisions, and public space.

The cultural policy of the Islamic regime was committed to creating an Islamic identity by deliberately reshaping space in public places through enforcement of a strict Islamic dress code: veiling of women in public, specific rules about interaction between men and women, and monitoring of proper moral conduct, directed mostly at women. As public space became the domain of state ideology, Tehran's large squares on occasion turned into controlled, enclosed spaces for religious and political activities. The space that was once the Tehran University tennis courts (1960s) was transformed into a Friday prayer site (1980s), where clerical leaders roused crowds with emotionally charged political speeches. The identity of the place and the space itself were transformed to symbolize an Islamic landscape.

Restructuring the identity of both space and its inhabitants to fit into an Islamic theocracy had a number of important implications for men and women. First, the government's control of spatial mobility established numerous boundaries separating men and women in public places, such as separate entrances to public buildings, separate space in the backs of buses for women although they share taxis with men, and separate sections in university classes, public theaters, mosques, prayer halls, and other public gathering places.

Second, the visual became a space controlled and at the same time selectively hidden from sight. Imposition of the veil and a strict Islamic dress code, with detailed instructions on the color of the veil (black), and the thickness of the fabric, the requirement of a long, loose overcoat (*roopoosh* or *manteau*), thick stockings, and flat shoes, and a prohibition of makeup, made the female body a site of state ideology. Even though these restrictions were later modified to allow colorful headscarves, shorter and tighter *manteaus*, high heels and makeup, state control remains a tool of arbitrary intimidation and harassment.

Third, the state began policing the "spatial separation" between unrelated men and women and regulating public space with strict gender-marked boundaries.[27] Held captive by state ideology, public space was transformed from a scene of active diversity to a regulated uniformity of veiled women and bearded men. The rapid disappearance of privacy and the right to anonymity in public space—where people had been able to interact without being monitored or harassed—caused a retreat to private space; people saw home as a refuge from the watchful eyes of disciplinary control. Foucault's concept of disciplinary power and the ways public places (such as prisons) are designed to allow public scrutiny captures the relationship between visibility, power, subjectivity, and discipline, explaining how people internalize social discipline as a result of fear brought on by constant surveillance.[28]

Gendered boundaries, controlled space, and bodies clothed in Islamic dress become instruments through which the Islamic regime keeps its hold on the society and regulates people's behavior. Paradoxically, the young men and women who have never experienced anything but disciplinary Islamic rules are more rebellious than the older generation. They find their own space, through a variety of transgressions, as a way of resistance. Improvisations such as car cruising, exchange of telephone numbers in the middle of a traffic jam, and meetings in religious gatherings, coffee shops, and Internet chat rooms allow them to make their way around restrictions of the social sphere. "The limitation of women's mobility in terms both of identity and space" and the assigned "woman's place" are crucial means of subordination.[29] A blogger who calls herself Goddess addresses her frustration at not being seen and asked:

> Our main problem in the work place has to do with male hegemony and cultural attitudes towards gender. I have a better education than some of my male coworkers and have no problem staying late for

long meetings or traveling alone for my work. I have an understanding husband whom I personally chose, but I am told "your problem
is that you are a woman." What is this fear of women, the archaic
belief in male superiority, these restricted laws and regulations, to
limit our social mobility and to take away our human identity?[30]

The generation that brought about the revolution of 1979 was a cohort
of idealists who committed their lives to the cause of revolution without
reservation. They fought the old regime for social justice and political freedom and were ready to sacrifice everything, including their lives, to achieve
their goals. This youthful idealism carried into the war with Iraq in 1980s.
A great mobilization of the population inspired hundreds of thousands of
young volunteers to sacrifice their lives for God and country. Motivated by
revolutionary slogans, chants, and war songs, they kept the flame of martyrdom ablaze.

But now the children of the revolution do not have any cause for idealism or a zeal for sacrifice. Many young people think the war was fought in
vain and feel betrayed by unfulfilled promises of the reform period of
Khatami's presidency (1997–2005). Angry and disillusioned, they mistrust
all authority, including parental authority, becoming skillful in the art of
survival and in subverting the controlled public space. They want individual
freedom, job security, and less intrusive political space, but they have no
desire for another revolution. As Nooshin Ahmadi Khorasani, a journalist
and founder of the Women's Cultural Center posted on her website :

The children of the revolution, who grew up in the period of so-
called "reconstruction" (after the Iran-Iraq war), have no interest in
a utopia or inclination toward the idealism of the past decades. In
contrast to the revolutionary generation, which was willing to sacrifice everything for an ideal or go to prison for a political flyer, they
are realists, opening their public spheres and expanding their social
horizons and possibilities in pragmatic ways to achieve their goals.
More than idealistic, they are angry. They are enraged by an uncertain future, by daily pressure and harassment, by thousands of
obstacles blocking their way. The young boys and girls who mock
authority with their heavy make-up, inappropriate clothes and

behavior in Ashoura carnivals (the ritual processions and mourning ceremonies for the martyrdom of Hossein, grandson of the Prophet) are far removed from past idealism. The same young people who have learned to maneuver their ways through the streets of Tehran, deal with the forces of oppression, through bribery or whatever else, can easily without any conviction repeat an empty slogan to get out of trouble. In truth, they don't think they are doing anything wrong because they feel, rightfully, that they are trapped in inhumane and unfair circumstances which they had no role in creating. Since childhood they have been taught both by figures of authority and family members, to be skeptical, to hide, to lie, and to pretend in order to survive.[31]

A young woman blogger responded:

The idealism of our generation is completely different from the idealism of our mother's generation. I cannot comprehend sacrificing one's life in the prime of one's youth for a political flyer. To believe in slogans like "From the martyr's blood, thousands of tulips grow," or "the revolution of the masses is victorious," is ridiculous and so far-fetched and alien that I cannot even imagine it. To lose one's life over an ideal is not acceptable to our generation; it is idiotic. Our generation looks for results, the outcome, and we are not willing to make sacrifices for nothing. And why should we, anyway? For whom, and for what? And with what results? It is absurd.[32]

The postwar generation cannot identify with the idealism of the revolutionary period; instead, it has become disillusioned with the system, and indifferent—even cynical—about the social restrictions imposed in the name of religion. Public education for a greater number of young Iranians from all walks of life (including traditional religious families), and the demographic change resulting from a decline in fertility starting in the mid-1980s have profoundly influenced the postwar generation. More important, the reduced size of families has contributed to a gradual change in relationships between parents and children, undermining the system of patriarchy.[33]

Throughout this process of change, Iranian women's wit and resilience, which can be seen in the ingenious ways they have found to circumvent gender barriers, is a testimony to their essential strength. Their defiance in the face of power has contributed to the gradual erosion of patriarchy and a weakening of the legitimacy of the state's ideology. A nineteen-year-old blogger called Pargolak reflects:

> Who says whatever our parents do, or decisions they make are the best? or that we have to accept every words of our elders as if it is a verse from Qur'an? I don't deny the benefits of experience, but that does not mean what they say are the ultimate words of wisdom. They are humans and make mistakes too! Such idealistic view of parents or elders, absolute obedience, and unquestioning respect only leads to dictatorial rule in the family.[34]

Benefiting from social and cultural transformation through higher education, the younger generation of women has established new relationship with their parents based on mutual respect.[35] A growing number of young women choose their own spouses rather than accepting their parents' choice. More women are not marrying, and, as noted before, a polled majority looks at work or career as the way to further independence.

The youthful ambience of Tehran can be seen as a reflection of Iranian society. While it is not clear whether there is potential for direct political change in the use of the Internet and new technology, the effortless proliferation of weblogs and independent news sites has offered a dramatic, liberating shift in the boundaries of Iranian public and social space.

Weblogestan, a lively, interconnected community and public space where self-expression, exchange of information and personal transformation can take place is a "street corner" of ideas with a vital potential. The borderless nature of the Internet has introduced an opportunity for public dialogue in a new communication environment—an interaction that opens the potential for transformation. By connecting local conditions to global forces by means of new media, young Iranians are challenging the authoritarian measures that limit individual rights and civil liberties. Concepts such as democracy, human rights, feminism and civil society are familiar to them, and they are open to debate and discussion through online journals and weblogs.

Many paradoxes play through the recent history and current events of Iran. Access to the Internet has intensified some of these dichotomies and focused attention on the urgent need for the right to privacy, agency, and, for women in particular, greater civil autonomy. The young generation's desire for personal freedom in such areas as relationships with the opposite sex and free association in public without harassment, and generally their wish to live their lives without interference, is in stark contrast with the Islamic regime's policy of regulating space and insistence on adherence to the prescribed Islamic identity. Such policy has alienated young Iranians and led them to "perceive the new political order as an anti-youth regime that is suspicious of all the desires they cherish."[36] Although Islam remains an integral part of their identity, young people also want religion to be a personal belief and value system, rather than a simple conformity to the external ideological propaganda and Islamic politics of the public sphere. The consequence of disillusionment with the officially prescribed religious policy has led to new interpretation of religion with "strong democratic bias," with emphasis on tolerance and desire for separation of politics from religion.[37]

The clerical rule—awash in privilege, unsure of popular support, resorting to force and intimidation to stay in power—is incapable of creative thinking to bring about democratic change. Any new discourse will emerge from within the Iran's young, educated, and wired population. The voice from this virtual public space rings with conviction:

> It's you and I. You and I will break the taboos one by one. You and I will build a generation for whom the subordination of women has no place. The era of leader worship and blind following is over. We are capable of taking charge of our lives and do not need guardians. This is the era of decentralized multiplicity of viewpoints and connecting networks. It is time to think of future perspective, to dialogue and critique.[38]

Although the political impact of digital, antihierarchal, and off-center voices in challenging the authoritarian regime is uncertain, there is evidence in women's blogs to indicate transformation in people's attitudes about sexuality, family, and society that challenges the rapport of domination and subordination and that can lead to political and social change. As Augustus Richard Norton states, "the horizontal proliferation of information" will eventually "undermine vertical lines of control."[39]

The capacity to resist and be independent, the ability to participate in dialogue and to establish rapport, the competence to navigate cyberspace, to interact and reassert identity—these attributes are the strength of the young women of Iran. Gianni Vattimo echoes this sentiment when he writes about the role of mass communication in the "dissolution of centralized perspectives." He argues that the new communication technology plays a "decisive role" in the emergence of "postmodern society." It is not that it makes society more "transparent," but more complex, even "chaotic"—and it is in this chaos that "our hopes for emancipation lie."[40]

Twenty-five years ago, the opposition used audiocassettes of Ayatollah Khomeini's lectures and sermons to stimulate the revolutionary movement against the monarchy. The success of the current Islamic theocracy is due partly to the use of personalized, small media and new technology.[41] Now the postrevolutionary generation is using the Internet to challenge the Islamic regime's intrusive rules, religious restrictions, and political control of the public space. But, compared to two and a half decades ago, despite widespread dissatisfaction with the Islamic regime, this is not a new generation of zealots demanding revolution; rather, it is an emerging digital cohort seeking gradual change from within the system.

The efforts of the younger generation may be more effective when it acts via communication networks and shared digital dreams. This generation's unwillingness to fight for slogans is matched only by its rebellious passion for freedom of expression and civil equality. Inevitably, a democratic shift in the political landscape will occur, and if external forces do not interfere to disrupt this process, it may well succeed.

Fereshteh Nouraie-Simone is a historian and professor at the American University Center for Global Peace. She teaches courses on gender and social change. Her current research interests include communication and social change with focus on global feminism and the emergence of civil society dynamics with emphasis on the Middle East and Iran. She was an associate professor and Dean of Women at Tehran

University and a broadcast journalist with the Voice of America. Her publications include a monograph on Malkam Khan, a constitutional reformist of the late nineteenth-century Iran, a textbook on U.S. history, and several articles including "The Constitutional Ideas of a Shia' Mujtahid: Muhammad Hossayn Nai'ni," and "Iranian Women, Reform, and Politics of Development in the 1970s." Nouraie-Simone is the founder of a joint lecture series for Middle Eastern women scholars at American University in conjunction with the African/Middle East Division of the Library of Congress.

Notes

1. http://www.golnaz82.com/archives/000660.html.
2. Marie-Laure Ryan (ed.), Introduction, *Cyberspace: Textuality, Computer Technology and Literary Theory* (Bloominton: Indiana University Press, 1999), p. 22.
3. http://www.farnaaz.com.
4. Scott Bukatman, *Terminal Identity: The Virtual Subject in Postmodern Science Fiction* (Durham, NC: Duke University Press, 1993), pp. 18–19.
5. Sherry Turkle, *Life on the Screen: Identity in the Age of the Internet* (New York: Touchstone Press, 1997).
6. Barbara Page, "Women Writers and the Restive Text: Feminism, Experimental Writing, and Hypertext," in Ryan (ed.), *Cyberspace Textuality*, p. 130, italics added.
7. http://www.zanan.co.ir/social/000092.html.
8. http://www.khorshidkhanom.com/archives/2001_11.php.
9. Ibid.
10. http://www.golnaz82.com/archives/000693.html.
11. http://www.blogcensus.net.
12. Postcards from Iran: "Surfing the Net," BBC News, February 13, 2004, http://news.bbc.co.uk/2/hi/middle_east/3486923.stm.
13. www.rsf.org/article.php3?idarticle=10733.
14. Andrew Shapiro, "Street Corners in Cyberspace," *The Nation*, July 3, 1995, pp.10–14.
15. Daniel W. Drezner and Henry Farrell, "Web of Influence," *Foreign Policy* November/December 2004.
16. http://fereshteh.blogfa.com.
17. Ibid.
18. http://shistory.blogspot.com.
19. http://www.khorshidkhanom.com/archives/2001_11.php.
20. Center for Women's Participation of the President's Office, draft of *The Socioeconomic and Cultural Needs of Iranian Women and Girls According to Geographic, Cul-*

tural, and Educational Divisions, Spring 2003, author's copy.

21. http://nifi50.persianblog.com/March.
22. Doreen B. Massey, *Space, Place, and Gender* (Minneapolis: Minnesota University Press 1994), p. 179.
23. http://www.khorshidkhanoom.com/archives/001300.php.
24. Massey, *Space, Place, and Gender*, p. 11.
25. Ibid, p.154.
26. Ibid., p.118.
27. Ibid., p.179.
28. Michel Foucault, *Discipline and Punish: The Birth of the Prison,* trans. Alan Sheridan (Harmondsworth Middlesex: Penguin, 1991).
29. Massey, *Space, Place, and Gender*, p. 179.
30. http://shistory.blogspot.com/2005_02_01_shistory_archive.html.
31. http://www.iftribune.com/news.asp?id=5&pass=114.
32. http://www.farnaaz.com.
33. Marie Ladier-Fouladi, "The Socio-Demographic Construction of Iranian Youth," paper presented at the Fifth Biennial Conference on Iranian Studies (Bethesda, MD, May 2004). Quoted with permission of the author.
34. http://pargolac.com. (She closed her weblog after she was briefly detained in late May, 2005.)
35. Ladier-Fouladi, "Socio-Demographic Construction of Iranian Youth."
36. Farhad Khosrokhavar, "Postrevolutionary Iran and the New Social Movements, " in Eric Hooglund (ed.), *Twenty Years of Islamic Revolution Political and Social Transition in Iran Since 1979* (Syracuse, NY: Syracuse University Press, 2002), p. 8.
37. Ibid., p. 12.
38. http://www.farnaaz.com.
39. Augustus Richard Norton, "The New Media, Civic Pluralism, and the Struggle for Political Reform," in Dale Eickelman and Jon W. Anderson, (eds.), *New Media in the Muslim World: The Emerging Public Sphere* (Bloominton: Indiana University Press, 1999), p. 23.
40. Gianni Vattimo, *The Transparent Society* (Baltimore: Johns Hopkins University Press, 1992), pp. 4–5.
41. Annabelle Sreberny and Ali Mohammadi, *Small Media, Big Revolution: Communication, Culture, and the Iranian Revolution* (Minneapolis: University of Minnesota Press, 1994); Eickelman and Anderson, (eds.), *New Media in the Muslim World.*

The Challenge of Globalization in Saudi Arabia

Mai Yamani

Introduction

Saudi Arabia's rulers have been battling the forces of globalization for the last decade. Gone are the robes they wore in the past—the symbol of an era in which the challenges of marrying tradition and modernity were met at least somewhat successfully. But the earlier strategy of shunning outside influences lingers on, and Saudi Arabia remains one of the most closed societies in the world.

Indeed, the regime clings to its hermetic habits. On the one hand, foreign journalists and other visitors are encouraged, but on the other, visas are difficult to obtain, and the authorities prefer that foreign ambassadors do not speak Arabic, for fear of their probing into hidden recesses of Saudi society. Camera cell phones are banned, because they might expose unveiled women.

The effectiveness of such measures has, however, clearly broken down under the onslaught of external forces rooted in globalization. As the climate of public opinion and sentiment changes, internal pressure is mounting, with the population steadily losing faith in its rulers' ability to address citizens' basic economic, social, and political aspirations. This dramatic loss of trust has increasingly exposed the splits and strains within Saudi society, threatening the cohesion of the state itself.

Three aspects of globalization have had a particularly devastating impact on the kingdom's totalizing adaptation of tradition, honor, and religion:

- *Growing economic interdependence,* framed by institutions such as the World Trade Organization—which Saudi Arabia has yet to join—has set off a fierce struggle within the royal family over whether to open the system or not.

- *Deterritorialization of political identity*, owing to the rapid development over the past decade of new trans-Arabian media—including 108 Arab satellite television channels and thousands of Internet sites—has eroded the national unity that is a key political resource for any regime.
- *The encroachment of the West*, in terms of politics, ideology, and force, owing to the emergence of the United States as the world's sole superpower.

Globalization's impact, while universally felt, has been especially profound in the Middle East, where nation-states continue to exist more in name than in reality. Relatively young states like Saudi Arabia, which was established in 1932, struggle even to control their borders in the face of enduring ethnic, tribal, and clan relations that transcend territorial boundaries. The rise of a transnational Arab identity, fueled by the technologies of globalization, has thus been accompanied by the persistence of strong subnational identities, with both undermining the nation-state.

The Search for Legitimacy

Even in the context of the Middle East, the Saudi authorities' continuing failure to come to terms with globalization is remarkable and reflects a uniquely severe clash between modernity and tradition. People's lives have been revolutionized by oil wealth and urbanization, but the state's legitimacy remains based on a dogmatic form of Islam, Wahhabism. Access to the outside world through travel, satellite TV, and the Internet has eroded the socialization process within the family and the educational system. As a result, the Saudi population knows that its rulers are incompetent and corrupt, and the rulers, knowing that the population knows, are scared to the point of paralysis, unable to reach any decision about reforms, much less devise a comprehensive strategy for the future.

In their desperate search for legitimacy, Saudi leaders are not moving forward, or even backward; they are simply trying to keep their heads above water by offering half-baked promises. For example, they have promised partial municipal elections—but with the exclusion of women. As Prince Mansour bin Miteb, the chairman of the General Committee for Municipal Elections, explained in January 2005, the elections are a new experience, and the short time given to prepare for them made it impossible to allow women's participation.

But municipal elections are not entirely unprecedented: the cities of Mecca and Medina held them regularly at the beginning of the twentieth century. More fundamentally, educated Saudi women have voiced their desire to vote, even if they have to do so by closed-circuit television—a staple of rigid sex segregation in the country's universities.

In fact, as on many other matters, the Saudi princes are in disagreement about whether to allow women to be elected—or even appointed—in this limited reform plan. Some have announced that women's participation may be possible in 2009. But the minister of interior, Prince Naif, remains adamantly opposed to the inclusion of women—a position that has exposed Saudi Arabia to international criticism and contrasts with almost every other Arab country that holds elections.

The inconsistent and aggressive policy of the United States is pushing the rulers deeper into their hole. The more that demands for reform come to be associated with American pressure, the stronger the resistance of the conservatives and hardliners. In reality, U.S. pressure is leavened by pragmatism. Simply put, as long as the oil continues to flow, it suits the United States to keep the hardliners placated, and thus under control.

The reality, however, is that the situation is increasingly out of control, because the political, economic, and cultural forces of globalization are causing the dream of a Saudi nation—a fantasy imagined solely by the ruling family and identified with it in the country's very name—to founder. The official narrative of identity is no longer tenable, because oil and patrimony are no longer sufficient to provide political and economic security. Globalization exposes everything.

The Resistant State

The Saudi rulers' dilemma is deepened by the highly resistant structure of the state and regime they have created. The connections between the al-Saud family and the Wahhabi religious authorities are numerous and deep, and have served as a pillar of the state since 1932. In many ways, the alliance resembles a coalition government. The princes handed out power and money, while the religious authorities provided a patina of divine legitimacy for the princes' actions.

The state was and continues to be set up accordingly. The Wahhabi clerics control some of the most important levers of official power, including the judiciary, the ministry of Islamic affairs, and the ministry of *hajj* (pilgrimage) and *awqaf* (religious endowments). They also intervene in people's lives more intimately through the formidably named Committee for the Promotion of Virtue and the Prevention of Vice. The committee's employees, the *Mutawa*—a force of thousands of religious police—roam the streets in government jeeps searching for sin and destroying satellite dishes. They patrol the shopping malls and wait outside girls' schools to make sure that women are securely veiled. In March 2002, they waited outside a girls' school in Mecca as the building burned, preventing the students from escaping because they were not properly veiled and their male guardians were not present. Fourteen young girls died as a result.

The religious establishment also controls the imams of the kingdom's seventy-one thousand mosques. Women—who are increasingly aware of their marginalization and exclusion from public life—are not allowed to pray in most mosques, the main exceptions being the Great Mosques of Mecca and Medina, and there they can pray only in areas assigned to them at the back.

Perhaps more significantly, the clerics control the religious educational system that constitutes up to 50 percent of students' curriculum. As a result, Wahhabi religious dogma penetrates every home and family in the country. It is, above all, an educational system designed to consolidate the traditionalist, patriarchal social order. Textbooks—pink for girls, blue for boys—emphasize the rules prescribed by the father of Wahhabism, Imam Muhammad bin Abdul Wahhab, and enforced by the al-Saud.

Indeed, the curriculum is little more than an arm of state control. Its main themes are *shirk* (idolatory in its various forms), sin, fear of the fires of hell, and rejection of the ways of the infidels. The textbooks memorized by secondary-school students sharply define the boundaries of virtue and provide guidelines of how to remain vigilant against the dangers of temptation and sin. The duties inculcated in young Saudis are summarized in the phrase *al-walaa' wal-baraa*, meaning loyalty to the system and hostility to nonbelievers.

Ironically, globalization has aided the export of this defensive ideology. Under Wahhabi influence, the Saudi royal family poured hundreds of millions of dollars into institutions feeding extremist ideology to students at home and in many parts of the Islamic world. This was little more than a fig leaf for their own impiety, but by the time some of these graduates had finished their studies, they no longer needed their original benefactors in Riyadh and duly turned against them.

The most glaring example of this is Osama bin Laden—a product of the Saudi educational and political system who speaks in religious terms but broadcasts his mission on the al-Jazeera and al-Arabiya satellite channels and trains his followers through the Internet. Newspapers across the globe turned bin Laden's image into a transnational antiglobalization icon, one that is now carried—interchangeable with Che Guevara—on mobile phones and T-shirts around the world. His success is built on his ability to unite the alienated and the embittered in common opposition to naked, illegitimate power.

Not only have the al-Saud come under direct threat from the very people they financed, trained, and trusted; by promoting the hard-line Wahhabis, the government has also alienated vast sections of Saudi society, including liberals and moderate Islamists. This has left the authorities ill equipped, to say the least, to face increasing violence and internal and external pressures for reform. After all, the religious establishment is not in the reform business.

A Tale of Two Saudis

For now, two broad trends—liberal-moderate and radical religious—define the population's response to globalization. We can examine what is at stake through biographical narratives of two young Saudi men.

Muhammad is moderate and pragmatic, accepting what the world gives him. He wants employment, civil rights, and increased political participation. He wants an education that will equip him to meet the demands of the global economy. Muhammad and what he represents offer the best opportunity to bring women—who represent 95 percent of unemployment and are still banned from driving cars—fully into Saudi society.

By contrast, Abdul is angry and seeks to fight the infidels. He is either at the mosque listening to the imams' sermons or at the computer linked to a website that connects him to the violent, subterranean world of Islam's radical fringe. Abdul uses the tools of globalization because of his revulsion against the corrupt leaders and their subservience to the United States.

Abdul was raised on Wahhabi dogma, but he has become disillusioned with the world he inherited. Al-Jazeera has introduced him to an imagined community of Arabs, a place defined by vivid images of Palestinian bloodshed and of Iraqis humiliated in Abu Ghraib prison and executed in Falluja mosques. Above all, such images, and the community of victimization they nurture, highlight the inaction and paralysis of Arab states and their rulers.

As a high-tech fanatic, Abdul prefers the virulent fatwas promulgated by his online peers to those of the old, blind members of the religious establishment. How can the late shaykh Abdul-Aziz bin Abdullah Bin Baz, who supported inviting U.S. troops into the kingdom in 1990 and once issued a fatwa stating that the earth is flat, hope to compare with the global power of radical Islamic websites?

Hundreds of these websites exist, the most extreme preaching the ideas of al-Qaeda and its ideological ilk. One includes the haunting celebration of a young man's imminent martyrdom by suicide bombing. Others, such as the Saudi-dominated www.geocities.com/um_anas, are less violent but have widened the scope of sin to include learning English and science permitting women to have access to the Internet without a male guardian present. Online fatwas harbor animosity not only toward the West but also toward other Muslims.

Abdul's story underscores in a perverse way what Václav Havel once called "the power of the powerless." Since demonstrations are illegal in Saudi Arabia and there are no other venues except the mosque, the Internet has created a worldwide community of alienated and embittered Abduls. By outlawing freedom of assembly and freedom of expression, the authorities did not eliminate pluralism or dissent but merely drove it underground.

Muhammad and Abdul have both suffered greatly: incompetent dictators have stifled their freedom, crushed their aspirations, and denied them a workable political identity. But each is alienated and deracinated in his own way. They both mistrust the rulers, but they perceive and deal with this situation differently.

The state should be encouraging Muhammad, celebrating his pragmatism, and channeling his energy into productive activities, especially as he does not intend actively to challenge or overthrow the regime. But the state is more afraid of the growth and empowerment of the Muhammads—and responds by repressing them with censorship and even jail—than appeasing the Abduls.

To be sure, the authorities have killed some of Abdul's more violent brothers in their "war against terrorism," but they fear that a wider crackdown, however necessary, would alienate important tribes and clans. For example the Ghamdi tribe, one member of which was a hijacker in the September 11, 2001, attack on the United States, has at least another thousand Abduls of exactly the same age. When the FBI tried to trace the young hijacker's relatives, a Google search simply confused matters more.

Such tribal links explain collusion with radical or violent *jihadis*, such as the terrorists who carried out the al-Khobar attack in May 2004, were trapped in a surrounded building, and somehow escaped. Loyalty cannot be bought with high oil prices, rising tribal employment, and higher salaries for the security forces and the police. A month after the Al Khobar attack, an ex-policeman became the head of al-Qaeda in Saudi Arabia.

Trans-state communication has further strengthened the links between tribesmen. When Americans talk about of foreign insurgents in Iraq, they don't realize that such groups' members are typically all from the same tribe. A man from Shammer may hold Saudi Arabian, Syrian or Iraqi nationality, but he regards himself as belonging to Shammer first and foremost and crosses these states' imaginary lines in the sand to fight with his brothers.

Conclusion

Saudi society now stands at a critical point, with the population moving in two opposing directions as a result of the state's conflicting demands for traditional order and reform. But society increasingly resembles Abdul, bearded and frowning in short robes, for the Saudi state is not set up to produce more Muhammads.

The outside world has done little to help Muhammad. The United States, in particular, has confused matters by continuing to place stability ahead of the democratic reforms it claims to support. This has blinded U.S. policy makers to the long-term threats—in the form of bin Laden's ideological children—implied by the current Saudi system, and it makes the United States indirectly responsible for these threats.

Saudi Arabia cannot survive without an entirely new vision of itself, which cannot emerge until the rulers enter a real dialogue with at least some sections of their population for the explicit purpose of nurturing a modern and moderate ethos. Globalization will destroy the old Saudi Arabia, but what will replace it remains highly uncertain.

Mai Yamani is an associate fellow at the Royal Institute for International Affairs (RIIA) in London. The first woman from Saudi Arabia to get her Ph.D. from Oxford, she works on the Middle East programs at RIIA as a social anthropologist. She is the author of several books and numerous articles. Her latest book is *Cradle of Islam: The Hijaz and the Quest for an Arabian Identity* (I.B.Tauris, 2004). Other publications include: *Changed Identities: The Challenge of the New Generation in Saudi Arabia* (RIIA, 2000) and *Feminism and Islam: Legal and Literary Perspectives* (ed.) (Ithaca Press, 1996).

Part Two

Gender, Communication, and Religion

Globalizing Equality: Muslim Women, Theology, and Feminism

Asma Barlas

I would like to engage the topic of Muslim women in the era of global com-munication from three different angles. First, I will critically address some common assumptions regarding the role of information technology (IT) in enabling democracy in Muslim societies. This will clarify some key issues and provide a context for my central argument, which is to define a Qur'an-ic hermeneutics of sexual equality that I believe needs to be at the heart of democratic reform in Muslim societies. Last, I join the debates on Muslim women as a way of engaging theological, secular, and feminist approaches to social change.

Although I make several arguments, my basic claim is that communica-tion technologies will only be able to transform Muslim women's (and men's) lives in meaningful ways if they accompany or, better yet, enable a fundamen-tal epistemic shift in how Muslims interpret and practice Islam. Such a shift would involve a willingness to read liberation from the same scripture that male authorities abuse to discriminate against women. Thus, like many other Muslims, I believe that "theology matters,"[1] and while it may not matter equal-ly for everyone or be a panacea for every problem, it is one of the most power-ful internal impulses for social critique and change in Muslim communities.

Some exculpatory caveats are in order here. I engage discussions of communication technology, feminism, and secularism only tangentially and to the extent that they are germane to my larger argument; I do not attempt to define them, since my more limited objective is to critique certain deployments of these terms. Also, the second of this essay draws on earlier work and is not all original.[2] I am learning rather providentially that some repetition is unavoidable while some things bear repeating.

Muslim Women, Information Technologies, and Democracy

I want to begin by querying the presumed links among information technologies (IT), Muslim women, and democracy and human rights, because I believe we need to theorize these relationships instead of taking for granted the interconnectedness of certain economic, religious, and technological factors and their impact on gender equality. For instance, many people assume that the fact that Muslim women are taking up careers in such future oriented sectors of society as IT, satellite TV, business administration, and so on, will have a democratizing effect on their societies that will push forward gender equality and fundamental human rights. Indeed, many people view technology itself—especially the Internet—as the harbinger of equality and democracy on the grounds that it has not only enabled borderless travel and cross-cultural dialogue but also transformed the nature of political participation. Muslim women, it is assumed, therefore only stand to benefit from access to such technologies, which many of them already are using to challenge culturally androcentric attitudes and institutions in their societies. Lastly, many people claim that by reinterpreting and reappropriating religious texts, Muslim women are already redefining patriarchal structures in their societies.

As a Muslim woman who is actively involved in the emerging dialogue surrounding these issues, I welcome this discussion and contribute to it by sharing (in the second part of this essay) one strategy for challenging androcentric and patriarchal epistemologies and institutions. Generally, I agree that the rapid pace of technological change is affecting people's lives in profound ways, that activists are using the Internet to forge real partnerships, and that, depending on where they live, more women are taking up careers that were once considered off-limits to them and by them. Women in many societies are also creatively reappropriating religious texts and struggling to broaden the political arena. These are universal occurrences that are unfolding in different societies in different ways, including, of course, in individual Muslim societies.

In the latter context, however, I am less sanguine that high-tech jobs for Muslim women will affect their social roles in such a way and to such an extent as to generate democratic societies that will push forward gender equality and fundamental human rights. This certainly was the developmental trajectory of "the West,"[3] but a domino theory of progress in which the West "works as a silent referent in historical knowledge"[4] is not very helpful for understanding postcolonial societies, as the spectacular failures of modernization theory attest. Consequently, rather than trying to universalize a Western teleology, we should work with models that can accommodate the specificities of Muslim societies, and I assume that some variant of postcolonial theory would offer such models.[5] As an aside, I should also note that there are no sound empirical referents for assuming that Muslim women are transforming the public sphere as a domain of equality and inclusion in Muslim societies. I am hard-pressed to find any countries, other than perhaps Iran, where this is happening, though not for a lack of effort on women's parts. However, when I think of my country of origin, Pakistan, I am less sure that women's struggles there are having, or will have, the same impact as those taking place in Iran.

Similarly, while I agree that technology is having an effect on Muslim women's lives, I believe we need to study this effect carefully rather than simply refer to the fact that we live in a technologically interconnected world. Such a blanket assumption, after all, says nothing about the nature of the technology, the connections it has enabled, or the world as we perceive it. The growing gap between the rich and the poor suggests that about 99 percent of people will never have access to such technologies as computers and thus to the rosy new worlds of borderless travel and participatory politics that the Internet is thought to have opened up. And, for the 1 percent that does have access, what precisely does it mean to travel via the Internet to observe others? Someone who has lived in, say, Turkey will tell you right away that one cannot recognize it from (what passes as) Turkish culture on the Internet,[6] in spite of the power of virtuality to make "the fake seem more compelling than the real."[7] This is obviously not the place to engage in an extended discussion about the nature of the real or of the simulacrum, but it may not be irrelevant to note that the function of the simulacrum, as Fredric Jameson argues, "lies in what Sartre would have called the derealization of the whole surrounding world of everyday reality."[8] To the extent that this derealization entails alienation, we need to problematize the realities and virtualities that the Internet opens up rather than uncritically celebrate them. The same goes for the concept of borderless travel. While the Internet does allow journeys without visas, this does not mean that technology has done away with borders; it has simply made the act of crossing them invisible. In point of fact, technologies are always in the process of remapping borders. (Incidentally, I also wonder at our collective investment in a borderless world, given that borders mediate our encounters with the real and thus constitute an integral aspect of our lived realities.)

Last, while I recognize the political potential of the Internet, I do not believe that we should treat the Internet as the signifier of a democratic global public arena by assuming that technology = borderlessness = participatory/democratic politics. The idea that the Internet is "a great tool for communication [that] can greatly enhance the democratic process,"[9] draws on a model of the public in which people are freely engaged in a mutually noncoercive dialogue out of which flows enlightened public policy. However, as theorists from C. Wright Mills to Jürgen Habermas have argued, this model was fractured long ago when a society of masses came to replace the community of publics.[10] If a public does not exist in any meaningful sense even in Western democracies, it has never existed in any sense in postcolonial Muslim states and clearly does not exist at the global level. Susan Buck-Morss puts it plainly: a "global public . . . does not yet exist. . . . We the multitude who might become that public, cannot yet reach each other across the excluding boundaries of language, beneath the power distortions of global media, against the muffling exclusions of poverty and the disparities in information." At best, we can be "members of partial publics."[11]

The absence of a global public also limits the democratic promise of the Internet, even if "every ethnicity, ideology, religion and fetish known to humankind is probably represented in cyberspace."[12] Variety and pluralism are not in themselves signs of democracy or even of tolerance, and even tolerance may be repressive. I have in mind Herbert Marcuse's brilliantly unsettling contention that "what is proclaimed and practiced as tolerance today, is in many of its most effective manifestations serving the cause of oppression."[13] This is because the dominant perspective continues to structure people's encounter with difference so that alternative ("minority") discourses get marginalized and "positioned as the exotic other."[14] Moreover, as Ulises Mejías argues, while the Internet allows "us to create spaces for the free discussion of ideas . . . these spaces co-exist with the corporate and government sources of information from which the majority of people still receive their news. But even with the alternative news sources . . . the machinery of the mass media has desensitized us to the possibilities and power of dialogue."[15]

If we cannot assume that dialogue, tolerance, or democracy is built into IT, we also cannot assume that technologies like the Internet are ubiquitous throughout the so-called Muslim world. Rather, it is the diasporan Muslims in the West who are using the Internet "for political purposes," points out Peter Mandaville.[16] For such Muslims, it provides "a forum for the conduct of politics *within* Islam"[17] that bypasses "traditional gatekeepers and adjudicators of interpretive rights, procedures and adequacy."[18] Thus, "in the absence of sanctioned information from recognised institutions, Muslims are increasingly taking religion into their own hands," although this does not mean that "anonymous computer personalit[ies]" will be able to chip away "the authority of the traditional scholars." Even so, the Internet is allowing diaspora Muslims "to create a new form of imagined community, or a reimagined *Umma*" and, more importantly, by admitting an element of syncretism, it is enabling the emergence of "new forms of Islam, each of which is redrawn to suit the unique set of sociocultural contingencies into which it enters."[19] I believe that this interface between theology and technology is utterly crucial to Muslim women. By allowing Muslims to take Islam into their own hands, IT is fragmenting the "traditional sources of authority such that the locus of 'real' Islam and the identity of those who are permitted to speak on its behalf [are becoming] ambiguous," allowing the rise of "a new breed" of Muslim intellectuals.[20] For the "new intellectuals, neither the transmission of knowledge nor the place of this transmission is institutionalized. Everyone is 'authorized.'"[21] To the extent that certain aspects of Muslim tradition—including certain readings of the Qur'an—are misogynist, such self-authorizations can indeed be revolutionary, if they are based in a liberatory hermeneutics.

I am therefore tempted to conclude, with Mejías, that "between Audre Lorde's belief that the master's tools will not dismantle the master's house, and Ani DiFranco's opinion that every tool is a weapon if you hold it right, there [is] . . . a productive space for technology and virtuality within praxis."[22] Like many Muslims, I am trying to identify an ethical and theological content of this praxis for Muslims, especially women. I do not assume that human rights, equality, and democracy will flow from the global economy (in truth, this economy is creating primarily low-end and badly paid jobs, held mostly by young girls). Nor do I feel that the sole political referents for Muslims should be "Western" history. Instead, I believe that Muslims must struggle to create "normative horizons specific to our existence and relevant to the examination of our lives and their possibilities."[23] As a believer, I look to Islam to provide such horizons and I contend that one such horizon, is a Qur'anic hermeneutics of sexual equality.

A Qur'anic Hermeneutics of Equality

Before I describe such a hermeneutics, I should explain why I even consider it relevant to a discussion of Muslim women's lives and to social change more generally. After all, as a Muslim woman who was born and raised in the world's second-largest Muslim country and lived in it most of my life, I know the hazards of ascribing the plight of Muslim women straightforwardly to Islam. For one thing, many of the social and cultural practices of Muslim societies have little or nothing to do with Islam, especially as it is embodied in the teachings of the Qur'an (the persistence of "honor" killings in Pakistan illustrates this graphically, as does the absence of widespread resistance to this revolting custom). In fact, it is unlikely that most Muslims even know what the Qur'an teaches, given that the vast majority of Muslims are illiterate. For another thing, women in Muslim societies lead dramatically different lives depending on a range of factors, especially social class, that determine the opportunities they will have throughout their lives. Therefore, it is difficult to generalize about women's experiences a single state, much less all Muslim societies. Yet, despite all their differences, Muslims everywhere regard men as ontologically superior to women, and most hold that the woman is obligated to submit to the man in his capacity as her "husband, father or brother."[24] This ideology of male supremacy infuses Muslim cultures and consciousness to such an extent that it has given rise to depictions of Islam as a religious patriarchy that "professes models of hierarchical relationships and sexual inequality and puts a sacred stamp [on] female subservience."[25]

What disturbs me most about misogyny in Muslim societies is not so much that it has been normalized or even that it has been wrapped in the mantle of religion; neither tendency, after all, is peculiar to Muslims. Rather, what I find intolerable is that Muslims project misogyny onto the scripture, hence onto the divine, on the basis of three or four words or phrases in the Qur'an, overlooking the egalitarian nature of the text as a whole. People who cannot read the Qur'an and do not live in accordance with its teachings will nonetheless throw about three words or parts of sentences from it to justify the mistreatment of women, ranging from outright abuse to forms of divorce and polygyny that distort and pervert the Qur'an's injunctions. I want to be clear: I am not accusing Muslims of purposely distorting the Qur'an. Nor am I calling all Muslim men oppressive; this is too much of a Western caricature to be true. What I consider more important than the actual number of men who engage in such practices is that there is religious sanction for them to do so, if they are thus inclined, in almost every Muslim community. That is why a reading of the Qur'an that challenges oppressive interpretations and demonstrates the egalitarian nature of its teachings on sexual equality can help challenge sexual discrimination among Muslims. That is the conviction that led me to write "*Believing Women*" *in Islam*.[26] In the rest of this section I summarize that book's main points.

Essentially, I do two things in the book. Part of my objective is to illustrate the truth of Leila Ahmed's claim that different readings of the same texts yield "fundamentally different Islams" for women,[27] and I do this by showing that what the Qur'an seems to be saying is a function of who reads it, how, and in what contexts. That is, I make visible the relationship between knowledge and the means of its production, particularly between knowledge and authority/method/gender (though I do not posit a fixed relationship between gender and reading). On this basis, I can argue that the reason Muslims have read the Qur'an as a patriarchal text has to do with who has read it (basically men), the contexts in which they have read it (basically patriarchal), and the method by which they have read it (basically one that ignores the hermeneutic principles that the Qur'an suggests for its own reading). Demonstrating the interconnectedness of hermeneutic and existential questions allows me to argue for a restructuring not only of Muslim religious knowledge but also of Muslim societies, on the grounds that knowledge is not produced in a vacuum.

The second part of the book involves reading the Qur'an by means of principles that I derive from the Qur'an itself. The first principle is to read the Qur'an in light of a sound theological understanding of God (or, rather, of divine self-disclosure; that is, how God describes God in the Qur'an), since for Muslims the Qur'an is God's speech, and we cannot understand it independently of how we visualize God. (Indeed, I regard God's self-disclosure as being at the heart of Qur'anic epistemology, as I term it.) To exemplify this approach, I draw on three aspects of God's self-disclosure. First, based on the doctrine of *Tawhid*, or divine unity, which says that God is one and that God's sovereignty is indivisible, I argue that theories of male privilege that set up men as rulers over women or as intermediaries between God and women encourage the worship of men, thereby undercutting divine sovereignty, which is a *shirk*, or heresy. We must therefore avoid reading such theories into the Qur'an. Second, since another aspect of divine self-disclosure is that God is Just and never does *zulm* to human beings (in the Qur'an, *zulm* primarily means to transgress against another's rights),[28] I argue that we also should not read *zulm* into the Qur'an. I contend that when patriarchies transgress against women's rights by oppressing them, they commit *zulm*, and we should therefore not read the Qur'an as advocating patriarchy since doing so ascribes *zulm* to God. Third, God is unlike anything created and unrepresentable, so we should not use similitude to describe God. I take this to mean that references to God as "He" are (faulty) linguistic conventions and not accurate statements about divine reality. (This is, of course, a more complex argument than I have conveyed here.)

The book's second principle is to read the Qur'an for its best meanings, as the Qur'an itself asks us to do. This injunction conclusively establishes that while we can derive different meanings from the Qur'an, not all meanings will be equally legitimate; in fact, the Qur'an provides criteria for judging the legitimacy of different readings. For instance, it emphasizes reading the text as a whole instead of piecemeal or in a decontextualized way, and privileging its clear verses over its allegorical ones. The Qur'an also allows us to contest the pervasive tendency to confuse divine speech with its male-authored interpretations by distinguishing between itself and its (mis)readings.

Finally, since part of my objective is to determine the Qur'an's position on patriarchy, I employ a very comprehensive definition of patriarchy that encompasses its historical/religious and modern/secular forms in reading the text. Historically, patriarchy was a form of rule by the father that derived its legitimacy from representing God as Father and the father/husband as sovereign over wives and children. That is, it drew parallels between God's sovereignty over men and men's sovereignty over women. I use this definition in reading the Qur'an because the text was revealed to a traditional patriarchy, and I seek to determine whether it endorses this mode of male authority by representing God as male or by teaching that God has a special relationship with men or that rule by the father/husband is divinely ordained and an earthly continuation of God's rule. Additionally, I ask whether the Qur'an teaches that men embody divine attributes and women are by nature weak, unclean, or sinful, as religious patriarchies claim. *evolution of patriarchy*

However, since male authority has been reconfigured in more modern ✳ and secular forms, I also define patriarchy as a politics of sexual differentiation that privileges males by "transforming biological sex into politicized gender, which prioritizes the male while making the woman different (unequal), less than, or the 'Other.'"[29] I apply this definition to the Qur'an because Muslims hold its teachings to be universal and thus applicable today, and I want to see if it endorses modern forms of male privilege by advocating dualisms, differentiations, or inequalities based on sex. Specifically, I want to see if the Qur'an privileges men over women as males, or treats man as the Self and woman as the Other, or views women and men as opposites, as modern patriarchal theories of sexual inequality do.

Based on a careful reading of the Qur'an's position on a wide range of issues, including the nature of divine ontology, human creation, moral individuality, mothers and fathers, wives and husbands, marriage and divorce, ✳ and sex and gender, I conclude that the Qur'an does not in fact endorse either form of patriarchy. ✳

To begin with, it does not represent God as male and in fact forbids sacralizing God as the Father. Nor does it valorize fathers or fatherhood as traditional and religious patriarchies do. In fact, the Qur'an suggests that there is a natural conflict between monotheism and patriarchy inasmuch as the former is based on God's sovereignty and the latter on man's. However, the Qur'an does recognize that patriarchies exist historically and that, in actual patriarchies, men are the locus of authority; this may be why it frequently addresses men. To address men, however, is not to condone or advocate patriarchy. The Qur'an repeatedly warns against "following the ways of the father," which can be read literally or metaphorically as cautioning against adherence to patriarchal tradition, rule by the father, or both.

I also show that the so-called misogynist verses—the ones dealing with "wife beating," divorce, and polygyny—can be read in different ways and that even if we are not happy with some of the Qur'an's provisions today, none of these verses establish men as being ontologically superior to women or entitled to demand their submission. On the contrary, the Qur'an teaches that God created woman and man from a single self (*nafs*), appointed them each other's friend and guide (*awliya*), and put love and mercy (*sukun*) between their hearts. It never says that men have attributes or faculties that women do not; indeed, the Qur'an does not even describe men and women in terms of masculine or feminine traits, because it does not associate sex with gender. That is, while the Qur'an recognizes biological differences, it does not assign them any gender symbolism. Not a single verse suggests that women's and men's gender roles are a function of their biology or that biological differences make them unequal or one subordinate to the other. Since sex and gender are not meaningful determinants of moral personality *in* the Qur'an, I argue that we also cannot ascribe sexual inequality *to* the Qur'an. On this basis, I contend that the Qur'an also does not support modern forms of patriarchy.

In arriving at this reading, I remain aware that the Qur'an treats women and men differently with respect to some issues. Nevertheless, while Muslims interpret this as a sign of inequality, the Qur'an itself does not tie its different treatment to the claim that women are like lesser or defective men or that the sexes are incompatible, incommensurable, unequal, or opposite. Moreover, difference does not always signify inequality, as many feminists who initially theorized women's liberation in terms of the identical treatment of women and men now argue.

I do not offer a theory of sexual equality based on my reading of the Qur'an, but I do offer elements of a Qur'anic framework for deriving such a theory—although I realize how difficult it is, especially for women, to undertake such a venture in Muslim societies. Regrettably, as Khaled Abou El Fadl argues, "interpretive communities do form around texts and at times they may hold the moral insights of the text hostage. [They] can stultify and imprison the text in an extremist paradigm that becomes very difficult to disentangle or dismantle and as a result makes it very difficult to restore the text's integrity."[30] Yet in order to be able to contest "culturally androcentric" and patriarchal institutions in Muslim societies, we have to retrieve the Qur'an's integrity by detaching God from sexual oppression. Such an endeavor is the first step in developing an egalitarian sexual praxis that will also allow Muslim women (and men) to experience the divine as a liberatory force in their lives. So long as men oppress women in God's name, neither

[margin handwritten note:] separate ≠ always ≠ equal

can hope to encounter God as full human beings, for the dialectic of oppression diminishes the humanity of both the oppressor and the oppressed.

Theology, Secularism, Feminism

Thus far, I have argued against a simplistic view of IT as the agent of democracy in Muslim societies, while also noting the opportunities that the Internet, for example, is making available for a democratic Muslim engagement with Islam. Additionally, I have illustrated the liberatory potential of theology for women by giving a reading of the Qur'an that challenges its appropriation by religious patriarchies. Although I have not linked these two arguments, my approach implicitly reveals the value of not positioning technology and theology against each other in the manner of much of the literature on women and social change in Muslim societies. In fact, this literature has become so polarized around binaries—theology versus social issues, Islam versus democracy, the Qur'an versus universal standards—that it keeps us from theorizing the "practical options . . . opened up or closed by the notion that the world has no significant binary features, that it is, on the contrary, divided into overlapping, fragmented cultures, hybrid selves, continuously dissolving and emerging social states," as Talal Asad argues.[31] In conclusion, therefore, I want to dwell on the options that we close down when we frame the problem of change in Muslim societies in terms of binaries, especially theology versus secularism. This will also allow me to link Muslim societies with global politics, albeit only illustratively.

danger in binaries

When I said earlier that theology matters, I was referring to an exchange between Abou El Fadl and Tariq Ali in the wake of 9/11. While Abou El Fadl's inclination is to try to separate 9/11 from Islam by defending the Qur'an's provisions on tolerance, his critics point to the injurious impact of U.S. foreign policies and the Israel-Palestinian conflict as a way of framing 9/11 as more than just a problem of Muslim intolerance and extremism. In this context, Ali argues that theology is "useless" for resolving the "real problems" of Muslims, who, he says, need to "move beyond discussing whether or not the Qur'an promotes tolerance and grapple with the urgent social and political problems that affect [them] today."[32] Abou El Fadl replies that for millions of believers, God is a "part of their moral and material universe. This is why theology matters. If theology does not matter, then they do not matter, and, ultimately I do not matter either. It would seem to me to be both unwise and immoral to imply that the perspectives of people whose theology is inseparable from their very existence simply do not matter." Moreover, at a practical political level, it is only by engaging theology that Muslims can deny fanatical "groups their Islamic banner and . . . challenge their claim to authenticity.[33]

In many ways, this exchange symbolizes the debate on Muslim women as well. On the one hand, people (like me) believe that liberatory theology can challenge and reform oppressive Muslim practices against women by critiquing Islam from within. This does not mean, however, that we all pin the entire project of sexual equality and women's rights on theology alone. On the other hand, others, mostly Marxists and secular feminists, believe that "so long as [Islamic feminists] remain focused on theological arguments rather than socio-economic and political questions, and so long as their point of reference is the Qur'an rather than universal standards, their impact will be limited at best."[34] This is Val Moghadam's conclusion in her essay "Islamic Feminism and its Discontents," in which she reviews the controversies (mainly within the expatriate Iranian community) about women's rights and the Islamic regime in Iran. She cautions Muslim women against trying to reform Islam from within an Islamic framework because it is "difficult to win theological arguments" and because attempts to do so can "reinforce the legitimacy of the Islamic system, help to reproduce it, and undermine secular alternatives."[35]

To understand and even sympathize with Moghadam's suspicion of Islam given the experiences of women in contemporary Iran and other Muslim states, to say nothing of the history of sexual discrimination in Muslim societies, is not, however, to agree with all her premises. First, in the vein of "modern European political" thinkers, Moghadam (and other Marxists) can only accommodate religious beliefs as "practices of so-called 'superstition.'" According to Dipesh Chakrabarty, this is because they view "the human [as] ontologically singular" and "gods and spirits . . . [as] 'social facts,' [as if] the social somehow exists prior to them." However, not only need we not assume "a logical priority of the social," but it is also difficult to find a society "in which humans have existed without gods and spirits accompanying them." Indeed, on some accounts, "being human means . . . discovering 'the possibility of calling upon God [or gods] without being under an obligation to first establish his [or their] reality.'"[36]

[handwritten marginalia: trying to tear down the master's house w/ the master's tools]

[handwritten marginalia: So. does that legitimate them?]

[handwritten marginalia: stupid.]

Second, and perhaps more to the point, I am not sure how feasible it is to draw neat lines between people's belief systems and their social and political conditions. In fact Marxists themselves point out that all systems of thought (ideology, philosophy, religious knowledge, commonsense) exist in symbiosis with economic and political structures and cannot be entirely dissociated from them. But since many Marxists also adhere to a unidirectional theory of change that sees it as proceeding from the economy to politics and ideology, they regard the latter as merely epiphenomenal. However, such determinism is problematic, as internal critiques of Marxism have revealed since at least Antonio Gramsci.[37] Moreover, even if religion and theology are not directly relevant to socioeconomic and political questions (though some classics of European thought, such as Max Weber's *Protestant Ethic and the Spirit of Capitalism*, would suggest otherwise), they can affect people's attitudes about social and economic issues and, more importantly, about women, thus affecting women's opportunities as well. Conversely, political and economic change may not always be able to secure women's interests in societies in which they are intrinsically held to count for less than men. While many non-Muslims also assign women a secondary status, to the extent that Muslims justify doing this in the name of Islam, a progressive theology may well be the most powerful corrective to their beliefs.

Even more important, framing the problems of Muslim societies in terms of sociopolitical issues versus theology ignores that not all theological or hermeneutic projects undercut attempts to secure civil liberties or representative governments. On the contrary, such projects can provide an incentive for change by showing that discrimination is not intrinsic to Islam and in fact subverts the Qur'an's egalitarianism. However, we close down this option in Muslim societies when we accept patriarchal readings of the Qur'an as the only authentic ones and, on this basis, position Islam against democracy and the Qur'an against "universal standards." The oppositional framing of Islam and democracy, supposedly meant to edge Muslims toward democracy, ensures that democracy is never presented as being compatible with Islam. Telling Muslims that the cost of joining the "universal community" is to abandon any sense of themselves as a specifically Muslim *umma* (community; faithfulness) can only evoke in them suspicion of this community, not veneration for it.

Problematically, the same people who put the onus of defending the relevance of our religion and our scripture to ourselves on Muslims feel no need to defend the secular alternatives they champion, since secularism already enjoys a certain currency. Robert Young, for instance, argues that all critical theory is "distinguished by an unmediated secularism, opposed to and consistently excluding the religions that have taken on the political identity of providing alternative value-systems to those of the west—broadly speaking, Islam and Hinduism." As an example, he points to the failure of postcolonial studies to consider Gandhi's spirituality "a form of anti-western political and cultural critique." In fact, in Young's view, "Gandhi's anomalous position brings out the extent to which, as a result of its Marxist orientation, an absolute division between the material and the spiritual operates within postcolonial studies. . . . Postcolonial theory, despite its espousal of subaltern resistance, scarcely values subaltern resistance that does not operate according to its own secular terms."[38]

This unmediated secularism not only obscures the epistemic violence of secularism in its garb of "universalizing reason,"[39] but it also keeps Marxists like Ali and Moghadam from realizing some simple truths about Muslims. One is that regardless of whether or how well Muslims read the Qur'an (and I said earlier that the majority does not), the Qur'an nonetheless abides in our consciousnesses so enduringly that we are unlikely to toss it aside in the name of sociopolitical values or "universal standards." Incidentally, the tendentious positioning of the Qur'an against "universal standards"—which disparages the Qur'an while removing these "standards" from the domain of political contestation by privileging them at the outset—reveals a paradox in how certain variants of Marxism treat ideology. On the one hand, traditional Marxism treats materialist ideologies as the most authentic expressions of the human condition and therefore as universally valid and beyond critique. On the other, it consigns religion-as-ideology to the netherworld of false consciousness. Yet in the end what concerns me are not the inner tensions in traditional Marxism, or even the double standards of many Marxists. Rather, it is that certain options are closed down for Muslims at the global level when Marxists and other secular theorists refuse to acknowledge the value of internal critiques of Islam in reforming Muslim practices. Of course, to recognize the efficacy of such critiques, one would need to recognize the power of Islam, and to recognize the power of Islam, one would need to engage it on its own terms, without trying to secularize or privatize it in the manner of Western religions. But this would mean legitimating Islamic discourses, if not Islam itself, in the global arena, and most secular theorists are loath to do this, preferring instead to silence "Islam as a political discourse, by reducing it to a religious practice . . . in effect closing off public discussion of how the many varieties of Islamism are challenging and extending the discursive field of political resistance," as Susan Buck-Morss puts it.[40] However, insists Buck-Morss, "Such a discussion . . . is there to be engaged within the *global* public sphere, as opposed to our own provincial one, and there is urgency to do so." The critique of George W. Bush from the left shows that secular commitments need not keep one from recognizing that what deserves respect is "the intellectually critical and socially accountable power of Islamism . . . not its instrumentalized uses by groups in power to garner unquestioning support and to silence internal opposition." The social power of "Islamism," as Buck-Morss realizes, lies in its function as an internal critique of Islam. "Just as in Western critical theory the great defenders of reason are those who criticize the rationalization of society in reason's name, so today's progressive Muslims are able to use Islam as an immanent, critical criterion against its own practice, with similar effects." Buck-Morss is able to recognize the power of "Islamism" as an oppositional discourse, partly because she realizes that "what is involved" in Muslim resistance to Westernization "is not freedom but dignity. And in a postcolonial context, dignity matters. Better put, dignity *is* freedom in a different sense, as liberation from Western hegemony." If "Western-defined freedom brings with it submission to Western power, the purported goal is undermined by the self-alienating means."[41]

To me, the most compelling aspect of Buck-Morss's argument is not so much its intelligent and audacious defense of "Islamism" (though I note that she is more at ease dealing with "political Islam" than with Islam as a religion), rather it is the fact that her gesture toward Islamism reveals the possibilities latent in the West to renew itself by engaging Islamism on its own terms. Thus in her hands Islamism also becomes a critical criterion against which the West too can measure its own practices and, in so doing, engage in a constructive self-critique. As she says:

Islamism as a political discourse embraces far more than the dogmatic fundamentalism and terrorist violence that dominate in the

Western press. It is also a powerful source of critical debate in the struggle against the undemocratic imposition of a new world order by the United States, and against the economic and ecological violence of neo-liberalism, the fundamentalist orthodoxies of which fuel the growing divide between rich and poor. This is to say that secularization is no guarantee against dogmatic beliefs, and that even foundational religious texts are open to multiple interpretations.[42]

The only choice before Western secular and critical theorists, then, is not an unmediated secularism or complicity in the West's hegemonizing projects ("universal standards"); they can also strive to articulate "a critical discourse adequate to the demands of a global public sphere, in which the hegemony of the colonizing discourses has been shaken."[43]

Like many other people, both Muslim and non-Muslim, I also believe that so long as colonizing discourses, especially U.S. discourses, remain intact, the global arena will not be conducive to equality and democracy. This is partly what I mean to convey by the title of this essay, "Globalizing Equality." To put it directly, we (the "partial publics" of Buck-Morss) cannot with a clear conscience speak about sexual equality in Muslim societies without speaking about equality in the global arena. The language of rights needs to be employed not only to ensure women equal rights in Muslim societies but also to ensure Muslim societies equal rights in an emergent global public sphere in which we can not only "think past" U.S. hegemony but actually move beyond it.

Nevertheless, by "Globalizing Equality" I also mean to refer to the need to ensure equality for Muslim women wherever they live. To my mind, such a project should not only ensure women's access to education, jobs, and information technologies, but also enable Muslims to evolve a sexual praxis that is based in "a discourse of gender equality and social justice that derives its understanding and mandate from the Qur'an and seeks *the practice* of rights and justice for *all* human beings in the totality of their existence across the public-private continuum."[44] This is how Margot Badran defines "Islamic feminism," based largely on her reading of both Amina Wadud's work and mine, even though neither of us claims that label for our work.

I have attempted to show the liberatory potential of women's reappropriation of theology and to point out that it is supported by—not solely enabled by, nor intrinsically antithetical to—the advances of information technology. By examining the impact of technology and a Qur'anic hermeneutics of equality side by side without directly connecting them, I have attempted to allow these two movements to illuminate each other while rejecting the simplistic tendency to embrace them in binary forms. Theology versus secular, east versus west, Islam versus democracy—all these polarizations ignore the complex, evolving dialogue about gender equality in a vigorous civil society.

For Badran, even being able to "speak of gender equality" means being able to transcend "private _and_ public . . . east _or_ west [since] we are speaking [of the] world." In fact, according to Badran, not only does "Islamic feminism" break down

> the east-west binary, it also dissolves the historically created religious-secular polarity. Islam (as religion and culture) is both _din wa dunya_, "religion and the world." Islamic feminism must and does concern itself with everyday life, with the workings of the mundane world. The aggressive constructing and labeling of Muslims "secularists" and "religious" in our day has been politically motivated and deployed. I say "in our day" because this intense polarity is _created_ in time and place—in the context of identity politics (another form of cross-demonizing).[45]

Moreover, inasmuch as "gender equality and social justice are embedded in the Qur'an we are not speaking of these principles as products of 'modernity' understood as _western_ modernity. People worldwide come to concepts of gender equality and social justice through different routes, through different texts—religious or secular." For Muslims, as Badran points out, "Ideas of gender equality and social justice were introduced in early seventh-century C.E. Arabia through the words that became enshrined in the Qur'an."[46]

While for this reason I prefer to label the sort of perspective Badran defines simply as Qur'anic and to call myself a believer rather than a feminist, I believe that for Muslim theology really to matter it needs to incorporate the discourse of gender equality that she associates with "Islamic feminism." This will allow those of us who wish to keep the "company . . . of

God"[47] to do so while also carrying out our charge to be socially accountable agents on earth. It is this aspiration that has encouraged me to join my voice to those of other Muslims who want to interpret Islam "in the light of moral humanistic commitments,"[48] as well as to those of non-Muslims who want to ensure that Islamic discourses are not "excluded from the global discussion because [their] premises are non-Western."[49]

Asma Barlas is professor of politics at Ithaca College, New York. She has a B.A. in English Literature and Philosophy and an M.A. in Journalism from Pakistan and an M.A. and Ph.D. in International Studies from University of Denver. She is the author of *Islam, Muslims, and the U.S.: Essays in Religion and Politics* (India: Global Media, 2004), *"Believing Women" In Islam: Unreading Patriarchal Interpretations of the Qur'an* (Austin: University of Texas Press, 2002), and *Democracy, Nationalism, and Communalism: The Colonial Legacy in South Asia* (Boulder, CO: Westview Press, 1995).

Notes
1. Khaled Abou El Fadl, *The Place of Tolerance in Islam* (Boston: Beacon Press, 2002), p. 104.
2. I have dispensed with quotation marks since many of these talks are unpublished.
3. I understand that this is a problematic term, but I retain it here as an indicator of an actually existing hegemony that characterizes itself as Western.
4. Dipesh Chakrabarty, *Provincializing Europe: Postcolonial Thought and Historical Difference* (Princeton, NJ: University Press, 2000), p. 28.
5. However, not all postcolonial theory might be suitable, as I point out in the third section.
6. I have this on the good authority of Demir Mikael Ahmed Barlas, who has lived in Turkey while also being an avid consumer of Internet culture.
7. Sherry Turkle, quoted in Ulises Ali Mejías, "Postmodernism, Virtuality, Globalization, and the (fragmented) Self," December 19, 2003, http://ideant.typepad.com/ideant/2003/12/postmodernism_v.html.
8. Fredric Jameson, quoted in ibid.
9. Ulises Ali Mejías, "The Limits of e-Democracy: Between Public and Mass," January 27, 2004, http://ideant.typepad.com/ideant/2004/01/edemocracy.html.
10. Of course, as Mejías points out, "the mass and the public are (as Mills argues)

extreme ends of a scale. We are neither one nor the other completely" (ibid.)

11. Susan Buck-Morss, *Thinking Past Terror: Islamism and Critical Theory on the Left* (London: Verso, 2003), p. 92.

12. Ulises Ali Mejías, "Virtual Freedom and Tolerance: The Perils of Uniform Diversity," February 8, 2004, http://ideant.typepad.com/ideant/2004/02/virtual_freedom.html.

13. Herbert Marcuse, "Repressive Tolerance," in Robert Paul Wolff, Barrington Moore Jr., and Herbert Marcuse (eds), *A Critique of Pure Tolerance* (Boston: Beacon Press, 1965), p. 81.

14. Stephen Brookfield, "Reassessing Subjectivity, Criticality, and Inclusivity: Marcuse's Challenge to Adult Education," *Adult Education Quarterly*, 52:4 (2002), p. 276.

15. Mejías, "Postmodernism, Virtuality, Globalization, and the (fragmented) Self."

16. Peter G. Mandaville, *Transnational Muslim Politics: Reimagining the Umma* (New York: Routledge, 2001), p. 167.

17. Ibid., p. 168.

18. Jon Anderson quoted in ibid.

19. Ibid., pp. 168–170.

20. Ibid., p. 176.

21. Roy quoted in ibid.

22. Mejías, "Postmodernism, Virtuality, Globalization, and the (fragmented) Self."

23. Chakrabarty, *Provincializing Europe*, p. 20.

24. Syed Abul-'Ala Maududi quoted in Mazhar ul Haq Khan, *Purdah and Polygamy*. (New Delhi, India: Harman Publications, 1983), pp. 61–62.

25. Fatima Mernissi, *Women's Rebellion and Islamic Memory*, (Atlantic Highlands, NJ: Zed, 1996), pp. 13–14.

26. Asma Barlas, *"Believing Women" in Islam: Unreading Patriarchal Interpretations of the Qur'an* (Austin: University of Texas Press, 2002).

27. Leila Ahmed, *Women and Gender in Islam: Historical Roots of a Modern Debate* (New Haven: Yale University Press, 1992).

28. See Toshihiko Izutsu, *God and Man in the Koran: Semantics of the Koranic Weltanschauung* (Tokyo: Keio Institute of Cultural and Linguistic Studies, 1964).

29. Zillah R. Eisenstein, *Feminism and Sexual Equality: Crisis in Liberal America*, (New York: Monthly Review Press, 1984), p. 90. In her later work, Eisenstein recognizes that differences don't mean inequality.

30. Abou El Fadl, Cohen, and Lague, *Place of Tolerance in Islam*, p. 105.

31. Talal Asad, *Formations of the Secular: Christianity, Islam, Modernity* (Stanford: Stanford University Press, 2003), p. 15.

32. Tariq Ali, "Theological Distractions," in Abou El Fadl, Cohen, and Lague, *Place of Tolerance in Islam*, p. 41.

33. Abou El Fadl, Cohen, and Lague, *Place of Tolerance in Islam*, pp. 104–105.

34. Val Moghadam, "Islamic Feminism and Its Discontents: Notes on a Debate," Iran Bulletin [n.d.], http://www.iran-bulletin.org/islamic_feminism_IB.html.

35. Ibid.
36. Chakrabarty, *Provincializing Europe*, p. 16.
37. For a review of Gramsci's approach to ideology, see Asma Barlas, *Democracy, Nationalism, and Communalism: The Colonial Legacy in South Asia* (Boulder, CO: Westview Press, 1995).
38. Robert Young, *Postcolonialism: An Historical Introduction* (Malden, MA: Blackwell, 2001) p. 338.
39. Asad, *Formations of the Secular*, p. 59.
40. Susan Buck-Morss, *Thinking Past Terror: Islamism and Critical Theory on the Left* (London: Verso, 2003) p. 42.
41. Ibid., pp. 46 and 47.
42. Ibid., p. 49.
43. Ibid., p. 101.
44. Margot Badran, "Islamic Feminism: Beyond Good and Evil, Beyond East and West," unpublished manuscript, 2003, p. 2.
45. Ibid., p. 7.
46. Ibid., p. 6.
47. Abou El Fadl, Cohen, and Lague, *Place of Tolerance in Islam*, p. 104.
48. Ibid., p. 104.
49. Buck-Morss, *Thinking Past Terror*, p. 44.

Feminist Theory, Agency, and the Liberatory Subject

Saba Mahmood

In the last two decades, one of the questions that has occupied many feminist theorists is how issues of historical and cultural specificity should inform both the analytics and the politics of any feminist project. While this questioning has resulted in serious attempts at integrating issues of sexual, racial, class, and national difference into feminist theory, questions of religious difference have remained relatively unexplored. The vexed relationship between feminism and religious traditions is perhaps most manifest in discussions of Islam. This is partly because of the historically contentious relationship that Islamic societies have had with what has come to be called "the West" and partly because of the challenges that contemporary Islamic movements pose to secular-liberal politics, of which feminism has been an integral (if critical) part. The suspicion with which many feminists tended to view Islamist movements only intensified in the aftermath of the September 11, 2001, attacks on the United States, especially the immense groundswell of anti-Islamic sentiment that followed them. If supporters of the Islamist movement were disliked before for their social conservatism and their rejection of liberal values (key among them "women's freedom"), their association with terrorism—now almost taken for granted—has served to further reaffirm their status as agents of a dangerous irrationality.[1]

In this essay, I will probe some of the conceptual challenges that women's participation in the Islamist movement poses to feminist theorists and gender analysts, through an ethnographic account of an urban women's mosque movement that is part of the Islamic Revival in Cairo, Egypt.[2] "Islamic Revival" is a term that refers not only to the activities of state-oriented political groups but more broadly to a religious ethos or sensibility that has developed within Muslim societies, particularly Egypt, since the 1970s.[3] I conducted two years of fieldwork with a grassroots women's piety movement based in Cairo. This movement is composed of women from a variety of socioeconomic backgrounds who gather in mosques to teach each other about Islamic scriptures, social practices, and forms of bodily comportment considered germane to the cultivation of the ideal virtuous self.[4] Even though Egyptian Muslim women have always had some measure of informal training in Islam, the mosque movement represents an unprecedented engagement with scholarly materials and theological reasoning that had been the province of learned men. Movements such as this one, if they do not provoke a yawning boredom among secular intellectuals, certainly conjure up a whole host of uneasy associations, such as fundamentalism, the subjugation of women, social conservatism, reactionary atavism, cultural backwardness, and the rest. My aim in this essay is not to analyze the reductionism of an enormously complex phenomenon that these associations entail, nor am I interested in recovering a redeemable element within the Islamist movement by recuperating its liberatory potential. Instead, I want to focus quite squarely on the conceptions of self, moral agency, and embodiment that undergird the practices of this nonliberal movement so as to come to an understanding of the ethical projects that animate it.

I want to begin by exploring how a particular notion of human agency in feminist scholarship—one that seeks to locate the political and moral autonomy of the subject in the face of power—is brought to bear upon the study of women involved in patriarchal religious traditions such as Islam. I will argue that despite the important insights it has provided, this model of agency sharply limits our ability to understand and interrogate the lives of women whose sense of self, aspirations, and projects have been shaped by nonliberal traditions. In order to analyze women's participation in religious movements such as the Egyptian mosque movement I describe, I want to suggest that we think of agency not as a synonym for resistance to relations of domination but as a capacity for action that historically specific relations of subordination enable and create. This relatively open-ended understanding of agency draws on a poststructuralist theory of subject formation but also departs from it, in that I explore those modalities of agency whose meaning and effect are not captured within the logic of subversion and resignification of hegemonic norms. As I will argue, only once the concept of agency is detached from the trope of resistance that a series of analytical questions are opened up that are crucial to understanding nonliberal projects, subjects, and desires whose logic exceeds the entelechy of liberatory politics. The second half of this essay is dedicated to elaborating this latter point through the analysis of an ethnographic example drawn from my fieldwork that juxtaposes two different modalities of agency and illuminates the difference each modality makes to how structures of gender inequality are lived.

Topography of the Mosque Movement

The women's mosque movement occupies a somewhat paradoxical place in relationship to feminist politics. It represents the first time in Egyptian history that such a large number of women have mobilized to hold lessons in Islamic doctrine in mosques, thereby altering the historically male-centered character of mosques as well as Islamic pedagogy.[5] This trend has, of course, been facilitated by the mobility and sense of entitlement engendered by women's greater access to education and employment outside the home in postcolonial Egypt. In the last forty years, women have entered new social domains and acquired new public roles from which they were previously excluded. A paradoxical effect of these developments is the proliferation of forms of piety that seem incongruous with the trajectory of the transformations that enabled them in the first place.[6] Notably, even though this movement has empowered women to enter the field of Islamic pedagogy in the institutional setting of mosques, their participation is critically structured by, and seeks to uphold, the limits of a discursive tradition that regards subordination to a transcendent will (and thus, in many instances, to male authority) as a coveted goal.[7]

According to the organizers, the women's mosque movement emerged in response to the perception that religious knowledge, as a means of organizing daily life, has become increasingly marginalized under modern structures of secular governance. The participants in this movement often criticize what they believe to be an increasingly prevalent form of religiosity in Egypt that accords Islam the status of an abstract system of beliefs that has no direct bearing on the way one lives and structures one's daily life. This trend, usually referred to as the secularization (*'almana*) or Westernization (*taghrib*) of Egyptian society, is understood to have reduced Islamic knowledge (as a mode of conduct and as a set of principles) to the status of "custom and folklore" (*'ada wa fukloriyya*). The women's mosque movement, therefore, seeks to educate lay Muslims in the virtues, ethical capacities, and forms of reasoning that the participants perceive as having become either unavailable or irrelevant to the lives of ordinary Muslims.

In Egypt today, Islam has come to be embodied in a variety of practices, movements, and ideas.[8] Thus some Egyptians view Islam as constitutive of the cultural terrain upon which the Egyptian nation has acquired its unique historical character, some understand Islam as a doctrinal system with strong political and juridical implications for the organization of state and society, and others, such as the women I worked with, see Islam as first and foremost individual and collective practices of pious living. This does not mean, however, that the women's mosque movement is apolitical in the wider sense of the term, or that it represents a withdrawal from sociopolitical issues. On the contrary, the form of piety it seeks to realize is predicated on, and transformative of, many aspects of social life.[9] The women's mosque movement has affected changes in a range of social behaviors among contemporary Egyptians, including how one dresses and speaks, what is deemed proper entertainment for adults and children, where one invests one's money, how one takes care of the poor, and by what terms public debate is conducted.

While at times the mosque movement has been seen as a quietist alternative to the more militant forms of Islamic activism, in many ways this movement sits uncomfortably with certain aspects of the secular liberal project promoted by the state.[10] These tensions stem in part from the specific forms of will, desire, reason, and practice this movement seeks to cultivate, and the ways it reorganizes public life and debate in accordance with orthodox standards of Islamic piety. It is therefore not surprising that the Egyptian government recently sought to regularize and sanction this movement, recognizing that the proliferation of this kind of Islamic sociability makes the task of securing a secular-liberal society difficult if not impossible.[11]

Agency, Resistance, Freedom

The pious subjects of the women's mosque movement occupy an uncomfortable place in feminist scholarship: they pursue practices and ideals embedded in a tradition that has historically accorded women a subordinate status, and they seek to cultivate virtues associated with feminine passivity and submissiveness (for example, shyness, modesty, perseverance, and humility—some of which I discuss below). In other words, the very idioms that women use to assert their presence in previously male-defined spheres are also those that secure their subordination. While it would not have been unusual in the 1960s to account for women's participation in such movements in terms of false consciousness or the internalization of patriarchal norms through socialization, there has been increasing discomfort with explanations of this kind. Drawing on work in the humanities and social sciences since the 1970s that has focused on the operation of human agency within structures of subordination, feminists have sought to understand the ways women resist the dominant male order by subverting the hegemonic meanings of cultural practices and redeploying them for their own interests and agendas. A central question explored within this scholarship has been: "How do women contribute to reproducing their own domination, and how do they resist or subvert it?" Scholars working in this vein have thus tended to explore religious traditions in terms of the conceptual and practical resources they offer which women may usefully redirect and recode to secure their "own interests and agendas," a recoding that stands as the site of women's agency.[12]

It should be acknowledged that the focus on locating women's agency when it first emerged played a critical role in complicating and expanding debates about gender in non-Western societies beyond the simplistic registers of submission and patriarchy. In particular, the focus on women's agency provided a crucial corrective to scholarship on the Middle East that for decades had portrayed Arab and Muslim women as passive and submissive beings, shackled by structures of male authority.[13] This scholarship performed the worthy task of restoring women's voices to analyses of Middle Eastern societies, showing women as active agents who have far more complex and richer lives than past narratives had suggested.[14]

While such an approach has been enormously productive in complicating the oppressor/oppressed model of gender relations, I would submit that it remains encumbered not only by the binary terms of resistance and subordination, but is also insufficiently attentive to motivations, desires, and goals that are not necessarily captured by these terms. Notably, the female agent in this analysis seems to stand in for a sometimes repressed, sometimes active feminist consciousness, articulated against the hegemonic male cultural norms of Arab Muslim societies. Even in instances when an explicit feminist agency is difficult to locate, there is a tendency to look for expressions and moments of resistance that may suggest a challenge to male domination. When women's actions seem to reinscribe what appear to be "instruments of their own oppression," the social analyst can point to moments of disruption of, and articulation of points of opposition to, male authority, either in the interstices of a woman's consciousness (often read as a nascent feminist consciousness) or in the objective effects of the women's actions, however unintentional they may be.[15] Agency, in this form of analysis, is understood as the capacity to realize one's own interests against the weight of custom, tradition, transcendental will, or other obstacles (whether individual or collective). Thus the humanist desire for autonomy and expression of one's self-worth constitute the substrate, the slumbering ember that can spark to flame in the form of an act of resistance when conditions permit.[16]

What is seldom problematized in such an analysis is the universality of the desire to be free from relations of subordination and, for women, from structures of male domination, a desire that is central for liberal and progressive thought, and presupposed by the concept of resistance it authorizes. This positing of women's agency as consubstantial with resistance to relations of domination, and its concomitant naturalization of freedom as a social ideal, I would argue, is a product of feminism's dual character as both an analytical and a politically prescriptive project. Despite the many strands and differences within feminism, what accords this tradition an analytical and political coherence is the premise that where society is structured to serve male interests the result will be either a neglect, or a direct suppression of, women's concerns.[17] Feminism, therefore, offers both a diagnosis of women's status across cultures and a prescription for changing the situation of women who are understood to be marginal/subordinate/oppressed.[18] Thus the articulation of conditions of relative freedom that enable women both to formulate and to enact self-determined goals and interests remains the object of feminist politics and theorizing. As in the case of liberalism, freedom is normative to feminism: critical scrutiny is applied to those who want to limit women's freedom rather than those who want to extend it.[19]

Feminist discussions about human freedom remain heavily indebted to the distinction liberalism draws between positive and negative liberty. In the liberal tradition, negative freedom refers to the absence of external obstacles to self-guided choice and action, whether those obstacles are imposed by the state, corporations, or private individuals.[20] Positive freedom, on the other hand, is understood as the capacity to realize an autonomous will, one generally fashioned in accord with the dictates of "universal reason" or "self-interest," and hence unencumbered by the weight of custom, transcendental will, and tradition.[21] While there continues to be considerable debate over the formulation and coherence of these entwined notions, I want to highlight the concept of individual autonomy central to both, and the concomitant elements of coercion and consent that are critical to this topography of freedom.[22]

The concepts of positive and negative freedom, with the attendant requirement of procedural autonomy, provide the ground on which much of the feminist debate unfolds.[23] For example, the positive conception of freedom seems to predominate in projects of feminist historiography (sometimes referred to as "herstory") that seek to capture historically and culturally specific instances of women's self-directed action, unencumbered by patriarchal norms or the will of others.[24] The negative conception of freedom seems to prevail in studies of gender that explore the spaces in women's lives that are independent of men's influence and possibly coercive presence, treating such spaces as pregnant with possibilities for women's fulfillment or self-realization. Many feminist historians and anthropologists of the Arab Muslim world have thus sought to delimit those conditions and situations in which women seem to autonomously articulate their own discourse (such as poetry, weaving, cult possession, and the like), at times conferring a potentially liberatory meaning to practices of sex segregation that had traditionally been understood as making women marginal to the public arena of conventional politics.[25]

A number of feminist scholars over the years have offered trenchant critiques of the liberal notion of autonomy from a variety of perspectives.[26] For example, while earlier critics drew attention to the masculinist assumptions underpinning the ideal of autonomy, later scholars faulted this ideal for its emphasis on the atomistic, individualized, and bounded characteristics of the self at the expense of its relational qualities, formed through social interactions within forms of human community.[27] Consequently, there have been various attempts to redefine autonomy so as to capture the emotional, embodied, and socially embedded character of people, particularly of women.[28] A more radical strain of poststructuralist theory has situated its critique of autonomy within a larger challenge posed to the illusory character of the rationalist, self-authorizing, transcendental subject presupposed by Enlightenment thought in general and the liberal tradition in particular. Rational thought, these critics argue, secures its universal scope and authority by performing a necessary exclusion of all that is bodily, feminine, emotional, nonrational, and intersubjective.[29] This exclusion cannot be substantively or conceptually recuperated through recourse to an unproblematic feminine experience, body, or imaginary (pace Beauvoir and Irigaray) but must be thought through the very terms of the discourse of metaphysical transcendence that enacts these exclusions.[30]

In what follows, I would like to push further in the direction opened by these poststructuralist debates. In particular, my argument for separating the notion of self-realization from that of the autonomous will is indebted to poststructuralist critiques of the transcendental subject, voluntarism, and repressive models of power. Yet, as will become clear, my analysis also departs from these frameworks insofar as I question the overwhelming tendency of poststructuralist feminist scholarship to conceptualize agency in terms of subversion or resignification of social norms, to locate agency within those operations that resist the dominating and subjectivating modes of power. In other words, the normative political subject of poststructuralist feminist theory often remains a liberatory one whose agency is conceptualized on the binary model of subordination and subversion. This scholarship thus elides dimensions of human action whose ethical and political status does not map onto the logic of repression and resistance. In order to grasp these modes of action that are indebted to other reasons and histories, I want to argue that it is crucial to detach the notion of agency from the goals of progressive politics.

The ideas of freedom and liberty as the political ideals are relatively new in modern history. Many societies, including Western ones, have flourished with aspirations other than these. Nor, for that matter, does the narrative of individual and collective liberty exhaust the desires of people in liberal societies. If we recognize that the desire for freedom from, or subversion of, norms is not an innate desire that motivates all beings at all times, but is profoundly mediated by cultural and historical conditions, then a question arises: How do we analyze operations of power that construct different kinds of bodies, knowledge, and subjectivities whose trajectories do not follow the entelechy of liberatory politics?

If the ability to effect change in the world and in oneself is historically and culturally specific (both in terms of what constitutes "change" and the means by which it is effected), then the meaning of agency cannot be fixed in advance but must emerge through an analysis of the particular concepts that enable specific modes of being, responsibility, and effectivity. Viewed in this way, what may appear to be a case of deplorable passivity and docility from a progressivist point of view, may actually be a form of agency— but one that can be understood only from within the discourses and structures of subordination that create the conditions of its enactment. In this sense, the capacity for agency is entailed not only in acts that resist norms but also in the multiple ways one inhabits norms.

It may be argued in response that this kind of challenge to the natural status accorded to the desire for freedom in analyses of gender runs the risk of Orientalizing Arab and Muslim women all over again—repeating the errors of pre-1970s Orientalist scholarship that defined Middle Eastern women as passive, submissive Others, bereft of the enlightened consciousness of their "Western sisters" and hence doomed to lives of servile submission to men. I would contend, however, that to examine the discursive and practical conditions through which women come to cultivate various forms of desire and capacities of ethical action is a radically different project than an Orientalizing one that locates the desire for submission in an innate ahistorical cultural essence. Indeed, if we accept the notion that all forms of desire are discursively organized (as much recent feminist scholarship has argued), then it is important to interrogate the practical and conceptual conditions under which different forms of desire emerge, including desire for submission to recognized authority. We cannot treat as natural and imitable only those desires that ensure the emergence of feminist politics.

Consider, for example, the women from the mosque movement that I worked with. The task of realizing piety placed these women in conflict with several structures of authority. Some of these structures were grounded in instituted standards of Islamic orthodoxy, others in norms of liberal discourse; some were grounded in the authority of parents and male kin, others in state institutions. Yet the rationale behind these conflicts was not predicated upon, and therefore cannot be understood only by reference to, arguments for gender equality or resistance to male authority. Nor can these women's practices be read as a reinscription of traditional roles, since the women's mosque movement has significantly reconfigured the gendered practice of Islamic pedagogy and the social institution of mosques. One could, of course, argue in response that, the intent of these women notwithstanding, the actual effects of their practices may be analyzed in terms of their role in reinforcing or undermining structures of male domination. While conceding that such an analysis is feasible and has been useful at times, I would nevertheless argue that it remains encumbered by the binary terms of resistance and subordination and ignores projects, discourses, and desires that are not captured by these terms, such as those expressed by the women I worked with.[31]

My argument should be familiar to anthropologists who have long acknowledged that the terms people use to organize their lives are not simply a gloss for universally shared assumptions about the world and one's place in it but are actually constitutive of different forms of personhood, knowledge, and experience.[32] For this reason, I have found it necessary, in what follows, to attend carefully to the specific logic of the discourse of piety: a logic that inheres not in the intentionality of the actors but in the relationships that are articulated between the words, concepts, and practices that constitute a particular discursive tradition.[33] I would insist, however, that an appeal to understanding the coherence of a discursive tradition is neither to justify that tradition nor to argue for some irreducible essentialism or cultural relativism. It is, instead, to take a necessary step toward explaining the force that a discourse commands.

Docility and Agency

In order to elaborate my theoretical approach, let me begin by examining the arguments of Judith Butler, who remains, for many, the preeminent theorist of poststructuralist feminist thought, and whose arguments have been essential to my own work. Central to Butler's analysis are two insights drawn from Michel Foucault, both quite well known by now. Power, according to Foucault, cannot be understood solely on the model of domination, as something possessed and deployed by individuals or sovereign agents over others, with a singular intentionality, structure, or location that presides over its rationality and execution. Rather, power is to be understood as a strategic relation of force that permeates life and produces new forms of desires, objects, relations, and discourses.[34] Second, the subject, argues Foucault, does not precede power relations, in the form of an individuated consciousness, but is produced through these relations, which form the necessary conditions of its possibility. Central to his formulation is what Foucault calls the paradox of subjectivation: the very processes and conditions that secure a subject's subordination are also the means by which she becomes a self-conscious identity and agent.[35] Stated otherwise, one may argue that the set of capacities inhering in a subject—that is, the abilities that define her modes of agency—are not the residue of an undominated self that existed prior to the operations of power but are themselves the products of those operations.[36] Such an understanding of power and subject formation encourages us to conceptualize agency not simply as a synonym for resistance to relations of domination, but as a capacity for action that specific relations of subordination create and enable.

Drawing on Foucault's insights, Butler asks a key question: "If power works not merely to dominate or oppress existing subjects, but also forms subjects, what is this formation?"[37] By questioning the prediscursive status of the concept of subject and inquiring instead into the relations of power that produce it, Butler breaks with feminist analysts who formulated the issue of personhood in terms of the relative autonomy of the individual from the social. Thus the issue for Butler is not how the social enacts the individual (as it was for generations of feminists) but what the discursive conditions are that sustain the entire metaphysical edifice of contemporary individuality.

Given Butler's theory of the subject, it is not surprising that her analysis of performativity also informs her conceptualization of agency; indeed, as she says, "the iterability of performativity is a theory of agency."[38] To the degree that the stability of social norms is a function of their repeated enactment, agency for Butler is grounded in the essential openness of each iteration and the possibility that it may fail or be reappropriated or resignified for purposes other than the consolidation of norms. Since all social formations are reproduced through a reenactment of norms, this makes these formations vulnerable because each restatement/reenactment can fail. Thus the condition of possibility of each social formation is also "the possibility of its undoing."[39]

There are several points on which Butler departs from the notions of agency and resistance that I criticized earlier. To begin with, Butler questions what she calls an "emancipatory model of agency," one that presumes that all humans qua humans are "endowed with a will, a freedom, and an intentionality" whose workings are "thwarted by relations of power that are considered external to the subject."[40] In its place, Butler locates the possibility of agency within structures of power (rather than outside them) and, more importantly, suggests that the reiterative structure of norms not only serves to consolidate a particular regime of discourse/power but also provides the means for its destabilization.[41] In other words, there is no possibility of "undoing" social norms that is independent of "doing" norms; agency resides, therefore, within this productive reiterability. Butler also resists the impulse to tether the meaning of agency to a predefined teleology of emancipatory politics. As a result, the logic of subversion and resignification cannot be predetermined in Butler's framework, because acts of resignification/subversion are, she argues, contingent and fragile, appearing in unpredictable places and behaving in unexpected ways.[42]

I find Butler's critique of humanist conceptions of agency and subject very compelling, and, indeed, my arguments in this article are manifestly informed by it. I have, however, found it productive to argue with certain tensions that characterize Butler's work, in order to expand her analytics to a somewhat different, if related, set of problematics. One key tension in Butler's work comes from the fact that while she emphasizes the ineluctable relationship between the consolidation and destabilization of norms, her discussion of agency tends to focus on those operations of power that resignify and subvert norms. Thus even though Butler insists time and again that all acts of subversion are products of the terms of violence they seek to oppose, her analysis of agency often privileges those moments that "open possibilities for resignifying the terms of violation against their violating aims" or that provide an occasion "for a radical rearticulation" of the dominant symbolic horizon.[43] In other words, the concept of agency in Butler's work is developed primarily in contexts where norms are thrown into question or are subject to resignification.[44]

Clearly Butler's elaboration of the notion of agency should be understood in the specific context of the political interventions her work is intended to effect. The theoretical practice Butler has developed over the last fifteen years is deeply informed by a concern for the violence that heterosexual normativity enacts and the way it delimits the possibilities of liveable human existence. Her theorization of agency therefore must be understood in its performative dimension: as a political praxis aimed at unsettling dominant discourses of gender and sexuality. An important consequence of these aspects of Butler's work is that her analysis of the power of norms remains grounded in an agonistic framework in which norms suppress and/or are subverted, are reiterated and/or resignified—so that one gets little sense of the work norms perform beyond this register of suppression and subversion within the constitution of the subject.

Norms are not only consolidated and/or subverted, however, but also performed, inhabited, and experienced in a variety of ways. I think Butler would not disagree with this; indeed, in her writings she often reverts to the trope of the "psyche" and the language of psychoanalysis to capture the density of ties through which the individual is attached to the subjectivating power of norms.[45] Nevertheless, Butler's exploration of this density often remains subservient, on the one hand, to her overall interest in tracking the possibilities of resistance to the regulating power of normativity, and on the other, to her model of performativity, which is primarily conceptualized in terms of a dualistic structure of consolidation/resignification, doing/undoing, of norms.[46]

The Subject of Norms

I would like to push the question of norms further in a direction that I think allows us to deepen the analysis of subject formation and also address the problem of reading agency primarily in terms of resistance to the regularizing power of structures of normativity. In particular, I would like to expand Butler's insight that norms are not simply a social imposition on the subject but constitute the very substance of her intimate, valorized interiority. But in doing so, I want to move away from an agonistic and dualistic framework—one in which norms are conceptualized on the model of doing and undoing, consolidation and subversion—and instead to think about the variety of ways norms are lived and inhabited, aspired to, reached for, and consummated. As I will argue below, this in turn requires that we explore the relationship between the immanent form a normative act takes, the model of subjectivity it presupposes (specific articulations of volition, emotion, reason, and bodily expression), and the kinds of authority upon which such an act relies. Let me elaborate by discussing the problems a dualistic conception of norms poses when analyzing the practices of the mosque movement.

Consider, for example, the Islamic virtue of female modesty (*al-ihtisham, al-haya*) that many Egyptian Muslims uphold and value. Despite a consensus about its importance, there is considerable debate about how this virtue should be lived and particularly about whether its realization requires donning the veil. A majority of the participants in the mosque movement (and the larger piety movement of which the mosque movement is an integral part) argue that the veil is a necessary component of the virtue of modesty because the veil both expresses "true modesty" and is the means through which modesty is acquired.[47] They posit, therefore, an ineluctable relationship between the norm (modesty) and the physical form it takes (the veil) such that the veiled body becomes the necessary means through which the virtue of modesty is both created and expressed. In contrast to this understanding, a position associated with prominent secularist writers argues that the virtue of modesty is no different than any other human attribute, such as moderation or humility: it is a facet of character but does not commit one to any particular expressive repertoire.[48] Notably, these authors oppose the veil but not the virtue of modesty, which they continue to regard as necessary to appropriate feminine conduct. The veil, in their view, has been invested with an importance that is unwarranted when it comes to judgments about female modesty.

The debate about the veil is only one part of a much larger discussion in Egyptian society wherein political differences between Islamists and secularists, and even among Islamists of various persuasions, are expressed through arguments about ritual performative behavior. The most interesting features of this debate lie not so much in whether the norm of modesty is subverted or enacted but in the radically different ways the norm is supposed to be lived and inhabited. Notably, each view posits a very different conceptualization of the relationship between embodied behavior and the virtue or norm of modesty: for the pietists, bodily behavior is at the core of the proper realization of the norm, and for their opponents, it is a contingent and unnecessary element in modesty's enactment.

Some of the questions that follow from this observation are: How do we analyze the work the body performs in these different conceptualizations of the norm? Is performative behavior differently understood in each of these views, and, if so, how? How is the self differently tied to the authority that the norm commands in these two imaginaries? Furthermore, what sorts of ethical and political subjects are presupposed by these two imaginaries, and what forms of ethico-political life do they make possible or impossible? These questions cannot be answered as long as we remain within the binary logic of doing and undoing norms. They require, instead, that we explode the category of norms into its constituent elements—that we examine the imminent form that norms take and inquire into the attachments their particular morphology generates within the topography of the self. My reason for urging this move has to do with my interest in understanding how different modalities of moral-ethical action contribute to the construction of particular kinds of subjects, subjects whose political anatomy cannot be grasped without applying critical scrutiny to the precise form their embodied actions take.[49]

In what follows, I will elaborate on these points by analyzing two ethnographic examples drawn from my fieldwork with the Egyptian women's mosque movement. The ethnographic here stands less as a signature for the "real" and more as a substantiation of my earlier call to attend to the specific workings of disciplinary power that enable particular forms of investments and agency.

Cultivating Shyness

Through my fieldwork, I came to know four lower-middle-class working women in their mid- to late thirties who were well tutored and experienced in the art of Islamic piety. Indeed, one may call them virtuosos of piety. In addition to attending mosque lessons, they met as a group to read and discuss issues of Islamic doctrine and Qur'anic exegesis. Notably, none of these women came from a devout family, and in fact some of them had had to struggle against their kin in order to become devout. They told me about their struggles, not only with their families but also, and more importantly, with themselves, in cultivating the desire for greater religious exactitude.

Not unlike other devout women I worked with from the mosques, these women also sought to excel in piety in their day-to-day lives—something they described as the condition of being close to God (variously rendered as *taqarrab allah* and *taqwa*). While piety was achievable through practices that were both devotional and worldly in character, it required more than the simple performance of acts: piety also entailed the inculcation of entire dispositions through a simultaneous training of the body, emotions, and reason until the religious virtues acquired the status of embodied habits.

Among the religious virtues (*fadail*) that are considered important to acquire for pious Muslims in general, and women in particular, is modesty or shyness (*al-haya*), a common topic of discussion among the mosque participants. To practice *al-haya* means to be diffident, modest, and able to feel and enact shyness. While all Islamic virtues are gendered (insofar as their measure and standards vary when applied to men and women), this is particularly true of shyness and modesty. The struggle involved in cultivating this virtue was brought home to me when, in a discussion about a chapter in the Qu'ran called "The Story" (*Surat al-Qasas*), one of the women, Amal, drew our attention to verse 25. This verse is about a woman walking shyly—with *al-haya*—toward Moses to ask him to approach her father for her hand in marriage. Unlike the other women in the group, Amal was outspoken and confident and seldom hesitated to assert herself in social situations with men or women. Normally I would not have described her as shy, because I considered shyness contradictory to candidness and self-confidence. Yet as I was to learn, Amal had learned to be outspoken in a way that was in keeping with Islamic standards of reserve, restraint, and modesty required of pious Muslim women. Here is how the conversation proceeded:

Contemplating the word *istihya*, which is form 10 of the substantive *hya*,[50] Amal said, "I used to think that even though shyness (*al-haya*) was required of us by God, if I acted shyly it would be hypocritical (*nifaq*) because I didn't actually feel it inside of me. Then one day, in reading verse 25 in *Surat al-Qasas* I realized that *al-haya* was among the good deeds, and given my natural lack of shyness, I had to make or create it first. I realized that making it in yourself is not hypocrisy, and that eventually your inside learns to have *al-haya* too." Here she looked at me and explained the meaning of the word *istihya*: "It means making oneself shy, even if it means creating it." She continued with her point, "And finally I understood that once you do this, the sense of shyness eventually imprints itself on your inside."

Another friend, Nama, a single woman in her early thirties, who had been sitting and listening, added: "It's just like the veil (*hijab*). In the beginning when you wear it, you're embarrassed (*maksufa*), and don't want to wear it because people say that you look older and unattractive, that you won't get married, and will never find a husband. But you must wear the veil, first because it is God's command (*hukm allah*), and then, with time, your inside learns to feel shy without the veil, and if you were to take it off your entire being feels uncomfortable about it."

To many readers, this conversation may exemplify an obsequious deference to social norms that both reflects and reproduces women's subordination. Indeed, Amal's struggle with herself to become shy may appear to be no more than an instance of the internalization of standards of feminine behavior that contributes little to our understanding of agency. Yet if we think of agency not simply as a synonym for resistance to social norms but rather as a modality of action, then this conversation raises some interesting questions about the relationships established between the subject and the norm, between performative behavior and inward disposition. To begin with, it is striking that instead of innate human desires eliciting outward forms of conduct, one's practices and actions determine one's desires and emotions. In other words, action does not issue from natural feelings but *creates* them. Furthermore, it is through repeated bodily acts that one trains one's memory, desire, and intellect to behave according to established standards of conduct.[51] Notably, Amal does not regard simulating shyness in her initial self-cultivation to be hypocritical, as it would be in certain liberal conceptions of the self, according to which a dissonance between internal feelings and external expressions is a form of dishonesty or self-betrayal (as captured in the question: "How can I do something sincerely when my heart is not in it?"). Instead, taking the absence of shyness as a marker of an incomplete learning process, Amal further develops the quality of shyness by synchronizing her outward behavior with her inward motives until the discrepancy between the two dissolves. This is an example of a mutually constitutive relationship between body learning and body sense—as Nama says, your body literally comes to feel uncomfortable if you do not veil.

Second, what is also significant in this program of self-cultivation is that bodily acts—like wearing the veil or conducting oneself modestly in social interactions (especially with men)—do not serve as manipulable masks detachable from an essential interiorized self in a game of public presentation. Rather, they are the critical markers of piety as well as the ineluctable means by which one trains oneself to be pious. While wearing the veil serves at first as a means to tutor oneself in the attribute of shyness, it is simultaneously integral to the practice of shyness: one cannot simply discard the veil once a modest deportment has been acquired, because the veil itself partly defines that deportment.[52] This is a crucial aspect of the disciplinary program pursued by the participants of the mosque movement, the significance of which is elided when the veil is understood solely in terms of its symbolic value as a marker of women's subordination or Islamic identity.

The complicated relationship among learning, memory, experience, and the self undergirding the model of pedagogy followed by the mosque participants has at times been discussed by scholars through the Latin term *habitus*, meaning an acquired faculty in which the body, mind, and emotions are simultaneously trained to achieve competence at something (such as meditation, dancing, or playing a musical instrument). While the term *habitus* has become best known in the social sciences through the work of Pierre Bourdieu, my own work draws on a longer and richer history of this term, one that addresses the centrality of gestural capacities in certain traditions of moral cultivation.[53] Aristotelian in origin and adopted by the three monotheistic traditions, this older meaning of *habitus* refers to a specific pedagogical process by which moral virtues are acquired through a coordination of outward behavior (bodily acts, social demeanor) with inward dispositions (emotional states, thoughts, intentions).[54] Thus habitus in this usage refers to a conscious effort at reorienting desires, brought about by the concordance of inward motives, outward actions, inclinations, and emotional states through the repeated practice of virtuous deeds.[55]

This Aristotelian understanding of moral formation influenced a number of Islamic thinkers, foremost among them the eleventh-century theologian Abu Hamid al-Ghazali (d. 1111), but also al-Miskawayh (d. 1030), Ibn Rushd (d. 1198), and Ibn Khaldun (d. 1406). The historian Ira Lapidus draws attention to this genealogy in his analysis of Ibn Khaldun's use of the Arabic term "*malaka*."[56] Lapidus argues that although Ibn Khaldun's use of the term *malaka* has often been translated as "habit," its sense is best captured in the Latin term *habitus*, which Lapidus describes as "that inner quality developed as a result of outer practice which makes practice a perfect

ability of the soul of the actor."[57] In terms of faith, *malaka*, according to
Lapidus, "is the acquisition, from the belief of the heart and the resulting
actions, of a quality that has complete control over the heart so that it commands the action of the limbs and makes every activity take place in submissiveness to it to the point that all actions, eventually, become subservient to
this affirmation of faith. This is the highest degree of faith. It is perfect
faith."[58] This Aristotelian legacy lives on in the practices of the contemporary
piety movement in Egypt. It is evident in the frequent invocation of Abu
Hamid al-Ghazali's (d. 1111) spiritual exercises and techniques of moral
cultivation, found in popular instruction booklets on how to become pious,
and often referred to by the participants of the Islamic Revival.[59]

To Endure Is to Enact?

In this section I want to explore different modalities of agency whose operations escape the logic of resistance and subversion of norms but which raise
interesting questions about what it means to endure and struggle against
structures of gender inequality. In what follows I will investigate how suffering and survival—two modalities of existence often considered the antithesis of agency—came to be articulated in the lives of women who lived under
the pressures of a patriarchal system that required them to conform to the
demands of heterosexual monogamy. Since these conditions of gender
inequality uniformly affect Egyptian women, regardless of their religious
persuasion, I am particularly interested in understanding how a life lived in
accordance with Islamic virtues affects a woman's ability to inhabit the
structure of patriarchal norms. What resources and capacities does a pious
lifestyle make available to women of the mosque movement, and how do
their modes of inhabiting these structures differ from those women whose
resources of survival lie elsewhere? In particular, I want to understand the
practical and conceptual implications of a religious imaginary in which
humans are considered only partially responsible for their own actions, versus an imaginary in which humans are regarded as the sole authors of their
actions. What interests me is not so much the epistemological repercussions
of these different accounts of human action,[60] but how these two accounts
affect women's ability to survive within a system of inequality and to flour-
ish despite its constraints.

One of the mosque-movement participants was a married woman in her mid-thirties named Nadia; she was a primary-school teacher and also taught the Qur'an to young children in a mosque as part of what she considered her social responsibilities in the ongoing work of piety. In one of my meetings with Nadia, I participated in a conversation she had with a friend of hers, Iman, who was in her late twenties and, by Egyptian standards, well past marriageable age. A married male colleague had asked Iman for her hand in marriage.[61] Iman was agitated, because although the man was very well respected at her place of work and she had always held him in high regard, he already had a wife. She was confused about what to do and asked Nadia for advice. Much to my surprise, Nadia advised Iman to tell the man to approach her parents formally to ask for her hand in marriage, and allow her parents to investigate his background to ascertain whether he was a suitable match for her.

I was taken aback by this response. I had expected Nadia to tell Iman not to think about the issue any further, since the man not only had broken the rules of proper conduct by approaching Iman directly instead of her parents but also was already married. So a week later, when I was alone with Nadia, I asked her the question that had been bothering me: Why did she not tell Iman to cut off all communication with this man? Nadia seemed a little puzzled and asked me why I thought that this was proper advice. When I explained, Nadia said, "But there is nothing wrong in a man approaching a woman for her hand in marriage directly, as long as his intent is serious and he is not playing with her. This occurred many times even at the time of the Prophet." I interrupted her and said, "But what about the fact that he is already married?" Nadia looked at me and asked, "You think that she shouldn't consider marriage to an already married man?" I nodded yes. Nadia gave me a long, contemplative look and said, "I don't know how it is in the United States but this issue is not that simple here in Egypt. If you are unmarried after the age of, say, late teens or early twenties—as is the case with Iman—everyone around you treats you like you have a defect (*al-naqs*). Everyone knows that you can't offer to marry a man, that you have to wait until a man approaches you. Yet they act as if the decision is in your hands! What is even worse is that even your [immediate] family starts to think in this way." Nadia acknowledged that single men were treated differently because, as she said, "the assumption is that a man, if he wanted to, could have proposed to any woman: if he is not married, its because he didn't want to, or there was no woman who deserved him. But for the woman it is assumed that no one wanted her because it's not up to her to make the first move."

When I asked Nadia what a woman could do about this situation, she replied: "You have to be strong; you must be patient (*sabira*) in the face of difficulty, trust in God (*tawwakali 'ala allah*), and accept the fact that this is what he has willed as your fate (*qada*); if you complain about it all the time, then you are denying that it is only God who has the wisdom to know why we live in the conditions we do, and not humans."

I asked Nadia if she had been able to achieve such a state of mind, given that she was married quite late. Nadia answered in an unexpected manner. She said, "O Saba, you don't learn to become patient (*sabira*) or trust in God (*mutawakkila*) just when you face difficulties. There are many people who face difficulties, and may not even complain, but they are not *sabirin* (patient, enduring). You practice the virtue of patience (*sabr*) because it is a good deed, regardless whether your life is difficult or happy. In fact, practicing patience in the face of happiness is even more difficult." I asked Nadia, "But I thought you said that one needs to have patience so as to be able to deal with one's difficulties." Nadia responded by saying, "*Sabr* is a condition of being: you practice it regardless of whether you are happy or sad. If it brings you solace from hardship, this is a secondary consequence of practicing the virtue of *sabr*. God is merciful, and he rewards you by giving you the capacity to be courageous in moments of difficulties. But you should practice *sabr* (patience) because this is the right thing to do in the path of God (*fi sabil lillah*)."

I came back from my conversation with Nadia quite struck by the clarity with which she outlined the predicament of women in Egyptian society— a situation created and regulated by social norms for which women were in turn blamed. While Nadia's response about having to make such choices resonated with other secular Egyptians, it was her advocacy of the cultivation of the virtue of *sabr* (roughly meaning perseverance in the face of difficulty without complaint) that seemed most problematic for them.[62] Insofar as *sabr* entails uncomplaining endurance in the face of hardship, it invokes in the minds of many the passivity women are often encouraged to cultivate in the face of injustice. Sana, a single professional woman in her mid-thirties who came from an upper-middle-class family and called herself a "secular Muslim," concurred with Nadia's description of how difficult life progressively became for single women in Egypt but strongly disagreed with her advice regarding *sabr*. She said, "*Sabr* is an important Islamic principle, but these religious types think it's a solution to everything. It's such a passive way of dealing with this situation." While for Sana too a woman needed a "strong personality" to be able to deal with such a circumstance, for her this meant self-esteem or self-confidence (*thiqa fi al-nafs wa al-dhat*). As she explained, "Self-esteem makes you independent of what other people think of you. You begin to think of your worth not in terms of marriage and men, but in terms of who you *really are*, and in my case, I draw pride from my work and that I am good at it. Where does *sabr* get you? Instead of helping you to improve your situation, it just leads you to accept it as fate—passively."

While Nadia and Sana shared a recognition of the painful situation single women face, they differed markedly in their respective engagements with this suffering, each enacting a different modality of agency in the face of it. For Sana, the ability to survive the situation she faced lay in seeking self-empowerment through the cultivation of self-esteem, as a psychological capacity that, in her view, enables one to pursue self-directed choices and actions unhindered by other's opinions. In contrast, for Nadia the practice of *sabr* does not necessarily empower one to be immune from others' opinions. According to her, one undertakes the practice of *sabr*, first and foremost, because it is an essential attribute of a pious character, an attribute to be practiced regardless of the situation one faces. Rather than alleviating suffering, *sabr* allows one to bear and live with hardship correctly as prescribed by one tradition of Islamic self-cultivation.[63] As Nadia says, if the practice of *sabr* fortifies your ability to deal with social suffering, this is its secondary, not essential, consequence. To explain this, Nadia gave the example of the figure of Ayyub (known as Job in the Bible) who she said is known not for his ability to rise above pain but precisely for how he lived his pain. Ayyub's perseverance did not decrease his suffering: it ended only when God had deemed it should. According to this view, the lack of complaint in the face of hardship counts as *sabr*, but it is the way in which *sabr* infuses one's life and mode of being also makes one a *sabira* (the one who exercises *sabr*).

It should be noted that Nadia's conception of *sabr* was linked to the idea of divine causality, the wisdom of which could not be deciphered by mere human intelligence. Thus, not unlike Sana, many secular Egyptians regard Nadia's approach as defeatist and fatalist, an acceptance of social injustice whose real origins lie in structures of patriarchy and social arrangements rather than in God's will manifest as fate (*qada*). In this logic, to hold humans responsible for unjust social arrangements allows the possibility of change that a divine causality forecloses. Note, however, that the weight Nadia accords to fate does not absolve humans from responsibility for the unjust circumstances single women face. Rather, as she pointed out to me later, predestination is one thing and choice another; while god determines your fate (for example, whether you are poor or wealthy), human beings choose how to deal with their situations (for example, you can either steal or use licit means to ameliorate your poverty); ultimately God holds humans accountable for their choices. What we have here is a notion of human agency defined in terms of individual responsibility, bounded by an eschatological structure on the one hand and a social one on the other.

Just as the practice of self-esteem structured the possibilities of action that were open to Sana, so did the realization of *sabr* for Nadia: enabling certain ways of being and foreclosing others. Notably, the exercise of *sabr* did not hinder Nadia from embarking on a project of social reform any more than the practice of self-esteem enabled Sana to do so. To recognize this is not to undervalue the project of reforming oppressive social conditions, something neither Nadia nor Sana could pursue for a variety of reasons. One should, therefore, not draw any hasty correlations between secular dispositions and the ability to transform conditions of social injustice. Beyond this point, I also want to emphasize that to analyze people's actions in terms of realized or frustrated attempts at social transformation is to necessarily reduce the heterogeneity of life to the rather flat narrative of succumbing to or resisting relations of domination. Just as our own lives don't somehow fit the demands of such a stringent requirement, it is also important to keep this in mind when analyzing the lives of women like Nadia and Sana, as much as movements of moral reform such as the one discussed here.

Finally, since much of the analytical labor of this essay is directed at the specificity of terms internal to the practices of the mosque movement, I would like to reiterate that the force of these terms derives not from the motivations and intentions of the actors but from their inextricable entanglement within conflicting and overlapping historical formations. My project is therefore based on a double disavowal of the humanist subject. The first disavowal is evident in my exploration of certain notions of agency that cannot be reconciled with the project of recuperating the lost voices of those who are written out of "hegemonic feminist narratives," to bring their humanism and strivings to light—precisely because to do so would be to underwrite all over again the narrative of the sovereign subject as the author of her voice and her story.

My project's second disavowal of the humanist subject is manifest in my refusal to recuperate the members of the mosque movement either as "subaltern feminists" or as the "fundamentalist Others" of feminism's progressive agenda. To do so, in my opinion, would be to reinscribe a familiar way of being human that a particular narrative of personhood and politics has made available to us, forcing the aporetic multiplicity of desires and aspirations to fit into this exhausted narrative mold. Instead, my ruminations on the practices of the women's mosque movement are aimed at unsettling key assumptions at the center of liberal thought through which movements of this kind are often judged. Such judgments do not always simply entail the ipso facto rejection of these movements as antithetical to feminist agendas; they also, at times, seek to embrace such movements as forms of feminism, thus enfolding them into a liberal imaginary.[64] By tracing the multiple modalities of agency that inform the practices of the mosque participants, I hope to redress current feminist political thought's profound inability to envision valuable forms of human flourishing outside the bounds of a liberal imaginary.

Conclusion

In conclusion, I would like to clarify the implications of this analytical framework for how we think about politics, especially in light of some of the questions posed to me when I have presented this essay in public. In pushing at the limits of the analytical project of feminism, I am often asked, have I lost sight of its politically prescriptive project? Does attention to the ways in which moral agency and norms function within a particular imaginary entail the suspension of critique? What, I am asked, are the "implicit politics" of this essay?

In some ways, these questions bespeak the tension that attends the dual character of feminism as both an analytical and a political project, in that no analytical undertaking is considered enough in and of itself unless it takes a position vis-à-vis the subordination of women. Marilyn Strathern observed as much when she wrote about the "awkward relationship" between feminism and anthropology. She argued, "Insofar as the feminist debate is necessarily a politicized one, our common ground or field is thus conceived as the practical contribution that feminist scholarship makes to the solution or dissolution of the problem of women. . . . To present an ethnographic account as authentic ('these are the conditions in this society') cannot avoid being judged for the position it occupies in this particular debate. By failing to take up an explicit feminist position, I have, on occasion, been regarded as not a feminist."[65]

While I appreciate Strathern's astute comments about the enterprise of thinking and writing on the double edge of analysis and advocacy, I also think the argument I offer here has repercussions for the way we think about politics. In this essay I have argued that the liberatory goals of feminism should be rethought in light of the fact that the desire for freedom and liberation is historically situated and its motivational force cannot be assumed a priori but needs to be reconsidered in light of other desires, historical projects, and capacities that inhere in a discursively and historically located subject. What follows from this, I would contend, is that in analyzing the question of politics, we must begin with a set of fundamental questions about the conceptual relationship between the body, the self, and moral agency as constituted within different ethical-moral traditions, and not hold any one model to be axiomatic, as progressive-feminist scholarship often does. This is particularly germane to the movement I discuss here, insofar as this movement is organized around self-fashioning and ethical conduct (rather than the transformation of juridical and state institutions), an adequate understanding of which must necessarily address what in other contexts has been called the politics of the body—namely, the constitution of the body within structures of power.

If there is one thing that the feminist tradition has made clear, it is that questions of politics must be pursued through an analysis of the architecture of the self, the social and technical processes through which the self's constituent elements (instincts, desires, emotions, memory) are identified and given coherence. While this insight has often been used to explicate how gender inequality works differently in various cultural systems, far less attention has been paid to how different modes of affective attachment

might parochialize left-liberal assumptions about the constitutive relationship between moral action and embodiment when discussing politics.
Women's embodied relationships to the world and to themselves, once
understood as an enactment of structures of inequality, often serve as the
theater in which already known projects, affects, and commitments play
out. Yet if it is conceded that politics involves more than rational argumen-
tation and evaluation of abstract moral principles, and that political judgments arise from the intersubjective level of being and acting, then it follows that this level must be engaged to think constitutively and critically
about what politics is or should be about.

For a scholar of Islam, none of these issues can be adequately addressed
without encountering the essential tropes through which knowledge about
the Muslim world has been organized, especially the trope of patriarchal violence and Islam's (mis)treatment of women. The veil, more than any other
Islamic practice, has become the symbol and evidence of the violence Islam
has inflicted on women. I have seldom presented my arguments in an academic setting, particularly my argument about the veil as a disciplinary practice that constitutes pious subjectivities, without facing a barrage of questions
from people demanding to know why I have failed to condemn the patriarchal assumptions behind the practice and the suffering it engenders. I am
often struck by my audience's lack of curiosity about what else the veil might
perform in the world, beyond its violation of women. These exhortations to
condemnation are only one indication of how the veil and the commitments
it embodies, not to mention other kinds of Islamic practices, have come to
be understood through the prism of women's freedom and subjugation to
the extent that to ask a different set of questions about this practice is to lay
oneself open to the charge of indifference to women's oppression. The force
this coupling of the veil and women's freedom—or lack thereof—commands
is equally manifest in arguments that endorse or defend the veil on the
grounds that it is a product of women's "free choice" and evidence of their
"liberation" from the hegemony of Western cultural codes.

What I find most troubling about this framing is the analytical foreclo-
sure it effects and the silence it implicitly condones regarding a whole host
of issues—issues that demand attention from scholars who want to think
productively about the Islamic practices undergirding the contemporary
Islamic Revival. I understand feminism's political demand for vigilance

against culturalist arguments that seem to authorize practices that under-write women's oppression. I would submit, however, that our analytical explorations should not be reduced to the requirements of political judg-ment, in part because the labor that belongs to the field of analysis is differ-ent from that required by the demands of political action, in both its tem-porality and its social impact. These two modalities of engagement—the political and the analytical—should not remain deaf to each other, but they should not be collapsed into each other either. By allowing theoretical inquiry some immunity from the requirements of strategic political action, we leave open the possibility that the task of thinking may proceed in direc-tions not dictated by the logic and pace of immediate political events.

Wendy Brown has written eloquently about what is lost when analysis is subjected to the demands of political attestation, judgment, and action. She argues:

> It is the task of theory . . . to "make meanings slide," while the lifeblood of politics is made up of bids for hegemonic representation that by nature seek to arrest this movement, to fix meaning at the point of the particular political truth—the nonfluid and nonnego-tiable representation—that one wishes to prevail. . . . [L]et us ask what happens when intellectual inquiry is sacrificed to an intensely politicized moment, whether inside or outside an academic institu-tion. What happens when we, out of good and earnest intentions, seek to collapse the distinction between politics and theory, between political bids for hegemonic truth and intellectual inquiry? We do no favor, I think, to politics or to intellectual life by eliminating a productive tension—the way in which politics and theory effectively interrupt each other—in order to consolidate certain political claims as the premise of a program of intellectual inquiry.[66]

I read Wendy Brown here as insisting on the importance of practicing a cer-tain amount of skepticism, a suspension of judgment if you will, toward the normative limits of political discourse. "Intellectual inquiry" here entails pushing against our received assumptions and categories, through which a number of unwieldy problems have been domesticated to customary habits of thought and praxis.

This argument gains particular salience in the current political climate, defined by the events of September 11, 2001, and the subsequent war of terror that the United States government has unleashed on the Muslim world. The long-standing demand that feminists stand witness to the patriarchal ills of Islam has now been enlisted in the service of one of the most unabashed imperial projects of our time. Consider, for example, how the Feminist Majority's international campaign against the Taliban regime was essential to the Bush administration's attempt to establish legitimacy for the bombing of Afghanistan—in what was aptly called "Operation Enduring Freedom." It was the burka-clad body of the Afghan woman—and not the destruction wrought by twenty years of war funded by the United States through one of the largest covert operations in American history—that served as the primary referent in the Feminist Majority's vast mobilization against the Taliban regime (and later in the Bush administration's war).[67] While the denial of education to Afghan women and the restrictions imposed on their movements were often noted, this image of the burka, more than anything else, condensed and organized knowledge about Afghanistan and its women, as if this alone could provide an adequate understanding of their suffering. The inadequacy of this knowledge has today become strikingly evident, as reports from Afghanistan increasingly suggest that the lives of Afghan women have not improved since the ouster of the Taliban and that, if anything, life on the streets has become more unsafe than it was under the old regime because of the increased sociopolitical instability.[68] Perhaps we need to entertain the possibility that had some analytical complexity been added to the picture that organizations such as the Feminist Majority presented of Afghan women's situation under Taliban rule—that is, had the need for historical reflection not been hijacked by the need for immediate political action—then feminism might have been less recruitable to this imperialist project.

The ethical questions that imperialist projects of this proportion pose for feminist scholars and activists are also relevant to the more sedate context of the women's mosque movement. To the degree that feminism is a politically prescriptive project, it requires the remaking of sensibilities and commitments of women whose lives contrast with feminism's emancipatory visions. Many feminists who would oppose the use of military force would have little difficulty supporting projects of social reform aimed at transforming attachments, commitments, and sensibilities of the kind that undergird the practices of the women I worked with, in order that these women may live a more enlightened existence. Indeed, my own history of involvement in feminist politics attests to an unwavering belief in projects of reform aimed at rendering certain life forms provisional if not extinct. But I have come to ask myself, and I would like to ask the reader as well: Do my political visions ever run up against the responsibility I incur for the destruction of life forms so that "unenlightened" women may be taught to live more freely? Do I even fully comprehend the forms of life that I want so passionately to remake? Would an intimate knowledge of lifeworlds distinct from mine ever question my own certainty about what I prescribe as a superior way of life for others?

It was in the course of the encounter between my own objections to the form-of-life the piety movement embodies and the textures of the lives of the women I worked with that the political and the ethical converged for me again in a personal sense. As I conducted fieldwork with the women's mosque movement, I came to recognize that politically responsible scholarship entails not simply being faithful to the desires and aspirations of my "informants" and urging my audience to "understand and respect" the diversity of desires that characterizes our world today. Nor is it enough to reveal the assumptions of my own or my fellow scholars' biases and (in)tolerances. As someone who has come to believe, along with a number of other feminists, that the political project of feminism is not predetermined but needs to be continually negotiated within specific contexts, I have come to confront a number of questions. What do we mean when we as feminists, say that gender equality is the central principle of our analysis and politics? How does my being enmeshed within the thick texture of my informants' lives affect my openness to this question? Are we willing to countenance the sometimes violent task of remaking sensibilities, lifeworlds, and attachments, so that women like those I worked with may be taught to value the principle of freedom? Furthermore, does a commitment to the ideal of equality in our own lives endow us with the capacity to know that this ideal captures what is or should be fulfilling for everyone else? If it does not, as is surely the case, then I think we need to rethink, with far more humility than we are accustomed to, what feminist politics really means. (Here I want to be clear that my comments are not directed at "Western feminists" alone, but also address "Third World" feminists and all those who are locat-ed somewhere within this polarized terrain, since these questions implicate all of us given the liberatory impulse of the feminist tradition.)

As for whether my framework calls for the suspension of critique regarding the patriarchal character of the mosque movement, my response is that I urge no such stance. But I do urge an expansion of the normative understanding of critique, one that is quite prevalent among many progres-sives and feminists (among whom I have often included myself). Criticism, in this view, is about successfully demolishing your opponent's position and exposing her argument's implausibility and logical inconsistencies. This, I would submit, is a very limited and weak understanding of the notion of critique. Critique, I believe, is most powerful when it leaves open the possi-bility that we might also be remade in the process of engaging another's worldview, that we might come to learn things that we did not already know when we undertook the engagement. This requires that we occasion-ally turn the critical gaze upon ourselves, to leave open the possibility that we may be remade through an encounter.

The above questions about politics should not be seen as a call to aban-don the struggle against what we consider unjust practices in the situated context of our own lives, or as advocating for the pious lifestyles of the women I worked with. To do so would only be to mirror the teleological certainty that characterizes some of the versions of progressive-liberalism that I criticized earlier. Rather, I suggest that we leave open the possibility that our political and analytical certainties might be transformed in the process of exploring nonliberal movements of the kind I studied—that the lives of the women with whom I worked might have something to teach us beyond what we can learn from the circumscribed social scientific exercise of "understanding and translating." If there is a normative political position that underlies this essay, it is the belief that we—my readers and I—must embark on an inquiry in which we do not assume that our political posi-tions will necessarily be vindicated or provide the ground for our theoretical analysis, but instead hold open the possibility that we may come to ask of politics a whole series of questions that seemed settled when we embarked on our inquiry in the first place.

Saba Mahmood teaches anthropology at the Un
Berkeley. Her research interests lie at the intersecti
of subject formation, secularism, religion, and gende
societies. She is the author of *Politics of Piety: The*
the Feminist Subject (Princeton, 2005). Her work ha
journals such as *Journal of Religion, Cultural Anthropology, Social
Research, American Ethnologist,* and *Cultural Studies.*

Notes

I would like to thank Princeton University Press for allowing me to reprint this excerpt
from my book *Politics of Piety: The Islamic Revival and the Feminist Subject* (Princeton:
Princeton University Press, 2005).

1. This dilemma seems to be compounded by the fact that women's participation in
    the Islamic movement in a number of countries (such as Iran, Egypt, Indonesia,
    and Malaysia) is not limited to the poor and middle classes (that is, the classes
    often considered to have a "natural affinity" for religion), but also from the upper-
    and middle-income strata.

2. There are three important strands that constitute the Islamic Revival: state-orient-
    ed political groups and parties, militant Islamists (whose presence has declined
    since the 1980s), and a network of socioreligious nonprofit organizations that pro-
    vide charitable services to the poor and perform the work of proselytizing. The
    women's mosque movement is an important subset of this network of socioreli-
    gious organizations and draws on the same discourse of piety (refered to as *da'wa*).

3. This sensibility has a palpable public presence in Egypt, manifest in the vast prolif-
    eration of neighborhood mosques and other institutions of Islamic learning and
    social welfare, in the dramatic increase in attendance at mosques by both women
    and men, and in marked displays of religious sociability. Examples of the latter
    include the adoption of the veil (*hijab*), brisk consumption and production of reli-
    gious media and literature, and a growing circle of intellectuals who write and
    comment on contemporary affairs in the popular press from a self-described Islam-
    ic point of view. Neighborhood mosques have come to serve as the organizational
    center for many of these activities.

4. My research is based on two years of field work (1995–1997) conducted in five dif-
    ferent mosques from a range of socioeconomic backgrounds in Cairo, Egypt. I also
    carried out participant observation among the leaders and members of the mosque
    movement in their daily lives. This was supplemented by a yearlong study with a
    shayk from the Islamic University of al-Azhar on issues of Islamic jurisprudence
    and religious practice.

osques have played a critical role in the Islamic Revival in Egypt: Since the 1970s, there has been an unprecedented increase in the establishment of mosques by local neighborhoods and nongovernmental organizations, many of which provide a range of social services to the Cairene, especially the poor, such as medical, welfare, and educational services. Given the program of economic liberalization that the Egyptian government has been pursuing since the 1970s and the concomitant decline in state-provided social services, these mosques fill a critical lacuna for many Egyptians.

6. Currently there are hardly any neighborhoods in this city of eleven million inhabitants where women do not offer religious lessons to each other. The attendance at these gatherings varies between ten and five hundred women, depending on the popularity of the teacher. The movement continues to be informally organized by women and has no organizational center that oversees its coordination.

7. This is in contrast, for example, to a movement among women in the Islamic republic of Iran aimed at the reinterpretation of sacred texts so as to derive a more equitable model of relations between Muslim women and men; see Haleh Afshar, *Islam and Feminisms: An Iranian Case-Study* (New York: St. Martin's Press, 1998) and Afsaneh Najmabadi, "Feminism in an Islamic Republic: 'Years of Hardship, Years of Growth,'" in *Islam, Gender, and Social Change* ed. Y. Haddad and J. Esposito (New York: Oxford University Press, 1998), p. 59-84.

8. For recent studies of the Islamic movement in Egypt, see Charles Hirschkind, *Ethics of Listening* (New York, Columbia University Press, 2006), forthcoming and "Civic Virtue and Religious Reason: An Islamic Counterpublic," in *Cultural Anthopology* 16 (1): 3-34, 2001; Mahmood, *Politics of Piety*; Armando Salvatore, *Islam and the Political Discourse of Modernity* (UK: Ithaca Press, 1997); and Gregory Starrett, *Putting Islam to Work: Education, Politics, and Religious Transformation in Egypt* (Berkeley: University of California Press, 1998).

9. Piety here refers more to one's practical (and thus "secular") conduct than to inward spiritual states, as the term connotes in the English Puritan tradition. For an analysis of the politics that the piety movement (and the mosque movement) has enabled, see Mahmood, *Politics of Piety*.

10. Secularism is commonly thought of as the domain of real life emancipated from the ideological restrictions of religion. As Talal Asad has argued, however, positing the opposition between a secular domain and a religious one (in which the former comes to be seen as the ground from which the latter emerges) provided the basis for a modern normative conception not only of religion but of politics as well. See Talal Asad, *Formation of the Secular: Christianity, Islam, Modernity* (Stanford, CA: Stanford University Press, 2003). This juxtaposition of secular and religious domains has been facilitated through the displacement of religious authority from the realms of the state and its institutions of law. To say that a society is secular does not mean that religion is banished from its politics, law, and forms of association. Rather, religion is admitted into these domains on the condition that it take particular forms; when it departs from these forms it confronts a set of regulatory

barriers. The ban on the veil as a proper form of attire for girls and women in Turkey and France is a case in point.

11. In 1996, the Egyptian parliament passed a law that aimed to nationalize the vast majority of neighborhood mosques, and the Ministry of Religious Affairs now requires everyone who wants to preach in a mosque to enroll in a two-year state-run program regardless of his or her prior training in religious affairs. See *al-Hayat*, "Wazir al-auqaf al-masri lil-Hayat: muassasat al-Azhar tu'ayyid tanzim al-khataba fi-al-masajid" (January 25 and 27, 1997). In addition, women's mosque lessons are regularly recorded and monitored by state employees. The government continues to suspend lessons delivered by women mosque teachers when the women make remarks critical of the state. For an analysis of the kind of politics the piety movement has made possible, see Mahmood, *Politics of Piety*, ch. 2 and 4.

12. In the Muslim context, see, for example Janice Boddy, *Wombs and Alien Spirits: Women, Men, and the Zar Cult in Northern Sudan* (Madison: University of Wisconsin Press, 1989); Mary Hegland, "Flagellation and Fundamentalism: (Trans)forming Meaning, Identity, and Gender through Pakistani Women's Rituals of Mourning," in *American Ethnologist* 25 (2): 240–66 (1998); Arlene Elowe MacLeod, *Accomodating Protest: Working Women, the New Veiling and Change in Cairo* (New York, Columbia University Press, 1991); and Azam Torab, "Piety as Gendered Agency: A Study of *Jalaseh* Ritual Discourse in an Urban Neighborhood in Iran," in *Journal of the Royal Anthropological Institute* 2 (2): 253–52 (1996). For a similar argument made in the context of Christian evangelical movements, see Elizabeth Brusco, *The Reformation of Machismo: Evangelical Conversion and Gender in Colombia* (Austin: University of Texas Press, 1995); and Judith Stacey, *Brave New Families: Stories of Domestic Upheaval in Late Twentieth Century America* (New York: Basic Books, 1991).

13. For a review of this scholarship on the Middle East, see Lila Abu-Lughod, "The Boundaries of Theory on the Arab World," in *Theory, Politics, and the Arab World: Critical Responses* ed. Hisham Sharabi (New York: Routledge, 1990), pp. 81–131.

14. In a sense, this trend within gender studies bears certain similarities to the treatment of the peasantry in new-left scholarship which also sought to restore a humanist agency (often expressed metaphorically as a voice) to the peasant in the historiography of agrarian societies—a project articulated against classical Marxist formulations that had assigned the peasantry a non-place in the making of modern history. The Subaltern Studies Project is a clear example of this scholarship. See, for example, Ranajit Guha and Gayatri Spivak, eds., *Selected Subaltern Studies* (Delhi: Oxford University Press, 1988). It is not surprising, therefore, that, in addition to the peasantry, Ranajit Guha, one of the founders of the Subaltern Studies Project, called for a new historiography that would restore women as agents, rather than instruments, of various movements. See Ranajit Guha, "The Small Voice of History," in *Subaltern Studies IX: Writings on South Asian History and Society* ed. S. Amin and D. Chakrabarty (Delhi: Oxford University Press, 1996), pg. 12.

15. Consider, for example, Janice Boddy's rich ethnographic work on women's *zar* cult

in northern Sudan, which uses Islamic idioms and spirit mediums. In analyzing the practices of these women, Boddy argued that the women she studied "use perhaps unconsciously, perhaps strategically, what we in the West might prefer to consider *instruments of their oppression* as means to assert their value both collectively, through the ceremonies they organize and stage, and individually, in the context of their marriages, so insisting on their dynamic complementarity with men. *This in itself is a means of resisting and setting limits to domination . . .*" (Boddy, *Wombs and Alien Spirits*, p. 345; emphasis added).

16. Aspects of this argument may also be found in a number of anthropological works on women in the Arab world, such as Susan Davis, *Patience and Power: Women's Lives in a Moroccan Village* (Cambridge: Schenkman, 1983); Daisy Dwyer, *Images and Self Images: Male and Female in Morocco* (New York, Columbia University Press, 1978); Evelyn Early, *Baladi Women of Cairo: Playing with an Egg and a Stone* (Boulder, CO: Lynne Rienner, 1003); Arlene MacLeod, *Accomodating Protest*; and Unni Wikan, *Behind the Veil in Arabia: Women in Oman* (Chicago: University of Chicago Press, 1991).

17. Despite the debates within feminism, this premise is shared across various feminist political positions including radical, socialist, liberal, and psychoanalytical ones, and marks the domain of feminist discourse. Even in the case of Marxist and socialist feminists who argue that women's subordination is determined by social relations of economic production, there is at least an acknowledgment of the inherent tension between women's interests and those of the larger society dominated and shaped by men. See Nancy Hartsock, *Money, Sex, Power: Toward a Feminist Historical Materialism* (New York: Longman Press, 1983) and Catharine MacKinnon, *Toward a Feminist Theory of the State* (Cambridge, MA: Harvard University Press, 1989). For an anthropological argument about the universal character of gender inequality, see Sylvia Yanagisako and Jane Collier, eds., *Gender and Kinship: Essays Toward a Unified Analysis* (Stanford, CA: Stanford University Press, 1987).

18. Marilyn Strathern, *The Gender of the Gift: Problems with Women and Problems with Society in Melanesia* (Berkeley: University of California Press, 1988).

19. For example, John Stuart Mill, a central figure in the liberal and feminist tradition argued, "The burden of proof is supposed to be with those who are against liberty; who contend for any restriction or prohibition. . . . The *a priori* assumption is in favor of freedom." John Stuart Mill, *On Liberty and Other Essays* ed. J. Gray (New York: Oxford University Press, 1991), p. 472.

20. Within liberal political philosophy, this notion (identified with the thought of Bentham and Hobbes) finds its most direct application in debates about the proper role of state intervention in the protected sphere of the private lives of individuals. This is also the ground on which feminists have debated the appropriateness of antipornography legislation proposed by a number of feminists. See for example Sandra Bartky, *Feminism and Domination: Studies in the Phenomenology of Oppression* (New York: Routledge, 1990); Catharine MacKinnon, *Only Words* (Cambridge, MA: Harvard University Press, 1993); Gayle Rubin, "Thinking Sex: Notes

for a Radical Theory of the Politics of Sexuality," in *Pleasure and Danger: Exploring Female Sexuality* ed. C. Vance (Boston: Routledge and Kegan Paul, 1984), pp. 267–319; Samois Collective, eds. *Coming to Power: Writings and Graphics on Lesbian S/M* (Boston: Alyson, 1987).

21. Isaiah Berlin, *Four Essays on Liberty* (London and New York: Oxford University Press, 1969); Thomas Hill Green, *Lectures on the Principles of Political Obligation and Other Writings* ed. P. Harris and J. Morrow (Cambridge: Cambridge University Press, 1986); Avital Simhony, "Beyond Negative and Positive Freedom: T. H. Green's View of Freedom," in *Political Theory* 21 (1): 28–54 (1993); and Charles Taylor, "What's Wrong with Negative Liberty," in *Philosophy and the Human Sciences: Philosophical Papers* 2 (Cambridge: Cambridge University Press, 1985), pp. 211–229.

22. See Ian Hunt, "Freedom and Its Conditions" in *Australasian Philosophy* 69 (3): 288–301 (1991); Gerald MacCallum, "Negative and Positive Freedom," in *Philosophical Review* LXXVI (3): 312–34 (1967); Simhony, "Beyond Negative and Positive Freedom"; and David West, "Spinoza 'On Positive Freedom,'" in *Political Studies XLI* (2): 284–96 (1993).

23. It is quite clear that both positive and negative notions of freedom have been used productively to expand the horizon of what constitutes the domain of legitimate feminist practice and debate. For example, in the 1970s, in response to the call by white middle-class feminists to dismantle the institution of the nuclear family, which they believed to be a key source of women's oppression, Native and African American feminists argued that for them freedom consisted in being able to form families, since the long history of slavery, genocide, and racism had operated precisely by breaking up their communities and social networks. See, for example, Beth Brant, *A Gathering of Spirit: Writing and Art by North American Indian Women* (Rockland: Sinister Wisdom Books, 1984); Patricia Hill Collins, *Black Feminist Thought, Knowledge, Consciousness, and the Politics of Empowerment* (New York: Routledge, 1991); Angela Davis, *Women, Race, and Class* (New York: Vintage Books, 1983); and Audre Lorde, *Sister Outsider: Essays and Speeches* (Trumansburg, Crossing Press, 1993). Similarly, "A Black Feminist Statement" by the Combahee River Collective, rejected the appeal white feminist appeal for lesbian separatism on the grounds that the history of racial oppression required black women to make alliances with male members of their communities in order to continue fighting against institutionalized racism. See Gloria Hull, Patricia Bell-Scott, and Barbara Smith, eds., *All the Women Are White, All the Blacks are Men, but Some of Us Are Brave: Black Women's Studies* (New York: Feminist Press, 1982).

24. For an illuminating discussion of the historiographic project of "herstory," see Joan Scott, *Gender and the Politics of Herstory* (New York: Columbia University Press, 1988), pp. 15–27.

25. Leila Ahmed, "Western Ethnocentrism and Perceptions of the Harem," in *Feminist Studies* 8 (3): 521–34, (1999) and Wikan, *Behind the Veil in Arabia*.

26. For an interesting discussion of the contradictions generated by the privileged posi-

tion accorded to the concept of autonomy in feminist theory, see Parveen Adams and Jeff Minson, The "Subject" of Feminism *m/f* 2:43–61, (1978).

27. In the first group, see Nancy Chodorow, *The Reproduction of Mothering: Psychoanalysis and the Sociology of Gender* (Berkeley and Los Angeles: University of California Press, 1978) and Carol Gilligan, *In a Different Voice: Psychological Theory and Women's Development* (Cambridge, MA: Harvard University Press, 1982); in the second, see Seyla Benhabib, *Situating the Self: Gender, Community, and Postmodernism in Contemporary Ethics* (New York, Routledge, 1992) and Iris Young, *Justice and the Politics of Difference* (Princeton, NJ: Princeton University Press, 1990).

28. Suad Joseph, ed. *Intimate Selving in Arab Families: Gender, Self, and Identity* (Syracuse: Syracuse University Press, 1999); Marilyn Friedman "Autonomy and Social Relationships: Rethinking the Feminist Critique," in *Feminists Rethink the Self* ed. D. T. Meyers (Boulder, CO: Westview Press, 1997), pp. 40–61 and *Autonomy, Gender, Politics* (New York: Oxford University Press: 2003); Jennifer Nedelsky, "Reconceiving Autonomy: Sources, Thoughts and Possibilities," in *Yale Journal of Law and Feminism* 1 (1): 7–36 (1989).

29. Judith Butler, *Bodies that Matter: On the Discursive Limits of "Sex"* (New York: Routledge, 1993); Moira Gatens, *Imaginary Bodies: Ethics, Power, and Corporeality* (London: Routledge, 1996); Elizabeth Grosz, *Volatile Bodies: Toward a Corporeal Feminism* (Bloomington: Indiana University Press, 1994).

30. For an excellent discussion of this point in the scholarship on feminist ethics, see Claire Colebrook, "Feminism and Autonomy: The Crisis of the Self-Authoring Subject," in *Body and Society* 3 (2): 21–41 (1997).

31. Studies on the resurgent popularity of the veil in urban Egypt since the 1980s provide excellent examples of these problems. The proliferation of such studies reflects scholars' surprise that, contrary to their expectations, so many "modern Egyptian women" have returned to wearing the veil. Some of these studies offer functionalist explanations, citing a variety of reasons why women take on the veil voluntarily (for example, the veil makes it easy for women to avoid sexual harassment on public transportation, lowers the cost of attire for working women, and so on). For examples of these studies, see Fadwa El Guindi, "Veiling Infitah with Muslim Ethic: Egypt's Contemporary Islamic Movement," in *Social Problems* 28 (4): 465–85 (1981); Valeria Hoffman-Ladd, "Polemics on the Modesty and Segregation of Women in Contemporary Egypt," in *International Journal of Middle East Studies* 19:23–50 (1987); Macleod, *Accomodating Protest*; Zeinab Abdel Radwan, *Zahirat al-hijab baina al-jami'at* (Cairo: al-Markaz al-qaumi lil-buhuth al-ijtima'iyya wa al-jinaiyya, 1982); and Sherifa Zuhur, *Revealing Reveiling: Islamist Gender Ideology in Contemporary Egypt* (Albany: State University of New York Press, 1992). Other studies identify the veil as a symbol of resistance to the commodification of women's bodies in imported Western media, and more generally to the hegemony of Western values. While these studies have made important contributions, it is surprising that their authors have paid so little attention to Islamic

virtues of female modesty and piety, especially given that many of the women who have taken up the veil frame their decision precisely in these terms. Instead, analysts often explain the motivations of veiled women in terms of standard models of sociological causality (such as social protest, economic necessity, anomie, and utilitarian strategy), while terms like morality, divinity, and virtue are accorded the status of the phantom imaginings of the hegemonized.

32. For an excellent exploration of the use of language in the cultural construction of personhood, see Steve Charles Caton, *"Peaks of Yemen I Summon": Poetry as Cultural Practice in a North Yemeni Tribe* (Berkeley and Los Angeles: University of California Press, 1990); Webb Keane, "From Fetishism to Sincerity: On Agency, the Speaking Subject, and Their Historicity in the Context of Religious Conversion," in *Comparative Studies in Society and History* 39 (4) 674–93 (1997); and Michelle Rosaldo, "The Things We Do with Words: Ilongot Speech Acts and Speech Act Theory in Philosophy," in *Language in Society* 11 (2): 203–37 (1982). Also see Marilyn Strathern's critique of Western conceptions of "society and culture" that feminist deconstructivist approaches assume in analyzing gender relations in non-Western societies. Marilyn Strathern, *Reproducing the Future: Essays on Anthropology, Kinship and the New Reproductive Technologies* (New York: Routledge, 1992).

33. The concept "discursive tradition" is from Talal Asad, *The Idea of An Anthropology of Islam* (Washington D.C.: Center for Contemporary Arab Studies, Georgetown University, 1986), occasional papers series. See my discussion of the relevance of this concept to my overall argument in Mahmood, *Politics of Piety*, ch. 3.

34. Michel Foucault, *The History of Sexuality: An Introduction* trans. R. Hurley (New York: Pantheon Books, 1978) and "Truth and Power," in *Power/Knowledge: Selected Interviews and Other Writings 1972–1977* ed. and trans. C. Gordon (New York: Pantheon Books, 1980), pp. 109–33.

35. Butler, *Bodies that Matter* and *Excitable Speech: A Politics of the Performative* (New York: Routledge, 1997); Michel Foucault, "Truth and Power" and "The Subject and Power," in *Michel Foucault: Beyond Structuralism and Hermeneutics* ed. H. Dreyfus and P. Rabinow (Chicago: University of Chicago Press, 1983), pp. 208–26.

36. An important aspect of Foucault's analytics of power is his focus on what he called its "techniques," the various mechanisms and strategies through which power comes to be exercised at its point of application on subjects and objects. Butler differs from Foucault in this respect, in that her work is not so much an exploration of techniques of power as of issues of representation, interpellation, and psychic manifestations of power. Over time, Butler has articulated her differences with Foucault in various places; see, for example, Butler, *Bodies that Matter*, pp. 248 n.19; *The Psychic Life of Power: Theories in Subjection* (Stanford, CA: Stanford University Press, 1997), pp. 83–105; *Gender Trouble: Feminism and the Subversion of Identity* (New York: Routledge, 1999), pp. 119–41; and Judith Butler and William Connolly, "Politics, Power, and Ethics: A Discussion Between Judith Butler and William Connolly," in *Theory and Event* 24 (2), http://muse.jhu.edu/journals/theory_and_event/v004/4.2butler.html (2000).

37. Butler, *The Psychic Life of Power*, p. 18.

38. Butler, *Gender Trouble*, p. xxiv, emphasis added.

39. Butler, "Further Reflections on Conversations of Our Time," in *Diacritics* 27 (1): 13–15 (1997). Butler explains this point succinctly in regard to sex/gender: "As a sedimented effect of a reiterative or ritual practice, sex acquires its naturalized effect, and, yet, it is also by virtue of this reiteration that gaps and fissures are opened up as the constitutive instabilities in such constructions, as that which escapes or exceeds the norm. . . . This instability is the *de*constituting possibility in the very process of repetition, the power that undoes the very effects by which sex is stabilized, the possibility to put the consolidation of the norms of sex into a potentially productive crisis." See Butler, *Bodies that Matter*, p. 10.

40. Seyla Benhabib, Judith Butler, Drucilla Cornell, and Nancy Fraser, *Feminist Contentions: A Philosophical Exchange* (New York: Routledge, 1995), p. 136.

41. Echoing Foucault, Butler argues, "The paradox of subjectivation (*assujetissement*) is precisely that the subject who would resist such norms is itself enabled, if not produced, by such norms. Although this constitutive constraint does not foreclose the possibility of agency, it does locate agency as a reiterative or rearticulatory practice, immanent to power, and not a relation of external opposition to power." See Butler, *Bodies that Matter*, p. 15.

42. See Butler's treatment of this topic in "Gender is Burning," in Butler, *Bodies that Matter*, and in "Doing Justice to Someone: Sex Reassignment and Allegories of Transsexuality," in *GLQ: A Journal of Lesbian and Gay Studies* 7 (4): 621–36 (2001).

43. Butler, *Bodies that Matter*, pp. 122 and 23. For example, in discussing the question of agency, Butler writes, "An account of iterability of the subject . . . shows how agency may well consist in opposing and transforming the social terms by which it is spawned" (see Butler, *The Psychic Life of Power*, p. 29). Note the equivalence drawn here between agency and the ability of performatives to oppose normative structures. Such oft-repeated statements stand in tension with her own cautionary phrases, in this case within the same text, when she admonishes the reader that agency should not be conceptualized as "always and only opposed to power" (Ibid., p. 17).

44. Amy Hollywood suggests that Butler inherits her valorization of resignification—the propensity of utterances and speech acts to break from their prior significations-from Derrida. But whereas Derrida, Hollywood argues, remains ethically and politically neutral toward this characteristic of language and signs, Butler often reads resignification as politically positive. See Amy Hollywood, "Performativity, Citationality, Ritualization" in *History of Religions* 42 (2): 93–115 (2002).

45. See, for example, Butler, *The Psychic Life of Power*.

46. Butler argues, for example, that Foucault's notion of subjectivation can be productively supplemented with certain reformulations of psychoanalytic theory. For Butler, the force of this supplementation seems to reside, however, in its ability to address the "problem of locating or accounting for resistance: Where does resist-

ance to or in disciplinary subject formation take place? Does [Foucault's] reduction of the psychoanalytically rich notion of the psyche to that of the imprisoning soul [in *Discipline and Punish*] eliminate the possibility of resistance to normalization and to subject formation, a resistance that emerges precisely from the incommensurability between psyche and subject?" (Butler, *The Psychic Life of Power*, p. 87).

47. See Muhammed Sayyid Tantawi, "Bal al-hijab farida islamiyya" in *Ruz al-Yusuf*, June 27, 68, (1994).

48. Said Muhammed Ashmawi, "Fatwa al-hijab ghair shar'iyya" in *Ruz al-Yusuf*, August 8 and 28 (1994). For an argument between these two groups about the veil and the virtue of modesty, see the exchange between the then-mufti of Egypt, Sayyid Tantawi, and the prominent intellectual Muhammed Said Ashmawi, who has been a leading voice for "Islamic liberalism" in the Arab world. See Said Muhammed Ashmawi, "al-Hijab laisa farida" in *Ruz al-Yusuf* June 13 and 22 (1994) and Tantawi, "Bal al-hijab farida islamiyya," 1994.

49. My analysis of the work that different conceptions and practices of the norm perform in the constitution of the subject draws heavily on Foucault's later work on ethics. See Michel Foucault, *The Use of Pleasure* in vol. 2 of *The History of Sexuality* trans. R. Hurley (New York: Vintage Books, 1990) and *Ethics: Subjectivity and Truth: Vol. 1 of Essential Works of Foucault, 1954–1984*, ed. P. Rabinow, trans. R. Hurley et. al. (New York: New Press, 1997). For my elaboration of this approach to understanding Islamist politics, see Mahmood, *Politics of Piety*, especially ch. 1 and 4.

50. Most Arabic verbs are based on a tri-consonantal root from which ten (sometimes fifteen) verbal forms are derived.

51. It is interesting to note that the women I worked with did not actually employ the body-mind distinction I use in my analysis. In referring to shyness, for example, they talked about it as a way of being and acting such that any separation between mind and body was difficult to discern. I have retained the mind-body distinction for analytical purposes, the goal being to understand the specific relation articulated between the two in this tradition of self-formation.

52. This concept can perhaps be illuminated by analogy to two different models of dieting: an older model, in which the practice of dieting is understood to be a temporary and instrumental solution to the problem of weight gain; and a more contemporary model in which dieting is understood to be synonymous with a healthy, well nourished lifestyle. The second model presupposes an ethical relationship between oneself and the rest of the world, and in this sense, is similar to what Foucault called "practices of the care of the self." The differences between the two models point to the fact that it does not mean much to simply note that that systems of power mark their truth on human bodies through disciplines of self-formation. In order to understand the force these disciplines command, one needs to explicate the conceptual relationship articulated between different aspects of the body and the particular notion of the self that animates distinct disciplinary regimes.

53. Pierre Bourdieu, *Outline of a Theory of Practice* trans. R. Nice (Cambridge: Cam-

bridge University Press, 1997). As a pedagogical technique necessary for the development of moral virtues, *habitus*, in the sense I discuss it, is not a universal term applicable to all types of knowledges, and neither does it necessarily serve as a conceptual bridge between the objective world of social structures and subjective consciousness, as it does in Bourdieu's formulation.

54. In *Nicomachean Ethics*, Aristotle makes a distinction between intellectual and moral virtues, and it appears that the pedagogical principal of *habitus* pertains to the latter but not the former: "Virtue, then, being of two kinds, intellectual and moral, intellectual virtue in the main owes both its birth and its growth to teaching (for which reason it requires experience and time), while moral virtue comes about as a result of habit, whence also its name *ethike* is one that is formed by a slight variation from the word *ethos* (habit). From this it is also plain that none of the moral virtues arise in you by nature; for nothing that exists by nature can form a habit contrary to nature . . . . For the things we have to learn before we can do them, we learn by doing them, e.g. men become builders by building and lyre players by playing the lyre; so too we become just by doing just acts, temperate by doing temperate acts, brave by doing brave acts . . . . By doing the acts we do in our transactions with other men we become just or unjust, and by doing the acts that we do in the presence of danger, and being habituated to feel fear or confidence, we become brave or cowardly." See Aristotle, *The Basic Works of Aristotle* ed. R. McKeon (New York: Random House, 1941), pp. 592–593. See Cary Nederman, "Nature, Ethics, and the Doctrine of 'Habitus': Aristotelian Moral Psychology in the Twelfth Century," in *Traditio* XLV: 87–110 (1989) for the emphasis the Aristotelian tradition places on the conscious training of various human faculties and assiduous discipline in the cultivation of *habitus*. For Bourdieu, *habitus* is primarily imbibed through unconscious processes. For a fuller discussion of this point, see chapter 4 in Mahmood, *Politics of Piety*.

55. In retaining the distinction between inward motives and outward behavior so often invoked by the mosque participants, I do not mean to suggest that it is an appropriate description of reality or an analytical principle. Instead, I am interested in understanding the different kinds of relationships posited between body/mind, body/soul, inner/outer, when such distinctions are used in a tradition of thought. For example, Plato's body/soul distinction suggested a metaphysical primacy of the soul over the body. Aristotle reworked this relationship, seeing the two as an inseparable unity whereby the soul became the form of the body's matter. The women I worked with seemed to regard the body almost as a material enactment of the soul whereby the latter was a condition of the former.

56. See O. N. Leaman, in *The Encyclopedia of Islam*. CD-ROM, version 1.0 (Leiden: Brill, 1999) for a discussion of the term *malaka* in the Islamic tradition.

57. Ira Ladipus "Knowledge, Virtue, and Action: The Classical Muslim Conception of *Adab* and the Nature of Religious Fulfillment in Islam," in *Moral Conduct and Authority: The Place of Adab in South Asian Islam* ed. B. D. Metcalf (Berkeley and Los Angeles: University of California Press, 1984), p. 54. Consider, for example,

Ibn Khaldun's remarks in *The Muqadimmah*, which bear remarkable similari
Aristotle's discussion: "A habit[us] is a firmly rooted quality acquired by doing a
certain action and repeating it time after time, until the form of that action is firmly fixed [in one's disposition]. A habit[us] corresponds to the original action after
which it was formed." See Ibn Khaldun, *The Muqaddimah: An Introduction to History* trans. F. Rosenthal (New York: Pantheon Books, 1958), p. 346.

58. Ladipus. "Knowledge, Virtue, and Action," pp. 55–56.

59. See, for example, Ahmed Farid, *al-Bahr al-raiq* (Alexandria: Dér al-imdén, 1990)
and Said Hawwa, *al-Mustakhlas fi tazkiyyat al-anfus* (Cairo: Dar al-salam, 1995).
A. H. al-Ghazali was critical of the Neoplatonist influence on Islam. See Majid
Fakhry, *A History of Islamic Philosophy* (New York: Columbia University Press,
1983), pp. 217–233. However, his ethical thought retained a distinctly Aristotelian
influence. On this point, see Mohamed Ahmed Sherif, *Ghazali's Theory of Virtue*
(Albany: State University of New York, 1975) and the introduction by T. J. Winter
in Abu Hamid al-Ghazali, *On Disciplining the Soul and on Breaking the Two Desires
The Revival of Religious Sciences* (Ihya 'Ulum al-din) bks. XXII and XXIII trans. T.
J. Winter (Cambridge, UK: Islamic Foundation, 1983), pp. xv–xcii. For A. H. al-
Ghazali's seminal work on practices of moral self-cultivation, see Abu Hamid al-
Ghazali, *Inner Dimensions of Islamic Worship* trans. M. Holland (Leicester, UK:
Islamic Foundation, 1983) and *The Recitation and Interpretation of the Qu'ran: al-
Ghazali's Theory* trans. M. Abul Quasem (London: KPI Press, 1984).

60. See, for example, Dipesh Chakrabarty, *Provincializing Europe: Postcolonial Thought
and Historical Difference* (Princeton, NJ: Princeton University Press, 2000) and
Amy Hollywood, "Gender, Agency, and the Divine in Religious Historiography"
in *The Journal of Religion* 84 (4): 514–28 (2004).

61. Islamic jurisprudence permits men to have up to four wives.

62. I have retained the use of *sabr* in this essay rather than its common English translation patience, because *sabr* communicates a sense not quite captured by the latter:
perseverance, endurance of hardship without complaint, and steadfastness.

63. I note the particularity of this tradition followed by the piety movement in Egypt,
which is quite distinct from other traditions of moral cultivation in Islam, such as
the *shi'i* or the *sufi* tradition.

64. On the former, see Haideh Moghissi, *Feminism and Islamic Fundamentalism: The
Limits of Postmodern Analysis* (London and New York: Zed Books, 1999). On the
latter, see Elizabeth Warnock Fernea, *In Search of Islamic Feminism: One Woman's
Global Journey* (New York, Doubleday, 1998).

65. Strathern, *The Gender of the Gift*, p. 28.

66. Wendy Brown, *Politics Out of History* (Princeton, NJ: Princeton University Press,
2001), P. 41.

67. On this subject, see Charles Hirshkind and Saba Mahmood, "Feminism, the Taliban, and Politics of Counter-Insurgency," in *Anthropological Quarterly* 75 (2):
339–54 (2002).

68. Amnesty International, *Afghanistan: "No one listens to us and no one treats us as*

ustice Denied to Women Amnesty International Reporters, AI
vember 23, 2003, http://www.web.amnesty.org/library/index/
3; Anna Badkhen, "Afghan Women Still Shrouded in Oppression:
use, Restrictions on Freedom Continue Almost Year After Fall of
an Francisco Chronicle October 14, 2002; Human Rights Watch,
ive as Humans": Repression of Women and Girls in Western Afghanistan
Human Rights Watch reports, vol. 14, no. 11 (C) http://www.hrw.org/reports/
2002/afghnwmn1202, 2002.

The Veil Debate—Again

Leila Ahmed

I want to begin this exploration with a quotation, or rather a collage of quotations made up of statements by three American Muslim college women in response to my inquiry about what wearing the hijab means to them: "I don't believe the Qur'an requires hijab," said one, "I believe it's a choice not an obligation. I wear it for the same reason that one of my Jewish friends wears a yarmulke: as a way of openly identifying with a group that people have prejudices about and as a way of saying yes we're here and we have the right to be here and to be treated equally." Another, also stating that she didn't believe the Qur'an required it, said she wore it just because she liked to and then added, "When people stare at me when I am on the T, I find myself thinking that, if there's just one woman out there who begins to wonder when she looks at me why she dresses the way she does and begins to notice the sexism of our society—if I've raised just one person's conscious-ness, that's good enough for me." A third said: "I started wearing it after I returned from a visit to my relatives in Palestine. I don't believe the Qur'an requires it—for me, wearing it is a way of affirming my community and identity, a way of saying that even as I enjoy the comforts we take for granted here and that people in Palestine totally lack, I will not forget the struggle for justice."

I come to this subject as someone who once studied in great detail the first major debate about the veil ever to occur in the Muslim world. It was triggered by a book which advocated unveiling, published in Cairo in 1899. Called *The Liberation of Woman* (*Tahrir al-Mara'a*), it was written by Qasim Amin, a French-educated, upper-middle-class Egyptian lawyer who was not so much a feminist as a modernizer, someone who was arguing that Muslims needed to follow in the paths of progress and civilization forged by Europe. There was nothing controversial about the practical measures he advocated for women—education, for example, to primary level, which was in fact already taking place not only in private schools but in government-sponsored schools. In any event Amin also now advocated this, arguing that this would enable women to become good wives and mothers in the way that European women were. Only his call for abandoning the "backward" and "uncivilized" practice of veiling and the arguments in which he framed this were controversial. "Do you imagine," he wrote, for instance, to give some sense of what his framing arguments were, "that the men of Europe who have attained such completeness of intellect that they were able to discover the force of steam and electricity . . . those intellects we so much admire, could possibly fail to know the means of safeguarding woman and preserving her purity? Do you think that such a people would have abandoned veiling if they had seen any good in it?"[1]

Clearly then this call for unveiling made at the end of the nineteenth century, came already marked with notions of who was civilized and who was not, and already replete with the markings of colonizer/colonized, European/non-European. And it came already marked, too, with class divisions, as the Western-educated and Westernizing upper classes, people such as Amin, now advocated unveiling: these were classes which were already, and in distinction to other classes, beginning to adopt the customs and dress-styles of Europe, and European ways of furnishing the home.

The moment at which this debate occurred, the end of the nineteenth century, was two decades into the British occupation of Egypt. And it was the era also when the British empire was at its height and the era of the common circulation of imperial discourses as to the proper hierarchies of peoples, races, customs, civilizations.

Amin's book in fact essentially reproduced the colonial narrative of the day as to the inferior Muslim Other, an inferiority and otherness symbolically connoted in European discourse by the veil. This narrative itself was a variant of the colonial trope designating other cultures and in particular the practices of other cultures in relation to women, as inferior—for Hindus for instance it was *suttee* that was the emblem of this, for Muslims—veiling. All of these were versions of the colonial trope that Gayatri Spivak famously called the trope of "white men saving brown women from brown men."

Besides reproducing the colonial narrative, Amin's book also reproduced the specific views on the veil of Lord Cromer, then the British representative in Egypt—the Paul Bremer as it were of his day. Cromer, who was
well known in England as the founder and first president of the Society of
Men Opposed to Women's Suffrage, in Egypt was passionate advocate of
the importance of unveiling. The veil, as he put it, was "the fatal obstacle"
standing in the way of Egyptian men's "attainment of that elevation of
thought and character which should accompany the introduction of Western civilization."[2]

For Cromer, then, the veil clearly did not signify merely male dominance or "patriarchy": Patriarchy and male dominance in their British,
Victorian forms at least were, indeed, clearly values that Cromer himself was
deeply committed to upholding—as president, for instance, of the Society
Opposed to Women's Suffrage. Rather, the veil, this visible emblem of
Islam, in Cromer's rhetoric and in colonial rhetoric more generally, was
essentially a sign of the backwardness of Islamic moral development and
civilization altogether—a shorthand signal for everything that was inferior
about Islam as moral order and civilization.

While some Egyptians, like Amin, admired Cromer, others hated him.
The topic of the veil and Amin's call for unveiling, echoing that of the colonizer, was clearly already, by this moment in history, fraught with other and
volatile issues—issues of class, of "superior" and "inferior" religions and civilizations, etc.—and all of these now were in evidence in the intense controversy around the veil that Amin's book ignited in Cairo and other Muslim
capitals. This first debate on the veil, then, was not merely the first but also,
as it were, the ur-debate on the subject, bringing together all the elements
that, henceforth, to some degree or other, would be at play whenever the
veil emerged as major issue: notions of civilized versus uncivilized, patriarchal versus liberated, colonizer or former colonizer versus Other; and then
also, as the Islamic counter-narrative began now to be articulated, as affirmation of Islamic purity and its God-ordained values versus the corruption
of the West—and all intertwined with class issues.

These elements are still often discernibly at play when the veil emerges
as focus of attention. The French ban, for instance, is clearly in some sense a
reiteration of elements of the colonial narrative, elements that France had
already acted on earlier in its history as it pursued the project of unveiling

women in Algeria through the early twentieth century, to the Algerian war of independence in the 1960s. And we saw elements of that narrative at play here, too, in our U.S. media, as we went to war in Afghanistan. As one journalist astutely observed, the burkah became "at once battleflag and moral justification for our going to war."[3] Its fleeting appearance on television could function as explanation enough of what we were doing and why we were at war—packaged into that one image were all those old notions of superior/inferior, saving the women, and moral rightness.

I wrote my analysis of that first debate in my book on women in Islam—a book I finished about fourteen years ago and in which I was, implicitly at least, distinctly not a supporter of veiling.[4]

Now we are in a different place, in the midst of events that compel rethinking. Most importantly we are living through the emergence of Muslims as minorities in Europe and the United States, among whom are women who wear hijab. New happenings are affecting their lives—bans on hijab, harassments or firings at work, and, since 9/11 in the United States, occasionally outright attack. Of course then I find myself first of all wanting to support unequivocally their right to wear whatever they wish. Moreover, since this is a country where Muslims are a minority, one anxiety about the veil is automatically removed—the idea, certainly present in Muslim majority countries, that if Islamists come to power, the veil (and with it, more importantly, a host of laws severely curtailing women's rights) might be imposed on all of us by law.

In the midst of this, though, I have found myself wondering as to how it came about that Muslim women, or some Muslim women anyway, growing up in the United States, came to assume and apparently to accept relatively easily the notion that hijab is somehow an important part of being Muslim. For, here, it is among the younger generation of Muslims most particularly that the practice seems to be prevalent and growing. In contrast to the reports from France of young girls being forced to wear it (and indeed in regard to France too such reports are being contested by other reports), here the more common stories one hears and reads of are of young women who choose to wear it, sometimes against parental wishes.

We are living now through this tumultuous, unfolding present, and the emerging and ever shifting realities and helter-skelter developments we are in the thick of are scarcely yet studied or documented. Some research on Muslim women in the United States. has been done and much more is currently in progress.[5] Inevitably though it will be years before we have documentation and studies available from which we can begin to glean and piece together some fairly rich and comprehensive notions of the nuanced complexity of the history we are living through and of what happened in our times—even with regard to this one matter of the veil, and why young women, members of a religious minority in the United States, are taking it up in this country. For surely there is no single or simple reason. Just to begin with, this is a minority made up of a rich variety of minorities with their own distinct histories, ethnicities, and different notions and experiences of the meanings of religious belief, and there is a range of possibilities as to the reasons, pressures, politics, and notions of self, of religion, of identity, of sexuality and so on, all of which must differently come into play in the decision of whether to veil or not to veil.

My readings of such studies as there are and my conversations with Muslim women in hijab and my general observations regarding veiling today in the United States confirm my sense that a vast variety of reasons, explanations, and motivations today shape the decision to veil. Besides my readings of such scholarship as is available on the subject, my preliminary conclusions on the matter are based on interviews I conducted over the years 2002 to 2003 with some sixteen college women in the Cambridge, Massachusetts, area who wear hijab; and also on innumerable informal conversations with students and colleagues who wear hijab, and with personal friends and acquaintances—daughters and parents; and on conversations I have had and observations I have made over the last six years during which I have been regularly attending the conventions of some of the major American Muslim associations and in particular that of the Islamic Society of North America (ISNA).[6] In addition too, of course, I have been an avid reader of the wealth of material, interviews, reports, and stories that our media, particularly since 9/11 has been fairly copiously generating on Muslim women in the United States and on the hijab.

As I looked into why the hijab seemed to have been accepted, by some Muslim women anyway, as a norm here in the United States, I found that there was, as it turned out, a direct connection (to my surprise initially) between that first debate in Egypt with which I began this essay, and how that debate had played out in that country in terms of political and class struggles, and the emergence in the United States in the late twentieth, early-twenty-first century of the notion of hijab as foundational to Islam. To be sure, in this era of the easy and constant crossing of borders between old world and new, many factors contribute to the shaping of Islam in the U.S. today. Therefore this connection between the struggle over the hijab in the past in Egypt and its use in the United States today is not by any means the sole reason that the practice appears to be becoming a norm today. Still, I think it is among the foundational and ongoing important reasons contributing to the routine assumption among some that the veil is a Muslim norm.

To sketch out this connection, I will take as my starting point the Egyptian elite's appropriation in the early twentieth century of the colonial narrative of unveiling as essential to the society's moving forward on the path of progress forged by Europe. The call for unveiling became, among this class, at once emblem both of the project of modernization and of the notion that the advancement of women was key to that project. When Huda Shaarawi, a member of a prominent political family and a well-known feminist, publicly abandoned the veil in the early 1920s, her gesture, which formally endorsed the process of unveiling that was already well under way, was important in that it signaled not only her own views but also the views and commitments of the governing classes on those subjects. And the government pursued those commitments by opening schools for girls at almost the same rate as those for boys, and opening the national university to women in 1928.

By mid-century the veil had all but disappeared from the country's major cities. After the 1952 revolution, which gave women the vote and equal access to schools and universities, Egypt embarked on the path of secular socialism. Through the 1950s and into the 1960s the veil steadily declined, declining seemingly beyond the possibility of return. In Egypt as in several other Muslim countries, unveiling had seemingly won out.

This of course was not the end of the story. Even as Shaarawi cast off her veil other movements had begun. In 1928 Hasan al-Banna founded the Islamist organization the Ikhwan Muslimeen, the Muslim Brotherhood. Opposed in every way to the government, which it saw as corrupt and subservient to the British, the Ikhwan took a stand against it with regard to the hijab as well as on other matters—affirming the hijab now as an essential part of Islamic dress.

Although it affirmed the hijab as essential, the Ikhwan did not oppose either women's education or their employment: On the contrary the importance of educating women and of enabling and even encouraging women to work was emphasized by several of the Ikhwan's ideologues. There was, however, a proviso: that women's work had to be understood within the framework of the primacy of women's duties as wives and mothers and within the framework of the notion, divinely ordained as they saw it, of men as the ultimate, deciding authorities in the family in all matters including, of course, whether women worked.

This stance on the part of the Ikhwan of both affirming the essentialness of the hijab and encouraging women's work within the framework of the divinely ordained patriarchal family, is important for us to note. The stance signaled that the Ikhwan stood not for old-style unreconstructed Islam but for something new: a restored, revived Islam that fully embraced modernity and the ideas brought in by the West of the importance of women's education and their active participation in society. The importance of women's full participation and even of women's rights they would in fact argue (within the framework always of the divinely ordained patriarchal family) had indeed been part of the founding Muslim society, and such rights were intrinsic to Islam. They were not in evidence in much of Muslim history (they would argue) only because Muslims had failed to attend to those aspects of their religion.

Fully and even eagerly embracing modernity then, the Ikhwan also embraced some basic elements of feminism—but of a feminism reconceived and redefined within strict, clear limits: a feminism rearticulated now within the framework of the divinely ordained patriarchal family. Even the style of veil they adopted was distinctly not that of any of the traditional veils of Egypt (all of which, in their variety, had distinct class connotations) nor indeed was it the traditional style of hijab of any other country. Rather it was distinctly a new and modern hijab divested of particular class or geographic associations: a style of hijab that signaled the movement's commitment both to modernity and in a way to feminism, but a feminism reconceived within the framework of a divinely revealed order of male dominance. It signaled more broadly the Brotherhood's affirmation of a revived

Islam, an Islam reconceived in response to the encounter with modernity. That, though, was not how this reconceived Islam represented itself—as a form of the religion that had been profoundly shaped and informed by the encounter with modernity. Rather, the shaping influence of modernity on this reconceived version of Islam was denied and erased: Those advocating and embracing this new Islam represented themselves rather as returning to a "pure" and "authentic" past Islam, an Islam that had freed itself at last of all cultural baggage, particularly the negative cultural baggage the religion had acquired (they asserted) through centuries of Islamic torpor and misinterpretation.

We have already emerging here, then, just in the varieties of meanings of hijab that I have identified in briefly sketching this history, three distinct meanings of the veil beginning with and following from the first attack on the veil conceived from within the bosom of colonialism and manifested in the debate of 1899. First, there was the meaning developed from within the imperial narratives of superior races, religions, civilizations, and of the white man's moral obligation to dominate, change and civilize: Within this narrative (whose outlook was exemplified in Cromer's perspective), the veil was symbol of the inferiority, comprehensively, of the Islamic Other.

Second, there was the somewhat different and indeed still always shifting and developing meaning of the veil that emerged when this thesis was adopted and rearticulated from the perspective and in the voice of the native Westernizing elites—from Qasim Amin to Huda Shaarawi and on through the twentieth century down to us and our contemporaries. Within this discourse, abandoning the veil signaled a commitment to the project of modernity and a commitment, with it, to a radical recasting and eventually of wholly reconceiving the position and rights of women. Over the twentieth century the commitment to unveiling and to women's rights has moved from Amin's (and Cromer's) Victorian patriarchal notion of reconceiving the position of women, through Shaarawi's more liberative notion of reforms to expand women's rights to, arguably, Nawal El Saadawi's notion of a continued staunch stand against the veil as signal of a commitment to women's full and equal participation without limit or qualification.

Third, there was the meaning that emerged in the Islamist response to the previous discourse, in which, countering the notion of unveiling as essential for progress and modernity, the veil was affirmed as a way of embracing modernity and feminism—but within the framework and limits set by what was understood to be a divinely ordained order of male dominance. This narrative too, like the narrative of unveiling as a necessary feminist goal, has continued and continues to shift its specific meanings and connotations into our own day. For instance, it is not uncommon now to hear young American Muslim women declare (as I will discuss further below) that they intend their habit of veiling to be understood as, among other things, a deeply feminist gesture.

These seem to be the three key master-narratives of the veil, the narratives that provide the foundational frameworks or scaffolding of the veil's meaning in our times. All of us today, those of us who attack it as irretrievably patriarchal, and those of us who attack it (and sometimes attack also the women who wear it) because it powerfully carries meanings of the inferior Muslim Other, and finally, too, those of us who wear it—all, to some degree, deriving our meanings and our responses to the veil from within the frameworks of these three master-narratives. Even when our intention and objective is to counter or reject those meanings—one or another of them—we are still grounded in and allowing ourselves and our perceptions and responses to this garment to be framed by this tangled history and these clashing, shifting, and intertwining narratives.

To return now to what happened in Egypt following the founding of the Ikhwan Muslimeen and to the connections between that history and the developments under way in the United States today. The Ikhwan grew rapidly through the 1930s and thereafter, drawing its membership primarily from educated men of the lower middle classes. The organization's goal was to bring down the government, through violence if necessary, and to institute a government that would bring about the Islamization of Egypt.

From early on, violence was perpetrated by both the Ikhwan and the government. In the 1940s, the elected prime minister of what was then a democratic Egypt, was gunned down by the Ikhwan, and the government, for its part, killed al-Banna, the Ikhwan's founder—and these were but two of many killings committed by both sides. The confrontation between the Ikhwan and the governments of Egypt would continue into the Nasser era and beyond. Since its founding this organization has been important to Egypt's history and indeed to world history. As Saad ed-din Ibrahim, an expert on Islamist movements, mentioned recently in a talk he gave at Harvard, the Ikhwan, is, "the mother of all Islamist movements in the world today."[7]

In cities like Cairo and Alexandria, from which the veil had essentially disappeared by the late 1950s, one might occasionally see back then—I speak now from memory—women wearing the hijab of the Ikhwan. The Ikhwan style of the hijab is now the commonplace style of hijab that one might see anywhere—whether in the United States, Egypt, or elsewhere: But, back then, it was new and distinctive—and quite different from traditional forms of the hijab. In a society in which Muslims were the majority, one did not, of course, think, at the sight of someone wearing it, "There goes a Muslim," nor even, in an era when most people thought of themselves as deeply religious in the things that mattered, did one think, "There goes a pious person." Rather, one thought, "There goes a member—or a relative of a member—of the Ikhwan Muslimeen." To the ordinary Muslim, that style of hijab denoted not greater piety but, quite simply and directly, membership in a politicoreligious organization, with very particular political goals and very particular understandings of the practices and requirements of Islam. (That style of hijab brought into currency by the Ikhwan no longer now implies membership in that organization.)

The Nasser era of the late 1950s and 1960s was among the most difficult politically for the Ikhwan. After discovering an Ikhwan plot to assassinate him, Nasser imprisoned many members of the group and executed some. Many Ikhwan fled the country and found refuge mainly in the Arab gulf and in particular in Saudi Arabia, whose form of Islam, Wahhabism, was closely allied to theirs.

In 1965 the United States changed its immigration laws, opening the way to Muslim immigration. Among those who came, often as students, were men with affiliations with the Ikhwan. Of the many Muslims who immigrated in that era, it was essentially men with connections to the Muslim Brotherhood who would become organizationally and religiously active in the United States. They, and men affiliated with similar organizations in other countries, set about founding Muslim student organizations, mosques, and Islamic centers. Today the most important and influential Muslim American organization—among them the Islamic Society of North America, and the Muslim American Student Association (MSA), the most influential Muslim organization on campuses—were founded by members of the Ikhwan and of similar organizations. In the United States, as throughout the world over the last three decades, funds from oil-rich countries helped support the growth and rapid expansion of such organizations and their mosques, centers, and schools.

These associations and the mosques and schools affiliated with them have been in charge of teaching Islam to the younger generation, and their teachings have reflected, naturally enough, the outlook and the religious and ideological commitments of those original organizations—including obviously their position on the veil.

Of course, organizations merely provide a framework for continuity within which change occurs as generation succeeds generation. Whatever beliefs informed the founding of ISNA and MSA, such beliefs are inevitably changing as the old guard is replaced by the new and as more and more of the latter are American-born.

I have been attending the conventions of different Muslim organizations over the last few years—from ISNA to al-Fatiha, which is a gay, lesbian, bisexual, transgender Muslim organization. At ISNA, despite the organization's conservatism, I listened to talks given by women committed to what I would certainly define as feminist goals. And at al-Fatiha I met young gay and lesbian Muslim activists who had grown up attending ISNA and had got their Islam from American mosque-schools.

With this for background let me now draw together a few final thoughts.

First, a brief point with respect to the French ban and its likely effectiveness in regard to curtailing the practice of veiling. Of course, the outcome of the law will depend primarily on the local, specific circumstances pertaining in France—in regard to political and socioeconomic conditions in matters of class, ethnic, and religious relations. But it is perhaps pertinent too to consider the evidence of history as to how the debates and passions mobilized by the issue of veiling have played out over the last hundred years or so—taking 1899 as starting point. That date marks the beginnings of the era in which colonizers and local elites began to make concerted efforts, through laws as well as in a variety of other ways, to stamp out the practice of veiling in Cairo, Istanbul, Tehran, and elsewhere.

A hundred years on now and more, the veil has returned in all those cities. In some, Tehran for instance, it is now required by law. In others, and this has been the more typical course, it has been adopted voluntarily (or more exactly perhaps, "voluntarily," in the sense that many of pressures and coercions, overt or insidious—political, social, religious, sexual—always go into shaping how people in any society dress). The veil is back now and making steady inroads even in Turkey, a country that many assumed had become a bastion of secularism several decades ago. Moreover, as we know, the practice of veiling is now commonplace and apparently on the rise in, for instance, Paris, London, Chicago, and New York—cities that are fast becoming centers of the production of meanings of the hijab and key loci now, along with—and perhaps now shortly to displace—Cairo, Tehran, and Istanbul as important centers of the hijab debate.

All of which could suggest that a state's banning the veil or conducting a campaign against it is not necessarily an effective tactic. On the contrary, in the long run, it is, rather, organized but informal, grassroots resistance to such bans and campaigns—resistance perhaps generated and invigorated by state opposition and the assaults on the veil by those in power—that have won out.

The cities of the United States and Europe are now fast becoming the centers of the production of meanings of the hijab. On the basis of the formal interviews I have conducted and the numerous informal exchanges and conversations that I have had on this subject with American Muslims, one fact above all is abundantly clear to me: that women's reasons for wearing it are as varied, multiple, complex, and shifting (and multiple, complex, and shifting for each wearer too) as are the women themselves, and the reasons that women—any women—choose to wear what they choose to wear. Human dress is all about symbolism and about signaling different and sometimes contradictory (whether deliberately or otherwise) meanings. The veil is only different—and also therefore infinitely more charged than most clothing—in its potential meanings, meanings which of course may be quite different for wearer and observer. Because of the historical meanings with which it has been imbued since the rise of European imperialism, it has the power, perhaps uniquely as a garment, to provoke, disturb, unsettle. For over a hundred years now it has served as perhaps the quintessential symbol and flag of civilizational clash, of clashing values, and of struggles between the powers of empire and those resisting imperial powers, and an emblem too of clashing classes and of the struggle between the haves and have-nots within a society. These at any rate are among its meanings in societies in which women are free to choose whether to wear it: In societies such as Saudi Arabia and Iran where it is by law compulsory dress for women, it has, of course, a whole other set of meanings.

But these are its grand, overarching meanings, meanings that we can observe as we analyze national and international political discourses on the veil, whether in France or the United States or Egypt or among the jihadis. (Just today for instance, July 9, 2005, there was a report in the news that jihadis in Iraq had thrown acid on women who wore Western dress and who defied the requirements set out by some group as to proper Islamic dress.)

Meanings such as these, however, were not at all in evidence among the young women in hijab that I spoke with and listened to. The reasons they gave as to why they wore the veil and as to its meanings for themselves were typically individualistic and post-modern in their multiplicity and in their inventive combining and recombining of old meanings in new ways. Strikingly too, those new meanings were critically inflected by the fact that this was the dress now, here, of people who belonged to a minority.

Wearing the veil or headscarf can be, for instance, at this moment in the United States, a statement of religious commitment, a statement of identity, of communal affiliation, national or international, a political statement, and an aesthetic and/or erotic statement. It can also be, to be sure, a statement of a commitment to a belief in men as the natural and God-ordained authorities in our societies, and it can be a silent but forceful rejection and even reversal of the veil as emblem of the inferior Muslim Other (much as the Afro was of African racial inferiority), and a stubborn affirmation, of, on the contrary, full moral equality. And of course too it can evoke and play on any combination of these—and many more—possible meanings.

Let me return now to the three interviewees I quoted at the beginning of this essay. All three began by saying that they did not believe that the Qur'an required the hijab: They wore it by choice, they said, not obligation. This response was striking to me in that it constituted a distinct and important departure from the position on the veil espoused by fundamentalist or

Islamist, Ikhwan-type Islam. I heard these statements as indicating that the speakers were tacitly distancing themselves from, and even that they were tacitly rejecting, the idea of the hijab as sign of a God-ordained patriarchy. Thus emptying the sign, first of all, of its patriarchal meanings, these three young women (whose responses were typical of responses I received from the majority of those I interviewed) then went on to imbue it with meanings of their own. And those meanings included, most saliently, meanings which in the first place gave visibility to Muslimness in societies where Muslimness is denigrated and where, therefore, Muslims might be expected, wherever possible, to choose invisibility. The women's intent in wearing it, moreover, was to give visibility to Muslimness in ways which foregrounded issues of ethnic, religious, and gender justice. For example, one woman compares her hijab to a yarmulke; another declares she wears it to signal her solidarity with the Palestinians and thus to signal her commitment to global justice; and a third declares that she hopes her hijab might raise the consciousness of observers as to the sexism of our society—the hijab here, far from being emblem of patriarchy, was evidently conceived of by its wearer as raising issues of gender justice.

It is clear from these meanings and the central importance of justice to all of them, that the fact that the hijab is now the dress of a minority has opened up distinctly new possibilities of meaning. In the first place, simply taking on a negatively charged garment in our society is an act of courageous defiance in the face of prejudice. Certainly in the wake of 9/11 simply putting on and venturing out in a hijab must have entailed daily acts of courage. It was ordinary to read in the news then of women attacked and spat on in the streets of the United States, of women who had beer bottles thrown at them from speeding cars, even of women (as I read in one report in any case) being dangerously forced off a motorway by another car. Evidently some of the American men in these times deemed it honorable and patriotic to attack women dressed in hijab—women marked by their dress as representatives of the Enemy and inferior Muslim Other. To dress in this way at such a moment in this society is to silently and yet insistently refuse the imputed meanings of the inferior Muslim Other—meanings first forged in the colonial era but still vitally alive in our times. Taking on that symbol rejects and inverts its meaning—in much the same way as the slogan "Black is beautiful" inverted and rejected racial stereotypes of the 1960s. Moreover the Afro, the visual sign and embodiment of that slogan, opened up whole other questions—about aesthetic preconceptions, for example. Thus the Afro simultaneously exposed the limits of conventional aesthetics and opened up new ways of seeing. Similarly, some women today quite self-consciously and deliberately intend the veil to open up aesthetic questions.[8] In taking on the hijab, then, some women—particularly the more intellectually engaged and more feminist among them—are also in effect performatively enacting their rejection of both the patriarchal and the colonial narrative of the veil—rejecting the totalizing narratives of both sides. Quoting, borrowing from, reiterating the symbols and narratives or fragments of the narratives of the past, they are also reinventing them. And so as we live through what looks like the return of the veil, we are living, too, through something quite new. Homi Bhaba's reflections on hybridity are pertinent here—"hybrid agencies," he writes, "deploy the partial culture from which they emerge to construct visions of community and versions of historic memory that give narrative form to the minority positions they occupy."[9]

Doubtless too, though, for many Muslims in the United States wearing the hijab is a sign of conformity and obedience to a belief in the God-given nature of male dominance and authority. There is, of course, some latitude in interpretations of these matters—there are important differences between the interpretations of the government of Saudi Arabia, for example, and that of Iran, and also in the Ikhwan's position on these matters. But in the end all agree that authority resides in men and that women ultimately are not free to make their own decisions as fully the equals of men. Such, however, were not the views I encountered among my interviewees.

In short, all of this indicates that while old meanings of the veil continue to be unquestionably present and alive in our society—its meaning as emblem of patriarchy, and as emblem of the inferior Muslim Other—new meanings, too, are emerging, meanings arising out of Muslim people's location as a minority in this society, meanings that are in conversation at once with old meanings and with daily events of our times as well as with our society's history and its underlying ideals and commitments.

Nor is it only among Muslims that the hijab or headscarf is taking on in our day new and sometimes unexpected meanings. For instance, as reports of attacks on women in hijab began to multiply in the wake of 9/11, groups of non-Muslim women in various towns across the United States declared "headscarf days" and took to wearing headscarves in solidarity with women in hijab who were now at risk because of their dress. In the words of Katrina, one of the organizers of a headscarf day, "We're standing up for Muslim women's right to wear hijabs when they want to." In this context the veil or headscarf clearly stands for—of all things—feminist sisterhood. As one woman put it as she tied a headscarf over dreadlocks: "I am wearing it because I understand how it marks you as an object of someone else's hatred. It's still the same fight, but the symbol means something different."[10]

These are clearly distinctly local and momentary U.S. meanings that arise and take their significance from specific events in this country—a country with very specific and particular commitments and history with regard to women and feminism. This is the case also with regard to the hijab being used to signal a call for and a commitment to justice—as in the responses of the interviewees I quoted. The hijab can emerge as emblem of a call for religious and ethnic justice, for justice for women and for global justice, only because these ideals and the struggle for them form part of the commitments and the history of *this* society.

The veil could not have these meanings in Saudi Arabia or Iran or any other place where there is no commitment to ideals of justice and equality for all. On the contrary, in many such countries the unequal treatment of women and minorities is seen by the ruling powers as the proper national, religious, and God-ordained order.

Meanings of the hijab, then, are intensely local. What it means in the United States, where Muslims are a minority about whom many in the majority have fierce prejudices, will inevitably be different from its meanings in countries where Muslims are the majority. But meanings of the hijab are also global and can follow dominant master-narratives, that are both forceful and international in their reach—compared to the local, specific meanings arising out of particular events and histories. And certainly the rightness of patriarchy and of male authority over women is one of these globally powerful meanings.

We are all mired in the meanings and histories of our times.

During the ISNA conventions members of the Young Muslim Women's Association (an affiliate of ISNA) put on evening performances of poetry, skits, plays, fashion-shows, for women-only audiences. The theme of the veil figured quite prominently on the evenings that I was able to attend. One evening the young women presented a series of short skits that made fun of the assumptions about the veil and its supposed constrictions. I recall one skit in particular: It showed two girls preparing for school in the early morning. Agonizing about what to wear, one girl changes from one outfit to the next, and having finally settled on something, she then puts on makeup and then redoes her hair endless times, despairing about how she looks— and finally she rushes out and is late for school. The other, after performing her prayers, eats breakfast and dresses smartly in Islamic gown and head-scarf, unworried about her hair or whether her clothes make her look fat, and leaves for school in good time. Which of these young women, after all—the skit asked—was more controlled and more driven by sexist assumptions and dress-requirements of our society: the one anxious to con-form to society's requirements of young women that they be attractive and sexy, or the one who could dress without having to endeavor to be attractive to men or to please and appeal to them?

I not only enjoyed these skits but also found their critique of the sexism of American dress for women entirely persuasive. It was a critique that harkened back, of course, to the critiques of women's dress of the U.S. femi-nists in the 1960s and 1970s—although I did not get the impression that the young Muslim women knew this and that they had any idea therefore of their debt to U.S. feminism. That, after all, had been what the 1968 protest at the Miss America contest had been all about (which included the tossing of bras, girdles, and other constrictive clothing into the trash can, a protest that gave rise to the "bra-burning" myth) as well as other gestures by some feminists of that era to wear corsets or shave their legs and other such things. Moreover, as I pointed out in my discussion of the debate over the veil in 1899, Western dress in that era, the dress that imperialists considered the only "civilized" dress which people of other cultures should adopt as they became civilized, was hardly unpatriarchal or non-sexist, consisting, as it did, of, among other things, corsets that literally cracked women's ribs (hence the frequent fainting) and high heels that damaged women's bodies. At least the veil, which imperialists denounced so fiercely, caused no physical damage.

And yet, though I found the young women's critiques of the American dress quite convincing, I found myself wishing too that they could make these critiques without, on the other hand, championing the veil. Given that it is emblem, in one of the globally powerful master-narratives of our day, of a reaffirmation of God-ordained patriarchy and the reaffirmation of God-ordained constraints as marking necessary limits to women's aspirations.

But we live in a world crisscrossed by master-narratives. Those of us who go bareheaded might as easily be accused of lending support, inadvertently if not deliberately, to the narrative which defines the Other, who is paramountly today the Muslim and whose symbol is the veil, as innately and irretrievably inferior. But arguably there is, in the end, a difference. The history and even the ongoing and contemporary record of this society in matters of freedom of thought and of justice and equality for all is, to be sure, far from exemplary and, indeed, it has at times been utterly, utterly bleak. But it is still a society that conceives of itself as a social experiment evolving into the future and radically open and committed to forthright criticism, struggle, dissent, and transformation—toward that project of justice for all.

Leila Ahmed is the Victor S. Thomas Professor of Divinity at Harvard Divinity School where she was appointed to the Women's Studies in Religion professorship in 1999, the first person to occupy that chair. Previously, she taught at the University of Massachusetts at Amherst in the Women's Studies Program (where she served as director of the Women's Studies Program from 1992–1995) and in Near Eastern Studies. She was a distinguished visiting professor at the American University in Cairo in 1993. In 1996–1997 she was a fellow at Clare Hall, Cambridge, where she was elected to life membership in 1997. Her many publications include *Women and Gender in Islam* (Yale University Press, 1992) and *A Border Passage* (Penguin Books, 2000).

Notes

1. Qasim Amin, *Tahrir al-mar'a*, in *Al-a'mal al-kamila li Qasim Amin*, 2 vols., Muhammad 'Amara (ed.) (Beirut: Al-mu'assasa al-arabiyya lil-dirasat wa'l nashr, 1976) Vol. 2, p. 67.
2. Earl of Evelyn Baring Cromer, *Modern Egypt*, 2 vols. (New York: Macmillan Co., 1908), 2: 538.

3. Polly Toynbee, "Was It Worth It?" *The Guardian*, November 13, 2002.

4. Leila Ahmed, *Women and Gender in Islam: Historical Roots of a Modern Debate* (New Haven: Yale University Press, 1992).

5. Among recent useful works of interest are: *The Muslim Veil in North America: Issues and Debates,* Sajida Sultana Avi and Homa Hoodfar (eds.) (Toronto: Women's Press, 2003), and Carolyn Moxley Rouse, *Engaged Surrender: African American Women and Islam* (Berkley: University of California Press, 2004).

6. I want to take this opportunity to thank the Ford Foundation and most particularly Dr. Constance Buchanan for the generous support which has enabled me to pursue this research.

7. This was a talk delivered at Harvard University by Dr. Saad Eddin Ibrahim, "Democracy, Autocracy and Terrorism in the Middle East," April 22, 2004.

8. See for instance the numerous articles and visuals on this subject in Azizah magazine.

9. Homi Bhabha, "Culture's In-Between," in Stuart Hall and Paul du Gay (eds.) *,Questions of Cultural Identity* (London: Sage, 1996), p. 58.

10 "Women Don Scarves in Solidarity with Female Muslims; Event at Wayne State Is like Ones Elsewhere," *Detroit Free Press*, October 18, 2001.

Between Religion and Secularism:
Islamist Women of Hamas

Islah Jad

While there is a considerable volume of writing on contemporary Islamic movements, there has only been sketchy reference to their gender ideology, and very little attention has been paid to women militants themselves.[1] Here, I intend to provide a voice for the Islamist women of Hamas (the Islamic Resistance Movement), who are not considered by many feminists to be part of the Palestinian women's movement. I argue that this is an important omission, particularly in view of their growing activism for civil society.

My aim is to contextualize and explore the changing discourse, structure, and gender ideology of the Islamic movement in the West Bank and Gaza and to examine Islamist women's activism within Hamas. The Islamists' emerging need for women to play a role in the public sphere resounded within the Islamic women's movement, resulting in a transformation from near-total apathy and inactivity to more inclusion and mobilization. I argue that secular feminist ideology influences the direction of the debate on gender and women's rights in the Islamic movement, and that many of the positions and views of the latter are formed in reaction to secular feminist movements. I have found it difficult to categorize any form of Islamist "feminism" without scrutinizing the rejoinders it offers to modern, secularist principles. Thus, the idea of a fixed "inner logic" of Islam explains the position of the Islamic movements less accurately than does an examination of how Islamist women engage with their secularist counterparts whose positions actively inform Islamist discourse.

Islamic movements entail a variety of forms of organization from declared political parties to underground organizations.[2] I use the phrase

"Islamic movement" to refer to a sociopolitical movement founded on an Islam defined as much in terms of political ideology as in terms of a religion.[3] I begin by contextualizing the Palestinian Islamists within the international debate on Islam and Islamists. One of the most important elements of the Islamic movement is the fusion between Islam as a religion and nationalism (whether pan-Arab or country specific) as a secular and modern construct. In this context, I analyze and critique the Palestinian debate over whether the Palestinian national movement is secular (modern) or conflates Islam and secularism (traditional).

The growing influence of Islamic movements in the Middle East is usually examined in the context of the states' withdrawal from providing vital social and economic services to its citizens. This frame does not fit in the case of Palestine, where a sovereign nation-state never existed. However, the socioeconomic and political transformations produced by the Israeli Occupation were important in promoting the Palestinian Islamists, directly or indirectly. Hamas thus shifted from an exclusionary religious movement into a powerful rival and alternative to the secular Palestinian national movement represented by the Palestine Liberation Organization (PLO) and the Palestinian Authority (PA). The Islamic movement's ability to shift to a nationalist position and broaden itself to exist nationwide was crucial for Hamas to reach wider constituencies, gain legitimacy, and expand its popular support. The conflation between Islam and nationalism was used deliberately by Hamas. Islam was "nationalized" and confined to the territorial context of Palestine; and Palestinian nationalism was "Islamisized."

By emulating the secular and leftist political groups—and by competing with them—the Islamists learned how to adjust their appeal to attract a wider constituency. With the collusion of the Israeli Occupation and the Jordanian regime (which I will discuss below), the Islamists in Palestine managed to build an impressive infrastructure of cultural, social, economic, and political institutions, which proved crucial in sustaining the Islamic movement.

The move from accommodating the Occupation to full-fledged resistance through spectacular military actions (which gained wide popularity) was a turning point in the history of the Islamists in Palestine. Once established as a broad, popular national movement, the Islamic movement altered its structure to act as a legal political party. The National Islamic Salvation Party (Khalas) was an important medium for the Islamists to seek a more sustained and organized constituency and the eventuality of power-sharing through democratic means (such as elections). This shift was crucial in compelling the Islamists to pay more systematic attention to recruiting and organizing women. In competition with the secularists and as a reaction to their stand on recruiting and integrating women to their organizations, the Islamists focused on women—particularly the highly educated—and integrated them into their party structure at all levels.

The link between religious fundamentalist movements and gender ideology is inseparable in the fundamentalists' quest to build a moral society based on the moral family. I examine what I term the gendered structure of Hamas and the evolving nature of Hamas gender ideology. The rigid, formal division of labor, confining women to the domestic sphere as the reproducers of a "moral" nation, gave way to more open-ended interpretations of texts, enabling women to occupy a wider space in the public arena. This shift was not haphazard; it was the outcome of the work of Islamist women within the movement, against the background of women's achievements, which were irreversible by the Islamists. It was also the outcome of pressure exercised by secular feminists who critiqued the Islamists' fixing of the gender order by instituting the immutable rules of *shari'a* law.

The phenomenon of *isteshhadeyyat* (female martyrs, or "suicide bombers" in the Western lexicon) in the Palestinian context has been explained by many scholars in religious and cultural terms to obfuscate any links between this phenomenon and the material forces of colonialism and socioeconomic and political oppression. In an attempt to transcend the gender barriers put up by Hamas's ideology, yet acting from within the same "traditional" gender order, I argue that Islamist women *istishhadeyyat*, in their act of fatal equality are in part attempting to hold Arab men and rulers accountable to their traditional gender roles of defending, protecting, and providing for women.

Israeli Occupation, the Islamist "Resurgence," and Hamas

Many studies have shown that the "resurgence" of Islam—which refers to a "return" to an Islamic lifestyle and a growing religiosity—can be seen in virtually all Muslim societies, affecting culture, social relations, economic affairs, and political life.[4] This phenomenon cannot be understood with reference to traditional systems of thought and action but represents an effort to generate and legitimate new forms of political and social action in radically changing societies. Thus, it is a novel and modern phenomenon.[5]

However, the Palestinian Islamic revival cannot be conflated with a broader revival in the rest of the Middle East. In Palestine, not only has there never been a state but there is also a further complication, in that Israel, as an occupying power, has been extremely interested in the elimination of the secular, nationalist PLO. As capitalist democracies supported Islamists who fought Communism during the Cold War, so the Israelis had an interest in nourishing the influence of the Islamists in order to weaken the PLO and ultimately break up the national movement.[6] Alongside these influences, Hamas has largely managed to mutate from being a religious, political movement into projecting itself as a broad-based national movement in which Islam becomes the core of Palestinian national identity.

It is against these economic, national, and political backgrounds that one can examine the fluctuating power and influence of the Islamic movement in the West Bank and, in particular, in Gaza, where it originated. The different types of social organizations that the Islamists established became important economic and social venues for young women looking for work and mobility.

The young were taught about self-sacrifice, pride in the simple life, obedience, and discipline. This took place during a phase of decline in the Palestinian economy, when the Israeli labor market was getting rid of thousands of Palestinian casual workers. Material services received an increased focus and appreciation. The Islamists instituted support programs such as funds for poor students in Gaza or abroad, aid to those suffering from housing demolitions by the Occupation army, and support for families whose breadwinners were imprisoned. They established many health clinics, occasional free medicine and a blood bank. The *mojam'a* (the Islamic center in Gaza, a branch of the Society of Muslim Brothers, transformed into the Islamic resistance movement Hamas) copied many activities that used to be provided by secular and leftist groups, such as voluntary work campaigns, summer sea camps, and sports training and competitions. Most of these activities were for men. The establishment of the Islamic University in Gaza was another important step in the spread of the Brothers' influence.

Competing with other groups also drew the Islamists' attention to what Ahmed Atawneh (the head of the Islamic Student bloc at Bir Zeit in the late 1990s) calls "the importance of the women's vote and how crucial the recruitment of female students is to the support of the Islamic blocs," especially in universities such as Bir Zeit, which "conservative families don't send their girls to" because the student body includes a lower percentage of "Muslim religious girls."[7]

The Islamists could neither hinder nor ignore the valuable lesson taught to the Palestinians after the 1948 *nakba* (creation of the state of Israel): that education, especially for rural girls, is the only guarantee against unpredictable change. For although Hamas's advocacy of education for women could lead to their gaining a new space in public life, it also enforced patriarchal norms through sex segregation. Yet the separation between the sexes led to new careers for educated women outside the realm of traditional professions (teaching, nursing, and so on), such as photographing and working as waiters at weddings, at which most veiled women, especially the unmarried, take off their veils.

The decline of the PLO and the Islamists ability to reinvent themselves as a nationalist movement were crucial factors in their growing popularity. While the PLO was effectively being transformed into a vehicle for the pursuit of diplomatic activity, Islamists wasted no time formulating a new ideology in which nationalism would be brought to the fore.

Thus, the transformation of Hamas into a militant national resistance movement brought the old national ethos, which fused struggle, sacrifice, and suffering invested with sacredness and inviolability, back into the very core of Palestinian national identity; within this formation, any act detracting from the struggle is considered sacrilege, if not treason. This reconstruction of Palestinian national identity goes against the PA's attempts to establish a political identity around narrow interpretations of loyalty and gains. Through struggle, women's purity once again becomes a keystone of the ethos of suffering, sacrifice, and noble conflict: women's immodesty dishonors the memory of the martyrs; women's preoccupation with trivia and fashion at a time of sacrifice and struggle is an insult to the fighters for liberation; and women's immodest dress and conduct unwittingly aids the enemy in its designs to corrupt the nation.[8] Islamists also rail against the ethos spread by the work of women's NGOs, which entail extravagant advertisements, conferences, high salaries, and donor funds (that is, profits) instead of sacrifice and suffering, while the Occupation rages on unabated.

In what follows, I will present an account of the conflict that erupted between a newly formulated nationalism that presented Islam as its essence and an old secular nationalism, in order to explore the impact of this conflict on women and their roles within it.

The Evolution of Hamas and Mainstreaming Gender "à la Islamism"

An overview of the Women's Action Department of the Salvation Party is important to explain the ways Islamists incorporate women into politics with the aim of creating the image of the "new Islamic woman."[9] Islamist women are presented with the need to meet two paradoxical expectations: They must be not only model mothers and obedient wives but also model political activists. It is the same dilemma that nationalist and secularist women are still struggling to solve.

Hamas's contradictory gender ideology, like that of the nationalists, stressed the accepted role of women in reproducing the nation. While the movement was keen to present the "new Islamic woman," it is apparent that this image potentially contradicts the usual conception of the Palestinian woman as a fertile "womb."

The party and its women's department opened its doors to the "new Islamic woman" who is highly educated, outspoken, *moltazemah* (veiled), and *modern* (a new form of veiling). Modernity is reflected in the fact that these women are educated, professional, and politically active. The veil is seen as a signifier of modernity, since it is different from traditional dress. The new Islamic dress (a long robe of plain color and a white or black head scarf) is seen as a uniform of conviction.

> It is different from the *thub* [traditional peasant woman's dress] which is used by our mothers and grandmothers. It is different in its meanings; it is a unifying symbol to our followers and members. If I see a woman wearing it, I will immediately realize that she is *ukhot* [a sister]. It indicates that we are educated and not like our mothers who are mostly illiterate. It gives us *heiba* [respect] as the dress of our *ulama* [religious leaders]. It is economical, simple, and modest.[10]

Implicit in the Islamist veiling style is participation in a national social movement that lends the wearer a heightened sense of status, both moral (vis-à-vis secularists) and social (vis-à-vis women who cover themselves, but do not veil). However, despite its political cachet, behind the social force of veiling "one can discern the familiar principle of *himaya* (guidance and protection) by (and from) men."[11]

Unlike some other Islamic countries—Turkey for example, where Islamist women, once married, lose their voice when they retreat to the security and seclusion of the patriarchal family[12]—the Salvation Party and its women's department provided an important venue for educated Palestinian women who have limited access to a restricted, male-dominated labor market. In this sense, it is important to trace the identity the party provides for women by allowing them to manage their dual roles as activist in the public sphere and as mother and caregiver.

The new participants brought into the Islamic movements by the party include university graduates, professional women, and future intellectuals, thus consolidating a new category that changed Hamas from a military, underground, male-dominated organization into a more popular political movement. The move to create an Islamic women's movement with the support of the party's top leadership is a significant marker in the history of the Palestinian women's movement. For the first time, women became a strategic concern for the Palestinian national movement, this time under the banner of Islam.

The Gender Ideology of Hamas

While Hamas's gender ideology rests on religious idioms, it is nonetheless possible to demonstrate that it is contradictory and in continuous flux. This is due to ordinary socioeconomic factors and, as I proposed, a reaction to the challenge presented by the discourse with feminist nationalist and secular women, as well as Islamist women's activism within the movement. The universalist discourse used by women in NGOs is alien not because it is "Western" but because it was not founded on a thorough knowledge of the situations of the women whose interests these organizations claimed to represent. This discourse was also reproduced and diffused in the absence of a power structure that could support it, through either the women's movement or the national secular political movement that lost strength or weakened in the aftermath of the Oslo Agreement.

The national secular movements of the 1970s and the 1980s, which led to the massive participation of women in the first Palestinian intifada, were weakened as the result of economic deterioration, massive unemployment, and the failure to find a viable political solution.[13] Starting in the mid-1970s, many Palestinian universities were established that attracted young girls from rural and poor backgrounds to higher education. University and secondary education have been steadily growing since 1975. The activism of the nationalist students in these universities was crucial in attracting young women into the secular national movement. By the 1990s many of the same women had adopted the veil.

The influence of Islamists can only be explained with reference to a series of interrelated factors: the decline of the Palestinian national movement, accompanied by the disappearance of grassroots service providers; the "NGOization" of women's organizations, which ruptured their organic links with the grassroots; and the "nationalization" of Islam and the "Islamisization" of the Palestinian national identity by the Muslim Brothers.

Central to this latter process was the Islamisization of gender. Rema Hammami has noted that the 1987 intifada was the first time "that an issue, specifically veiling, once relegated to the arena of religious behavior, had been mobilized as a nationalist issue."[14] Hammami rightly points out that this campaign showed Hamas's ability to conflate its social ideology with Palestinian nationalism, wielding the threat and use of violence against women to impose the veil. Women gained little support from the national leadership of the intifada, which failed to stop this campaign in time.[15]

From this, it may seem that Hamas's gender ideology was a fixed entity stemming from a conservative and misogynist religious platform. According to this view, women were the victims on whom something unwanted was imposed. While this might be true for some women in the leftist organizations, it is still important to understand why it was difficult to reverse the course of events. This was true after the establishment of the PA, and even after the national leadership of the intifada issued many leaflets, with the consent of Hamas, condemning the attacks on women. In other words, why do we witness an increase in the number of veiled women and girls if veiling is a symbolic form of—if not a signifier of—adherence to the textual tradition of Islam advocated by Hamas? In her study on PFWAC (Palestinian Federation of Women's Action Committees), Frances Susan Hasso indicated, for example, that 80 percent of her sample presented themselves as religious.[16] She showed that many were wearing the veil in response to social pressure since the first intifada, but that some also indicated that they wore it out of conviction. While Hasso researched the secular leftist women's group, I shall focus on a group of women whom as far as I know, have not yet been researched and who don't perceive themselves as victims of the veil, but rather as full-fledged agents in disseminating its principles.

In order to understand the gender agenda of Hamas, factors that link gender and nationalism must be explored. Hamas's gender ideology cannot be separated from the colonial use of gender and its rivalry with the other nationalist groups and, to a lesser extent, scriptural texts. However, other factors such as the conservative elements of Palestinian nationalism in its secular form, as explained above, could be invoked to elucidate the slide into Hamas's gender ideology. There is apart from the conservatism in the Palestinian national secular ideology in which women were portrayed as the producers for and the carers of the nation, a portrayal that eased Hamas's work in essentionalizing these roles as the main task for women.[17]

I would argue that the orthodoxy displayed by Hamas in the first intifada cannot be explained as a misrecognition of indigenous culture that arose in reaction to the increased intimidation of women brought about by the Israeli Occupation. Hamas, contrary to Fateh (the largest faction of PLO, founded in and started its military action in 1965), spelled out its gender agenda at an early stage. This is a common feature of religious movements that place a great deal of emphasis on the family unit. The Israeli writer Amnon Cohen, in his well-known work "The Moslem [sic] Brothers," said the movement had "fixed repressive ideas about women and how they were expected to conduct themselves. Women were not permitted to use makeup or to over-adorn themselves, they were to veil their faces, and were not to appear in public 'half naked.' This, the Brothers maintained, was clearly laid down by Islam."[18] Contrary to claims made by authors such as Cohen, the intimidation against women is a kind of artefact of the occupation rather than a "fixed"conservative culture which oppresses women.

Chandra T. Mohanty warns against the analytical leap of seeing the widespread practice of veiling as indicative of women's sexual oppression and control. Rather, she urges us to understand it analytically by questioning its meaning and function in various cultural and ideological contexts.[19] Hammami showed that the spread of veiling during the first intifada had a national meaning—that in the face of the calamity, death and destruction inflicted by the Israeli Occupation, women had to show respect for the martyrs.[20]

During the first intifada, a new formulation of the issue of women's piety and modesty was deemed essential in order to protect the nation . . . The insistence on veiling as a moral code for women can be explained as a tool in the Islamists' rivalry with secularist, nonveiled groups. Veiling is a unifying cultural marker for the movement and a signifier of its growing strength among Hamas followers—or, as Nikki R. Keddie suggests, it may be a way of asserting communal identity rather than a strong religious marker.[21] Veiling can also become an important political symbol employed to forge new social *modern* (identity) and a concrete tool in opening new possibilities for women within and outside the movement.

The different meanings of the veil should not be seen as the only marker of Hamas's gender ideology. Rather, its ideology changes as the power of the Islamist women evolves within the movement.

In 1988, Hamas published its *mythaq* (charter) in which its formal position on gender was spelled out in articles 17 and 18. Article 17 states: "Muslim women have a role in the liberation struggle that is no less important than the role of men: the woman is the maker of men, and her role in guiding and educating the generations is major."[22] In the same article, women were presented as passive targets for Freemasons, Rotary Clubs, and intelligence networks—all centers of destruction and saboteurs: "And the Islamists should play their role in confronting the schemes of those saboteurs, i.e. protecting them."[23]

Article 18 stressed again that "the woman in the house of the *Mujahid* and the striving family, be she a mother or a sister, has the most important role in caring for the home and raising the children with the ethical character and understanding that comes from Islam."[24] The woman was advised to be economical, to avoid carefree spending, and to "keep in mind that money is blood that must flow only in the veins to sustain the life of children and parents equally." Women were thus advised to give to their family and nation instead of taking, a notion that Hamas stresses to differentiate Islamist women from the secular activists. In this vision, women are portrayed as dependent on men, confined to their homes, and segregated from public space. However, this was not what Islamist women and female students were actively doing in the students' blocs of Hamas or in Islamist associations. The tension between Hamas's gender vision and what Islamist women actually do will be presented in the following sections. Through their own involvement in the movement, these women were able to change this vision to make a space for themselves.

Demobilization in Mobilization: Hamas's Gendered Structure

In this section, I analyze the contradiction between the marginalization of women in Hamas's organizational structure and their mobilization in civil society. Islamist women were a crucial force in widening Hamas's constituencies in the student movement, although this activism was not recognized within the movement's structure in the West Bank. I argue that this gendered form of structure might have been an important factor in demobilizing women in these areas, especially when Hamas became a hegemonic political power in the Palestinian polity during and in the aftermath of the first Palestinian intifada.

Hamas's structure for the inclusion of women varies in the West Bank and Gaza. The Salvation Party has no bodies parallel to those in Gaza in the West Bank, nor any mobilizing and organizing structures for other social groups, such as students and workers. While party members were seen in the different activities of the intifada (strikes, funeral processions, confrontations with the Israeli army, and so on), female Hamas members at the time were not visible as participants. (The veiled women participants were not necessarily Islamists.) The reason for this absence could be explained by the fact that Islamist organizations target males.

I did not find any indications in documents or interviews that women were participants or targeted for recruitment, whether as candidates or as electors. Islamist women had to wait until the establishment of the Salvation Party at the end of 1995 to be incorporated into Hamas. The activism shown by Islamist women in universities flowed not from the organizational structure of Hamas but from the efforts of male students, competing for votes in the universities.

In the West Bank, once a female student leaves the university, she has no place to go in the structure of the Islamist movement. The same situation applied to Gaza, where the growing number of female students in the Islamic university, and later al-Azhar University and other colleges, had no place to go except to work in the social institutions belonging to the Muslim Brothers. In late 2003, the Hamas leaders announced their intention to form an Islamic women's movement. That is when female students joined forces with mainstream political organizations like the Salvation Party in Gaza.

Organizing students and linking them to political parties is crucial in Palestine, where the youth in general and students in particular play an important role in boosting the national movement and the struggle against the Occupation. In answer to why the Islamists did not seek to organize female students in their mainstream political parties, whether under the name of the Muslim Brothers, Hamas, or the Salvation Party, it must be acknowledged that these institutions carried the imprint of the conservative gender ideology of the movement from its inception. This was especially true when it came to young unmarried females.

The absence of mobilizing structures for the Islamists in the West Bank could be mitigated by the apparent coordination among Islamists in the different regions in the West Bank in the underground militant, all-male Hamas structure. Islamist women are not part of the underground structure (all the Islamist women interviewed claimed no connection to Hamas). There is no legal, official unifying structure, as in the case of the Salvation Party in Gaza; however, it was difficult to determine whether the absense of any unifying body for Islamist women is due to the lack of interest in organizing Islamist women in the West Bank (in contrast to Gaza) or due to the women's own priorities. When Islamist women in the West Bank were asked if they coordinated their activities or programs, the answer was negative. However they asserted that "when possible, we attend each other's rallies and conferences."[25]

Women's charitable societies belong to a general union of charities, of which Islamist societies form a part, but they do not have a coordinating body. The delay in having a structure similar to that of the Salvation Party could be attributed to the PA's continuous disruption of the party activities. The same treatment is inflicted on the Islamist "figures" in the West Bank, alongside the targeted assassination of their leaders by the Israeli Occupation forces. Besides, the Israeli policy of separating Palestinian cities and villages is creating more obstacles for the Islamists to establish unifying structures like those in Gaza. The limitation of any involvement in political activism may be attributed to the absence of a mobilizing body for Islamist women, who are dependent on the goodwill of their husbands, not on the commitment of the party. I will show below that a unifying and organizing structure for Islamist women plays an important role in changing the "formal" gender ideology of the Islamists and that women's power was crucial in pushing the boundaries of its meanings.

The Ever-Evolving Gender Vision: "The Text Does Not Prohibit"

The observation "the text does not prohibit" was a recurrent theme in my interviews with Amira, Maysoon, Samira, and many other female militants. They meant that religious texts are open-ended, making it possible to forge a wider legitimate space for women in the public arenas. A critique of the status quo, supporting an expanded daily reality for women eager for work, education, and political participation, grew gradually within the movement. Islamist women, while fully complicit in disseminating the movement's gender ideology, are also the first to push its boundaries and stretch their public space.

These developments accompanied a change in Hamas strategy after the "peace process" began, when it transformed from a military underground organization into a political party. In what follows, I give an account of the impact of this transformation on women's activism within Hamas, relying on papers presented at many conferences organized by Islamist women activists in Gaza.

The Salvation Party started to widen its popular base more systematically by recruiting women. As it began to emphasize the legal political struggle like other national and secular organizations, it could not ignore the conditions in which women lived or prevent them from joining political life. Yet the movement strenuously attacked the claims for women's rights made by other nationalist and secularist women's organizations. Internal factors pressured Hamas to deal with women's issues, while external pressures—from feminists' demands and the equal rights discourse—offered a serious challenge to Islamist discourse.

What, then, are women's rights from an Islamic perspective? Here the answer will come not from the male leadership of the party but rather from its women. I draw on the contributions to a workshop and three conferences that clearly illustrate the shift in these positions, as well as Islamist women's experience within the party and their daily practices.

The first conference concentrated on one women's group delegitimizing others in order to present itself as the "true" and "authentic" voice for women's interests. The second conference admitted that the Islamists had no vision or agenda for women's issues, but at the same time it attempted to reinterpret the religious texts in order to allow a new reading that incorporated women's achievements thus far due to modernization processes. It is astonishing to note that in the process of formulating a new reading for religious texts, a parallel process of "de-lslamisizing" the discourse on women's rights took place. As will be explained, the Islamists adopted new terms (such as "sustainable development") predominantly used by donors and feminist activists. The third conference scrutinized the concept of sustainable development and questioned its relevance to Palestinian society. Also, for the first time, a modern and feminist critique of the liberal-rights approach was used. These conferences were landmarks for Hamas gender ideology in its passage from utter rejection of feminism to borrowing and selectively incorporating positions advocated by feminists. This resulted in their recuperation by the Islamists (that is, the women were Islamisized) even as their Islamic discourse was de-Islamisized and integrated into the present framework.

From Rejection to Engagement

The Women's Department of the Islamic Salvation Party proved energetic and active in pushing the boundaries of the Islamist women's space within the party structure and in society at large. On April 24, 1997, it published a booklet presenting the findings of a one-day workshop called "Palestinian Woman . . . Where Next?" The booklet, for the first time in the Brothers' history in Palestine, fills the gaps of their gender agenda and inverts some of their previous positions. The introduction to the booklet clearly states that the raison d'être of the whole discussion was that it "became a preoccupying issue for those many who are keen to see women occupying a distinguished position in the society side by side with men."[26]

Many prominent male and female Hamas cultural leaders presented papers throughout the workshop in a systematic attempt to delegitimize the non-Islamic women's groups. They did this by linking women's NGOs to the West, depicting them as a ploy of the West to weaken the nation and betray it by "smothering" Israel's existence in the heart of the *umma* (Islamic community of believers). It rejected the call for a gender agenda as inappropriate when the national agenda was still unresolved.

In interviews, many Islamists women expressed the same skepticism vis-à-vis universal rights for women. Maysoon, for example, stated:

> Isn't it weird to hear the same discourse all over the Arab world and the Islamic world by many women's organizations? How come that all women's needs and aspirations are all the same all over a spectrum of different societies with different contexts and needs? Where is the specificity of each society, where are the variations between them and among women themselves? This is a standard blueprint strategy pushed not by women but by foreign donors.[27]

However, the April 1997 workshop could not reject outright the prevailing discourse on women's rights. There were nuances among women's-rights activists. Some feminists (mainly those from Gaza) called for the prohibition of polygamy and the right to divorce within *shari'a* law; others called for restrictions on polygamy without outright prohibition. There was an appeal not only to establish a study center but also to direct more intellectuals' and researchers' attention to the laws, ideas, visions, and studies proposed by secularist women.

A paper presented by Khitam Abu Musa, an Islamist woman, inverted the gender vision of the Hamas Charter of 1988. Abu Musa interprets Islam as the religion that gives the woman all her rights: education, free choice of a husband, inheritance (widely denied by custom), mobility (to participate in the call for the rule of God and jihad), proselytizing, and social or professional work.[28] In interpreting religion and *shari'a* in this manner, she invokes the authority of the religious text to stress that "the urge of women to develop *intilaq* [to flourish] and participate in social life," and to promote the concept of public good by emphasizing that "Islam *mandates* that women go out and participate in social life because the opening up of public work for women is for the good (*al-khayr*)."[29]

This vision is not shared by all Islamist women in the party; it seems more pertinent to the needs of educated women who want to abolish sex segregation code to benefit from more opportunities in the labor market. Less educated women say, rather: "In the party they are irritated when we insist on being separate. The party says that since this is a developmental party there is no harm in mixing, but this is against our traditions."[30]

In these conferences, meticulous attention was paid to the demands and visions of Palestinian feminists concerning legislation, work, education, political participation, and women in the media and communication, all areas in which the Islamic vision is formulated in response to other platforms. The concluding vision crystallized around refuting the idea that religion is the cause of women's subjugation and dismissing civic legislation as recourse for women. It was stated that Islam is the path to "fairness and justice."[31]

Nevertheless, in these conferences many ideas were formulated to present a more progressive gender vision stemming from *al-shari'a*. While the starting point is the text, the call for new interpretations is always linked to the needs of society and the spirit of the age (*roh al-'assr*). In this way, the discussion moved gradually away from religious discourse toward a more "modern" and temporal discussion. The usual empty, repetitive religious discourse about other women's groups was criticized as a "traditional" Islamic stand.

The conclusions of these conferences can be encapsulated in two main points. First, they argued, Islamists should change, anticipate Islamic reform, and take the lead in uplifting (*nahda*) women—otherwise others will lead. Second, it should be stressed that "the mission to liberate women and activate their role falls primarily on women. Women have to claim their rights and struggle for them in the light of the proper understanding of the tolerant *shari'a*."

The third conference was dedicated to outlining more specifically the differences between *shari'a* and international conventions. Organized by the Women's Action Department, the conference provided a more thoughtful critique of the women's rights discourse as figured in international conventions. Using critical feminist thought, the papers presented at this conference questioned for the first time the viability not of the women's rights discourse altogether, but of its liberal, utilitarian, individualistic, and Western aspects.[32]

Thus the discourse on women's NGOs based on liberal rights was contested by another Western, feminist discourse based on the notion of active citizenship. Islamist critiques of liberalism, like the socialist feminist ones, question the morality of narrowly defending the principle of individual rights and allowing it to take precedence over the question of social responsibility. Citizenship, as I elaborate elsewhere, is conceived of solely as the exercise of key rights. In political terms, it is reduced to the practice of voting, which reflects an impoverished view of social membership. Instead there is a need for a more substantive version based on participation and social responsibility, known as social citizenship.[33] Haroun argues that "in our Islamic vision, the individual is seen in relation to the collective. That is why the notion of individual rights, in Islam, is formed in the context of duties that help to awaken in the individual the desire to 'give' and not only to 'take.'"[34]

The stress in Islamic discourse on giving and taking is linked to the specific situation of the Palestinian people, which is not cultural but rather national, and quite complex—a dimension that is very much missing in the feminist NGOs' discourse. They should see the stress on "giving to the nation" in the context of the now absent national agenda. The women's movements in Palestine should see it in a context in which the audible voice became a feminist one, claiming rights and obscuring what should be given to the nation under the continuing Occupation.

Thus, in the absence of a clear national agenda drawn by the nationalist, secularist women's movement, the Islamists link women's rights with the national and social needs of the Palestinian people in asking women, as did the old nationalist discourse, to serve the nation, à la Islamism this time, and to produce more men.[35]

Islamist women have managed to build impressive, well-organized women's constituencies among highly educated and professional women, at times using more modern discourses based on sustainable development and women's rights as well as new textual interpretations. The question arises as to how these new readings reflect themselves in daily practices within the party. I point to an increasing tendency to foster gender equality, not just complementarity, and more egalitarian social ideals. I argue that Islamist women, empowered by their skills, their education, and the newly acquired legitimacy opened by reinterpreting the Qur'an, are given a greater opportunity to subvert the "complementarity" attributed to women in Islam and convert it into total equality—at least in public life.

The efforts of the Women's Action Department in the Salvation Party opened a space for such common ground by moving gender issues into the political mainstream of an Islamic party. The success of the department in effecting this important change within the Islamic movement went hand-in-hand with demands for equal pay. The case of *istishhadeyyat* (female conscience martyrs) is another example and highlights the involvement of women in military activities. This suggests that there are differences not only between Islamist men and women but also among women. In the following section, I will present a case of "fatal equality," in which the notion of equality takes a deadly path.

Fatal Equality: Islamists and *Istishhadeyyat*

Islamists are depicted by Orientalists, old and new, as "other" and "uncivilized." This wildness is used as an excuse for control and subjection. The renowned Zionist historian Benny Morris recently added a new dangerous element to his discourse, representing Palestinians as pathological serial killers.[36] This criminality is a genetic abnormality, according to Morris.

The *istishhadeyyat* add a new dimension to what is seen as the abnormality of so called pathological terrorists. This abnormality and criminality is again explained in cultural terms in which Islam, Islamism, and Islamic and Arab culture in general are demonized. Alternatively, the *istishhadeyyat* raise another question about women's role in the armed resistance, a role that many Palestinian national and religious groups, in particular Hamas, see as an important source of legitimacy.

Even though *istishhadeyyat*, like their male counterparts, are very much linked to Islamism and fundamentalism, Hamas was late to begin recruiting women for this kind of action. The date was January 15, 2004, when the first *istishhadeyya* recruited by Hamas and the military wing of Fateh (*kataeb shuhada al-aqsa* or al-Aqsa Martyrs Brigades) took action, marks the change in Hamas's strategy. Hamas's refusal until that time to recruit women to its military operations was consistent with numerous studies that have shown that women are discriminated against in states that reinforce a strong military. V. Spike Peterson and Anne S. Runyan write, "Most male-dominated societies have constructed elaborate sanctions and even taboos against women's fighting and dying in war. As a result, men have gained almost exclusive control over the means of destruction worldwide, often in the name of protecting women and children, who are either discouraged from or not allowed to take up arms to protect themselves."[37] As I have said, Hamas would, in this matter as in others, change its position on women's role.

In the book *Shahidas: Les femmes kamikazes de palestine*, Barbara Victor presents and analyzes the lives of five "*shahidas*" or "female martyrs."[38] She concludes after examining their social backgrounds, that these women were doubly victimized: by the gender order in general, which slights women, and in particular by their own marginal and unstable circumstances. In addition to being victimized, they were manipulated by cowardly, fanatical patriarchs.[39] In the same vein, *istishhadeyyat* have been portrayed as indoctrinated by the PA, which undertook a very public campaign of programming its women to see themselves as potential *istishhadeyyat*.[40] On the other hand, the majority of sympathetic writers see suicide bombers in general and women in particular as committing an act of desperation provoked by an Occupation they see no way out of. In brief, they are seen as "dead-enders." As for Palestinian women in the national secular movement, *istishhadeyyat* are regarded as invoking the right of self-defense. Rabiha Diyyab of Fateh and the Palestinian Women's Union emphasizes that the actions of Wafa Idris (the first *istishhadeyya*) show the "determination of the Palestinian woman to participate as a full partner in the national struggle, alongside her brothers."[41] The same is true for many young girls who see this act as their right.

Based on these women's testaments (*wassaya*), I argue that their acts were committed out of a sense of empowerment and uniqueness, and that they were in full control of their actions and their agency. Contrary to claims that the motive is desperation or dead-endedness, these women were driven by a wish to open up a new space not only for their gender but more importantly for their men to help them regain their lost manhood. Through their acts, and from within the hierarchical gender order, they wish to transcend the power relations that exist between the Arab (*peoples*) and their leaders and between Arabs and Israelis. I argue that their acts do not seek a total equality with Arab men, let alone Hamas men, but aim to supersede men to activate their lost role as their women's protectors. In summary, through what I call a fatal equality, they rise above the male order and gain power over all structures of power, whether patriarchy, despotism, or Occupation.

Twenty-four women have volunteered for such an act, and another sixteen have given logistical support. Out of this number, eight women have managed to detonate themselves (out of 157 martyrs). All were sent by the national secularist Fateh's al-Aqsa Martyrs Brigades or *saraya al-qodus* (Jerusalem Armies of Islamic Jihad). Until the last *istishhadeyya*, Reem

Rayashi, the first from Gaza, detonated herself amid a group of Israeli explosives experts at the Gaza checkpoint Eriz, Hamas and its military wing, Ezz el-Din al-Qassam, refused to send women on such operations. This refusal reflects Hamas's contradictory vision of what roles are suitable for women. The rationale given by Hamas leaders is that "women can be active in other fields, whether political, social, economic or educational. Our strategy now is not to involve women in such activities [*istishhad*, martyrdom] since women need to travel inside Israel, and women are not allowed by their religion to do that without a guardian [*mohram*]."[42]

In saying this, Aisha al-Shanti, who is also a member of the *shoura* in the Salvation Party, was repeating the official gender politics of Hamas without paying attention to the ever-growing pressure by women to turn this vision upside down. When Hamas was denounced for using a mother of two small children as an *istishhadeyya*, it answered its critics (Palestinian journalists close to the PA) by claiming to be the first to ask women to work side-by-side with men in the struggle.

Although each *istishhadeyya* had a different life history, what was common between all of them was their strong character, sociability, sensitivity, and relative affluence. All were driven by a strong feeling of injustice, as is evident from Dareen Abu Aisha's testament: "Criminal Sharon wants to kill our children in their mothers' wombs at his checkpoints, but we will survive."[43] They all seek revenge, and they all state that they are not less than but equal to men. In Dareen's words, "Muslim women's role is not less than that of our brother mujahedeen. . . . All Zionist tyrants have to know that they are worth nothing in the face of our pride and determination . . . that the Palestinian woman's role is no longer just weeping for her husband, brother or father, but that she will transform her body into a human bomb to destroy the illusion of security for the Israeli people."[44] Dareen was a student in her final year at Najah University in Nablus before turning to Fateh for help with her act. In 1999, she had already asked one of Hamas's leaders in Nablus if she could join the military wing, but she was rejected and told that "when we finish with men we will ask women to come in."

The different statements left by all these women do not confirm the theory of despair or depression. Ayyat el-Akhras's mother, for example, recalls, "My daughter was distinguished in her study, was engaged, lived an easy life, and was not suffering from poverty or depression. She sat an exam in which she got full marks just before committing her act. She was full of life, loving it and she even chose with her fiancé the names of their future children" in her will. Ayyat el-Akhras, after asserting that she was driven to her act by the "call of martyrs, blood, orphans and orphans' mothers and all those oppressed [*mostad'afeen*] on earth," turned to address the Arab rulers. Ridiculing them, Ayyat states, "Enough torpor, enough relinquishing of your duties in defending Palestine. I scorn your armies that watch Palestinian girls who fight in your name while you watch them on your TVs. This is my call to you and let each proud Arab Muslim hear me." Similarly "Andalib Taqataa" wrote, "I said with my body what Arab rulers could not say with their tongues."

The provocative tone of the words addressed to rulers who are supposed to protect their people reached their destination. In response to her words and others like them, the Islamist Egyptian writer Fahmi Heweidi, astonished by these "iron women with steely hearts and nerves, solid like mountains," stated: "In the past the cry of an Arab woman to the al-Mu'atassem (the last Abbasid ruler) moved armies to her support, but in our bad times, the call of Reem and her kind fall on deaf ears." Another male writer expresses bitterly, "I felt ashamed as a man as if she wants to say: I am the frozen honor in your veins. I apologize that my femininity pressured me to sneak out behind your masculinity to blow itself up in the face of your murderers. I did what I did in the hope that my act will wake you up, will help to stop your snoring which fills Arab space. I hoped to waken the buried consciences in your hearts." He concludes by calling Reem "a feminine mine who embarrassed the bursting masculinity in all Arab tribes. She wrote a deep message to you with her blood."

Thus, the acts of suicide bombers carry many meanings: a refusal of their fathers' and mothers' tears and a rebuke of their passivity; a celebration of their femininity in the face of the impotence of male Arab rulers; and the stretching of the boundaries of the meaning of sacrifice—the instrument of their sacrifice being not their freedom but their lives. They don't seek to imitate men, but in all their testaments they seek a full replication of their femininity not only as something that can be protected (in the traditional sense) by Arab men and rulers, but also something that can defend them until the men wake up.

The symbolic use of femininity to shame Arab men by casting doubt on their manliness is a spectacular act of self-sacrifice for not only Palestine but for all the Arab and Muslim nations. Without entering the debate over the morality or utility of this form of action, *istishhadeyyat* are trying through their deaths to be superempowered women, to achieve what their men did not (in mobilizing the Arab rulers and masses to support them). In this respect, it is a rational, political act of self-sacrifice undertaken for the survival of the nation.

Shari'a Politics and a Possible Common Ground

I have argued that it is not the religious text but the political context that determines the Islamist discourse. The ever-evolving version of *shari'a* displayed by Hamas raises two issues. On the one hand, it challenges the feminist NGOs' discourse based on a liberal, individualistic notion of rights that ignores the nation's plight under Occupation. By putting Islam at the center of a modified notion of Palestinian nationalism, the Islamists managed to delegitimize the feminist women's discourse, which they portrayed as nonnational and alien. On the other hand, it also challenges the rather ambivalent Palestinian secularism that used Islam as a source of its legitimacy. By "Islamisizing" Palestine and "nationalizing" Islam, the Islamist proved successful in forging a brand of nationalism in which Islam was integral and mobilized the masses.

In such a context, the secularists, while pressuring and challenging the Islamists, are nonetheless losing ground by advocating the discourse of rights in isolation from the national agenda and in the absence of a mobilizing organization. NGO activism, based on short-lived projects, does not have the potential to constitute an alternative. By becoming an opposition movement against all violations of civic and human rights, the Islamists have developed a political organization. In contrast, women in NGOs have no organized constituency and any support they have is derived from a decaying, discredited authority.

However, I have highlighted two instances in which *shari'a*, a guiding principle for women's rights, was used in contradictory ways. In the debate provoked by the feminist women's organizations, *shari'a* was used first, by the Islamists, as a fixed, divine, and immutable idiom to delegitimize and to silence the non-Islamic women's groups and at the same time to discredit the notion of popular sovereignty advocated by the PA as the basis for new legislation. It is still uncertain whether the Islamists want instead to establish a sovereignty belonging to God, since their state project has yet to be spelled out.

The same debate on *shari'a* triggered discussion within the Islamist movement. The Islamists' search for an alternative to the secular feminist platform brought them into continuous engagement with it. I showed that highly educated and professional Islamist women used the total equality approach to defend equal rights for women in the public sphere (at least in work and political activism) and in their daily practice.

The top male leadership reacted swiftly to "fix the *Shari'a*"[45] in another set of laws concerning the penal code, again to silence and discourage feminist and secularist women's groups from suggesting any reforms. The motive of the top male leadership emphasizing the *shari'a* is not only about women's rights but also asserts a hegemonic power for the Islamist in society and vis-à-vis the PA. It could also be about the still uncertain nature of any future Palestinian or Islamic citizenship.

In this respect, Maxine Molyneux warns, "social citizenship understood as community activism, participation or moral regeneration is not always or indeed necessarily linked to projects for democratic reform or greater social cohesion. In some countries it is manipulated by 'fundamentalists' who seek to create a political community to further objectives leading to an authoritarian, theocratic and highly gendered state."[46] This will not necessarily happen. My data show that Islamists, in their quest for a platform as a national movement, were obliged to borrow and incorporate new visions to be inclusive and broaden their constituency. Challenges from opponents pushed the Islamists to act on notions such as pluralism, women's rights, the public good, sustainable development, the social self versus the individual self— all issues borrowed from the secular context and co-opted by the Islamists. The evidence shows that certain arenas of civil-society activism, such as the students' movement, included women militants in a positive way and that the party structure incorporated women marginalized by the national leadership, which overrepresented the elite.

However, while there are moments of opening and engagement, there are also many contradictions that might lead to a potential closure and a retreat into interpretations of Islam that would affect women negatively. The Islamists could return to an insistence on the role of women as repro-

ducers of the nation. The stand on polygamy is not yet cle
heated debate on the "suitability" of women for military
sort of "Islamic" state this activism might lead to depends
on the general context the secularists set.

The Islamist women's discourse stems not only from ~~.~~ but
also from positive engagement with the discourses of other groups whether
secular feminists or nationalists. This engagement inspires Islamist women
to go back to the religious text and look for possible new readings to
respond to the challenges posed by other women's groups. Islamist
women's discourses rely not solely on religious texts but also on what other
women's activism and discourses provide. This engagement could also be
the common ground on which Islamist, secularist, and nationalist women
unite by pushing for new readings of the religious texts, as well as by
engaging in the daily realities of women in a context of the unsolved
national struggle. This mutual accommodation requires each party to be
vigilant in attending to the changes in the approaches and discourses of the
other, instead of maintaining the stance of total rejection exemplified by
the posture of women's NGOs.[47]

Islamists have had to build on women's modern gains in areas such as
education and work opportunities. The kind of state they might claim will
not only depend on the blueprint of a religious text but also evolve in the
context of existing conditions of the state, society, and the visions and challenges posed by other significantly popular and widely supported nationalist
and secularist groups.

Islah Jad is a Palestinian scholar and associate professor at Bir Zeit
University. She currently teaches in Cultural Studies Department and
Women's Studies Institute. She is one of the founders of the Women
Studies Institute at Bir Zeit (1994). She is a women's rights activist in
the Palestinian women's movements. She has many articles and chapters
in edited books on the history of the Palestinian women's movements and
political participation.

Notes

1. Khalid Hroub, *Hamas: Political Thought and Practice* (Washington, D.C.: Institute for Palestine Studies 2000), and "Obstacles to Democritisation in the Middle East." *Contention* 14, pp. 81–106; Jawad Hamad and Iyad Burguthi, *Derassa fi fikr harakat al-moqawamah al-islameyya hamas* (A Study in the Political Ideology of The Islamic Resistance Movement, Hamas, 1987–1996) (Amman: Middle East Study Centre, 1997); Khaled Abul-Omrein, *Hamas: The Islamic Resistance Movement in Palestine* (Cairo: Marqaz al-Hadara al-Arabeyya [The Arab Civilisation Center], 2000); Nurel-Din Al-Taheri, *Hamas: harakat al-moqawamh al-islameyya fi falastine* (Hamas: The Islamic Resistance Movement in Palestine) (Casablanca: *Dar el-'itissam* Publishing House, 1995); Ziyad Abu 'Amr, Ziad, *Islamic Fundamentalism in the West Bank and Gaza Strip: Muslim Brotherhood and Islamic Jihad* (Bloomington: Indiana University Press, 1994); Meir Litvak, *The Islamization of Palestinian Identity: The Case of Hamas*, (Tel Aviv: Moshe Dayan Center for Middle Eastern and African Studies, 1996); Zeev Schiff and Ehud Yaari, *Intifada: The Palestinian Uprising* (New York: Simon & Schuster, 1991); Hillel Frisch, *Countdown to Statehood: Palestinian State Formation in the West Bank and Gaza* (Albany: State University of New York Press, 1998); Henry Munson "Islam, Nationalism and Resentment of Foreign Domination," *Middle East Policy* 10.2 (2003).

2. Joel Beinin and Joe Stork (eds.), *Political Islam: Essays from Middle East Report* (Berkeley: University of California Press, 1997).

3. Mitchell, 1969, quoted in Olivier Roy, *The Failure of Political Islam*, trans. Carol Volk (London: I.B. Tauris, 1999), p. 39.

4. John Esposito, *Voices of Resurgent Islam.* (New York: Oxford University Press, 1983); Ira M. Lapidus, "Islamic Political Movements: Patterns of Historical Change," in Edmund Burke, Ira Lapidus and Ervand Abrahamiam (eds.), *Islam, Politics, and Social Movements* (Berkeley: University of California Press, 1998); Sami Zubaida, "Trajectories of Political Islam: Egypt, Iran and Turkey," *Political Quarterly* 71.1 (2000), pp. 60–78; Roy, *The Failure of Political Islam*; Azza Karam, *Women, Islamisms and the State: Contemporary Feminisms in Egypt* (New York: St. Martin's Press, 1998); Nazith Ayubi, *Political Islam: Religion and Politics in the Arab World* (London: Routledge, 1991); Beinin and Stork (eds.), *Political Islam*; Shireen Hunter (ed.), *The Politics of Islamic Revivalism: Diversity and Unity* (Indianapolis: Indiana University Press, 1998); Yvonne Haddan and John L. Esposito (eds.), *Islam, Gender, and Social Change* (New York: Oxford University Press, 1998).

5. Burke and Lapidus (eds.), *Islam, Politics, and Social Movements*; Zubaida, "Trajectories of Political Islam"; Hrair Dekmejian, "Islamic Revival: Catalysts, Categories, and Consequences" in Hunter (ed.), *Politics of Islamic Revivalism*; Deniz Kandiyoti, *Women, Islam and the State* (Basingstoke: Macmillan, 1991); Roy, *Failure of Political Islam*; Karam, *Women, Islamism, and the State*; Ayubi, *Political Islam*; Beinin and Stork (eds.), *Political Islam*.

6. Graham Usher, "What Kind of Nation? The Rise of Hamas in the Ocupied Territories," in Beinin and Stork (eds.), *Political Islam*; Schiff and Yaari, *Intifada*.

7. Abul-Omrein, *Hamas*, p. 187.
8. Rema Hammami, "Women, the Hijab and the Intifada," *Middle East Report* 20:3–4 (1990), pp. 24–28; Valentine Moghadam, "Introduction: Women and Identity Politics in Theoretical and Comparative Perspective," in Moghadam (ed.), *Identity Politics and Women: Cultural Reassertions and Feminisms in International Perspective* (Boulder, CO: Westview Press, 1994); Lisa Taraki, "Islam Is the Solution: Jordanian Islamists and the Dilemma of the 'Modern Woman,'" *British Journal of Sociology* 46.4 (1995), pp. 643–661.
9. Jenny B. White, *Islamist Mobilization in Turkey: A Study in Vernacular Politics* (Seattle: University of Washington Press, 2002).
10. Amira Haroun, interview, Gaza in January 10, 2000, Youssra Hamdan interview, Gaza in January 10, 2000; Maysoon el Ramahi, interview, Ramallah in November 1, 2003; Kholod el Massri, interview, Nablus in October 4, 2004.
11. White, *Islamist Mobilization in Turkey*, p. 223.
12. Ibid.
13. Lisa Taraki, "Mass Organizations in the West Bank," in Naseer H. Aruri (ed.), *Occupation: Israel Over Palestine*, 2nd ed. (Belmond, MA: Association of Arab-American University Graduates, 1989); Islah Jad, "From Salons to the Popular Committees: Palestinian Women, 1919–1989," in Jamal R. Nassar and Roger Heacock (eds.), *Intifada: Palestine at the Crossroads* (New York: Praeger, 1990); Frances Susan Hasso, "Paradoxes of Gender/Politics: Nationalism, Feminism, and Modernity in Contemporary Palestine," Ph.D. thesis, University of Michigan; Hammami, "Women, the Hijab and the Intifada"; Eileen Kuttab, "Palestinian Women in the Intifada: Fighting on Two Fronts," *Arab Studies Quarterly* 15.2 (1993), pp. 69–85.
14. Hammami, "Women, the Hijab, and the Intifada," p. 194
15. Ibid., p. 194.
16. Hasso, "Paradoxes of Gender/Politics," p. 259.
17. Jad, "From Salons to the Popular Committees"; Joseph Massad, "Conceiving the Masculine: Gender and Palestinian Nationalism," *Middle East Journal* 49.3 (1995), pp. 467–483; Hammami, "Women, the Hijab, and the Intifada"; Musa K. Budeiri, "The Nationalist Dimension of Islamic Movements in Palestinian Politics," *Journal of Palestine Studies*. 24.3 (1995), pp. 89–95.
18. Amnon Cohen, *Political Parties in the West Bank under the Jordanian Regime, 1949–1967* (Ithaca: Cornell University Press, 1982).
19. Chandra T. Mohanty, Ann Russo, and Lourdes Torres (eds.), *Third World Women and the Politics of Feminism* (Bloomington: Indiana University Press, 1991), pp. 66–67.
20. Hammami, "Women, the Hijab, and the Intifada."
21. Nikki R. Keddie, "The New Religious Politics: Where, When, and Why Do 'Fundamentalisms' Appear?" *Comparative Studies in Society and History* 40.4 (1998), pp. 696–723.
22. Harakat al-Muqawamah al-Islamiyah (Hamas), Charter of the Islmamic Resistance Movement, Gaza, August 1988.

23. Hamas, Charter, Article 17.

24. Hamas, Charter, Article 18.

25. Maysoon el Ramahi, interview, Ramallah, January 11, 2003.

26. WAD Women's Action Department (1997), *al-Marah al-Falastineyya ila Ayn* (Palestinian Woman: Where?). Workshop and conference proceedings, Gaza, the Islamic National Salvation Party, "Introduction" (1997), p. 1.

27. Maysoon el Ramahi, interview, Ramallah, January 11, 2003.

28. Khitam Abu Musa, "*al-Marah fil Tasawour al-Islami*" (Women in Islamic Thought), paper at the workshop *al-Marah al-Falestineyya ila Ayna* (Palestinian Woman: Where?), Gaza, April 1997.

29. Ibid., pp. 17–21 and 22.

30. Fatmeh Abdel Rahman, interview, Ramallah, January 12, 2003.

31. Samira Qur'an, interview, Al-Bireh, July 2, 2001.

32. Anne Phillips, *Democracy and Difference* (Cambridge: Polity Press, 1993).

33. Maxine Molyneux, "Women's Rights and the International Context in the Post-Communist States," in Mónica Threlfall (ed.), *Mapping the Women's Movement: Feminist Politics and Social Transformation in the North* (London: Verso, 1996), p. 6.

34. Amira Haroun, "*al-Marah al-Falestineyya wal Tahawlat al-Ijtema'eyya*" (Palestinian Woman and Social Change), paper presented at the Third Women's Conference, Gaza, August 2000.

35. Floya Anthias and Nira Yuval-Davis, "Introduction," in Floya Anthias and Nira Yuval-Davis, Floya Anthias, and Jo Campling (eds.), *Woman-Nation-State* (New York: St. Martin's Press, 1989).

36. Ari Shavit, "Survival of the Fittest," *Haaretz*, January 9, 2004, http://www. haaretz-daily.com/hasen/pages/shart.jhtml?itemNo-38098.

37. V. Spike Peterson and Anne Sisson Runyan, *Global Gender Issues* (Boulder, CO: Westview Press, 1998), pp. 81–82.

38. Barbara Victor, *Shahidas: Femmes kamikazes de Palestine* (Montreal: Flammarion Québec, 2002), p. 12.

39. Ibid.

40. Marcus, "Promoting Women Terrorists" *Jerusalem Post* Op-Ed., October 9, 2003.

41. Rabiha Diyyab in www.al-gazeera.net /lilnissa' fakat (only for women).

42. Ibid.

43. Dareen Abu Aisha's testimony, www.palestine-Info.jnfo, February 27, 2002.

44. Ibid.

45. Sami Zubaida, *Law and Power in the Islamic World.* (London: I.B. Tauris, 2003), p. 1.

46. Molyneux, "Women's Rights and the International Context," p. 6.

47. Hudson, "Obstacles to Democratisation in the Middle East," *Contention* (1996) 14: pp. 81–106; Augustus Richard Norton, "The Future of Civil Society in the Middle East," *The Middle East Journal* (Spring 1993) 47.2: pp. 205–16; (ed.) *Civil Society in the Middle East*, Vols. I and II. (Leiden: E.J. Brill, 1997). Ghassan Salame, ed., *Democracy without Democrats? The Renewal of Politics in The Muslim World* (London: I. B. Tauris, 2001).

Part Three

Women and Citizenship in an
Information Society

The Prospects for Democracy: Women Reformists in the Iranian Parliament

Elaheh Koolaee

The victory of Mohammad Khatami in the 1997 presidential election and the subsequent victory of the reformists in the 2000 parliamentary election radically altered the Iranian political terrain. By emphasizing a national identity that exceeds strictly religious identity, the notion of rights over the notion of duties, and individual and social freedom over intolerance and lack of compassion, the reformists shifted the political discourse from the religious language of a nondemocratic version of Islam to a pluralist and tolerant Islam and democratic ideals. Women were an intrinsic part of that movement toward reform and democratization.

Compared to other Middle Eastern women, Iranian women have experienced a unique involvement in the development of their society. They played an influential role in the Islamic revolution and the formation of the new political regime. They have sought a paradigm for retaining all aspects of their cultural and national identity while promoting women's rights. Women's mass participation in the revolution of 1979, their continued active presence in the public sphere, and their involvement in the Iran-Iraq war and its aftermath throughout the 1980s all laid the ground for the reformist movement, the impressive election victory of President Khatami, and a new empowerment of civil society. In Iran, as in many developing countries, women have been the victims of dual oppression. Like men, they were victims of despotic regimes, but also trapped in the patriarchal system.[1] After the Islamic revolution, women increased their efforts to improve their conditions but as in many developing countries, they faced rigid obstacles to progress.

In the early years of the new regime, beginning with the Iran-Iraq war and Saddam Hussein's invasion of Iran, the situation deteriorated, and the fulfillment of revolutionary ideals seemed distant. Women played a constructive and positive role during those eight years of defending the country.[2] They were recruited as revolutionary guards and provided ideological support for the men at the front. The war took an enormous toll on human life and left behind many widows and fatherless children. When the war was over, women were given jobs to support their families as the head of the household and employed in reconstruction projects. Thus, during those years and after the end of the war, their constructive role was critical. Women's political participation embodied the revolutionary spirit promoted by the spiritual leader of the Islamic revolution, Ayatollah Khomeini.[3] He made several rousing speeches on women's importance in securing victory in the war against Iraq. Many of his speeches raised women's awareness, expectations, and demands. Women moved on from the war with Iraq to demand their rightful place in the postwar era by establishing various NGOs, human-rights networks, and welfare institutions. As grassroots activists, they challenged the state's gender policies to the extent that state officials found themselves constantly entangled in gender discourse.

Although the reinstatement of the civil code based on the Islamic law, or *shari'a*, after the Islamic revolution limited women's human rights, their political rights remained intact, and the opportunity for social participation increased. A woman's vote remained equal to a man's, making political participation an equal-opportunity civic duty. Women realized the power of the ballot box and by their massive participation in local and national elections showed their influence as voters, challenging the political system to come up with suitable answers to their needs and demands as citizens.

The active participation of women who voted en masse for reform and the development of civil society challenged the stereotype of Iranian women as subservient, passive, veiled creatures controlled by Islamist ideologues. Indeed, without the active and massive support of women and the youth, the reformist candidates could not have defeated the conservative traditionalists in the 1997 presidential election and the 2000 parliamentary election. I was one of thirteen women who were elected to the Parliament in June 2000, and benefited from the mass participation of women and the youth in the election. Indeed, both the presidential and the parliamentary election showed the power of the women's vote, which constitutes half of the voting population, and which, it was discovered, could determine the fate of male candidates.

During the era of the reform program, the Sixth Parliament was the setting for many discussions of women's rights and the democratization of Iran. The female members of this Parliament were leaders working for social change. We were articulate, committed advocates for reform who made our voices heard loud and clear from the parliamentary tribunal.

There were a number of committees in the Sixth Parliament, including the Women's Faction, which came to be one of the most influential and active groups in the Iranian Parliament in the period after the Islamic revolution.[4] Collective action in politics is a new experience for Iranian women. Besides working together as the Women's Faction, the female Parliamentarians attempted to implement their agenda individually through different committees. However, there was a gap between the ideals of the Islamic Republic and the reality of women's status and rights. This was in direct contrast to the progressive teachings of Ayatollah Khomeini, who promoted women's rights and true dignity by asserting women's high status and their important role in revolutionary Iran. Women realized in dismay that instead of support for their rights, they faced the resistance of the conservative forces who, under the influence of traditional Islam and the patriarchal system, opposed their human rights. Women in the Sixth Parliament realized that the Islamic gender policies and discriminatory laws had to be challenged from within the Islamic framework by relying on the teaching of Ayatollah Khomeini and the principles of the Islamic constitution.

The Women's Faction was motivated by a desire to simultaneously capitalize on the many positive aspects of Islamic thought and reduce the barriers and restrictions faced by women in many parts of Iranian society. We worked within the existing constitutional framework to implement reform. The coalition of female MPs was supported by the majority of the Parliament, which was dominated by the reformists. On occasion, the conservatives also supported particular proposals to amend the civil code.

We hoped to eliminate some of the deep-rooted problems in the Iranian society, especially those that had emerged after the revolution and affected family law and civil and penal codes. The reformist women tried to use the Islamic principles of the revolution to amend regulations on behalf of women and reverse rulings of the executive and judiciary institutions.

During those challenging years, the Women's Faction tried to change women's legal status by focusing on laws regarding such issues as inheritance, divorce, child custody, and insurance. We called on the government to ratify the Convention on Elimination of All Forms of Discrimination Against Women (CEDAW). Through the continuous efforts of female deputies, and after much debate and hard work, the motion to adopt CEDAW was approved by the Cultural Affairs Committee of Parliament. However, faced with staunch opposition and under threat of veto by the Guardian Council (an appointed conservative clerical body that oversees all elections and reviews all laws approved by the Parliament), CEDAW was not ratified.

We believed that, if approved, the Convention would strengthen women's rights by eliminating discriminatory laws such as women's legal testimony given half the legitimacy in court as that of men; gender-biased insurance laws; the law of retribution, and the so-called blood money, which essentially counts a woman's worth at half that of a man's, irrespective of the degree of her injury and bodily harm. There is no doubt that the primary means of changing people's attitudes and behavior are factors internal to the society, but with recent world developments and expanded global relationships among people and countries, adopting international conventions is an influential method for improving domestic affairs by taking advantage of the experience of different countries.[5]

The Women's Faction made efforts to point out that passing of CEDAW would also enhance the Islamic Republic's international image and standing. Joining countries that had already approved this convention could improve the Islamic Republic's negotiating position internationally and counter much negative propaganda regarding Iran's "anti-women's rights" status. But opposition from the Guardian Council was rigid and steady. In an attempt to bypass a stalemate with the Guardian Council, approval of CEDAW was taken directly to the Expediency Council, the authority which decides on legislation when there is disagreement between Parliament and the Guardian Council. There were hopes that the Expediency Council would support Parliament's efforts and approve CEDAW for its national and international benefits. Unfortunately, there was not enough time to rally support and the legislation passed over into the Seventh Parliament, where it was not taken up again.

The Women's Faction focused primarily on amending civil codes, where many barriers and limitations for women's social and economic advancement are to be found. We addressed both marriage and divorce laws, by attempting to amend the civil code so that women would have the same rights as men in seeking divorce in court. This bill also defined alimony by giving women the right to demand allowances for housing and health care. There was also the principle of *ojrat-ol mesl*, which had been amended and passed prior to the Sixth Parliament. It stipulates that when a man files for divorce, his wife can ask to be compensated for the housework she has carried out during the marriage. Although for the bill to become law it had to pass the Guardian Council's approval, its ratification by the whole assembly was considered the beginning of the realization that reforms were necessary to improve women's rights and that challenges to the male-dominated legal system were to come.

As the majority of the reformist women had university degrees, we paid particular attention to educational discrimination against women, especially the limits on the number of scholarships available to girls who wished to study abroad in foreign universities.[6] In the early years of the revolution, only men had access to this opportunity. Many gifted young women were deprived of this opportunity, just because they were female. One of the first steps in Parliament was to change this discriminatory law. It also reversed an earlier ban on women studying supposedly male subjects such as mining, technical sciences, engineering, and agriculture. According to the Islamic constitution, the government is obliged to abolish every type of discrimination against men and women alike. This is one of the duties of the Islamic state, but there are real cultural and historical obstacles to carrying out these principles. Many people still cannot imagine that a woman can take care of herself without the help of a man.

Our efforts later in the term were less successful. We worked to quash a quota system, promoted by the Ministry of Health, that would have limited the number of women permitted to study medicine, dentistry, and pharmacology. The ministry claimed that the number of female students had risen too much in these scientific disciplines in the universities. With the cooperation and support of Parliament's education committee, the Women's Faction proposed a bill prohibiting the use of any gender-based quota system in university admissions.

This is revealing and underscores the need for societal changes in male attitudes toward women. The significant presence of girls in different disciplines in the universities is one of the most honorable achievements of the Islamic Republic.[7] But proposing a fifty-fifty quota in admission to medical schools, for example, erodes victories based on women's hard work. Trying to limit the number of women in these disciplines is obviously a violation of the Islamic constitution, which stresses that it is the state's task to eradicate all kinds of unacceptable discrimination. The decreasing number of men in the universities is the result of a chain of causes that requires careful analysis. Also, this is not the exclusive experience of Iran. Similar trends have arisen in many countries, both developed and underdeveloped. It is an unavoidable fact that over 60 percent of new students enrolled in universities in Iran are female. In fact, the impressive accomplishments of women in higher education and their political participation at both local and national levels can be considered the most important achievement by Iranian women in the postrevolutionary era.

Even though the number of educated women increased and their school enrollment exceeded that of men, the employment record for women has remained rather dismal.[8] Women seeking jobs face cultural barriers to gainful employment. It is therefore crucial to increase the capacities of the labor market and recognize the necessity of expanding the role of women in the labor force. In the 2002 budget, provisions were made based on the notion of gender justice, to expand the role of women in the public sector and in the growth and development of the country. These realities require consideration, not laws discouraging the advancement of women.

Family law was also an area of great concern for the Women's Faction of the Sixth Parliament. One of our early works supporting the institution of family was a group of amendments to the regulations regarding working women and female judges. Changes to the law had been made to reverse the ban on women becoming judges, including provisions for recruitment of female police officers. We worked to create guarantees that professional married couples would be able to work in the same city and keep their families intact. During the debates on the budget, changes were instituted to exempt women's dower (*mahr*) from taxation. Financial support was provided for war widows and disabled veterans, and entitlements for surviving spouses were upheld, even if they remarried.

Another improvement in women's lives was made when the Women's Faction amended an article of the law regarding state employees' wages. The faction supported women's health care, through amendments regarding the wages and working conditions of pregnant women. In case of remarriage, women could also receive financial help for their children's expenses.

Throughout our four years in office, the Women's Faction led groundbreaking attempts to create bridges between secular and religious experts to reform laws in favor of women's rights. Both the Women's Committee and the Youth Affairs Committee were actively involved in this effort.[9] Meetings and roundtables were held to study various problems and challenges facing women. Petitions were sent to top clerics demanding equal compensation for crime victims, regardless of their gender. Some of these efforts were successful, and the Women's Faction used the results of these discussions to further improve women's status. It is, however, important to consider the success or failure of these efforts within the realities of a transitional society like Iran.[10] The limits to, and opportunities for, women's rights and citizenship were determined by the Islamic constitution, but their implementation depended on the political will of various officials of state machinery to uphold them.

We worked hard and played an important role in calling attention to gender discourse during the period of reform. We were successful in increasing the minimum legal age for marriage. In this case, the Expediency Council ruled with some modification in favor of Parliament's amendment, over the Guardian Council's objections. The law was changed, increasing the age of marriage to thirteen for girls and fifteen for boys. (In reality, the average age of marriage for both males and females in Iran is over twenty years old.)

In part as a result of many centuries of a male-dominated culture and legal framework, issues relating to marriage and divorce posed special problems for women. The proposed standard marriage forms passed in an earlier period enabled women to negotiate the terms and conditions of their marriage contracts. Amendments were proposed for widows, establishing financial support to be provided by the estate of the deceased. The women MPs also considered reforms to the civil code in divorce laws, such as reinstatement of women's conditional rights to divorce; the requirement that alimony be set according to the rate of inflation at the time of divorce; the right to health insurance and medical care, now stipulated as a duty of the husband. This amendment also gave women an equal right to go to the family courts and request a divorce on the grounds of abuse.[11]

With the support of the majority of Parliament, the Women's Faction was able to pass the Protection of Youth and Children's Rights Act. This law provided protection against all sorts of violations of the rights of children and the youth, including financial support for runaway and homeless children. It is important to note the influential role of Nobel Peace Prize winner Shirin Ebadi in getting this legislation passed. The enactment of child custody law and recognition of the mother's right to retain custody was another important part of the family-law reform.

Inheritance law was another area the Women's Faction addressed. We attempted to reduce the burden of working women inside and outside the home, especially in rural areas.[12] In these regions, women play the roles of wife, mother, housekeeper, and farmer, often without receiving a fair share of the family properties after the husband's death. The faction met with top clerics and judicial experts on this matter, and, with their guidance, attempted to change a portion of the civil code that deals with inheritance regulations.

According to Article 946 on this code, a woman cannot inherit her deceased husband's entire estate, especially land or other immovable property. This is clearly discriminatory in cases where, after many years of living with a man, a woman cannot inherit property to whose establishment she has contributed during the marriage. Despite the faction's attempts to show the flexibility of Islamic thought in answering the needs of society with changing times, the Guardian Council rejected all substantial changes to this amendment. Our efforts to alter other parts of the inheritance law were also vanquished. Under the current civil code, sole surviving men can inherit their deceased wife's full estate, but women cannot inherit all their husband's estate, even as the only surviving family member. The Guardian Council rejected attempts to amend this part of the law, and the current Parliament put it aside! And so our efforts were thwarted in some cases, even after the benefit of consultation with top clerics who had had close relationships with the late Ayatollah Khomeini.

The Women's Faction worked tirelessly to prove that Islam had the capacity for change and that the constitution was able to protect women's rights and respond to the evolving demands of a modern society. Naturally the resistance from the traditional, male-dominated society was very strong, but this resistance never stopped our work on behalf of women.

In response to the deep and vast changes in social structures, especially in family relationships during recent years, women in Parliament presented a plan to reform some parts of the civil code in a package titled "Plan to Solve Family Disputes."[13] This package combined many amendments to protect women's rights and maintain strong family relationships. Some articles of this package, as described above, were approved, but many were rejected by the Guardian Council.

An amendment to improve the condition of Iranian women who had been married to foreign men, in particular those married to Afghan men, was proposed. But there was very strong resistance to these efforts, due to fears of an influx of immigration of Afghan men wishing to take advantage of this opportunity. However, administrative bodies promised to consider Iranian women in this respect and aid them in remaining in Iran with their families.

To secure the health and protection of the family institution, the faction proposed conditions that made it more difficult for husbands to annul their marriages. A bill was also introduced granting permission for abortion if the life of the mother was in danger.

Families abandoned by men were not forgotten by the Women's Faction. We put forward a proposal to help women retain custody of their children. The faction aimed to offer different services to these women, such as job training, social services, cultural activities, and financial support, within the framework of a variety of programs. The plan called for all the administrative branches of government to play a role in improving these women's quality of life.

Due to the rapid, broad changes in Iranian society and the structure of the family, especially relating to women's awareness of their rights and the feminist movement, the issues of reform of the civil code and amendment of the family law have become essential for Iranian women in the era of globalization.[14]

The Sixth Parliament made a notable pro-woman move in the first year when it created a gender-based analysis as part of the Fourth Program for Social and Economic Development.[15] In the first year of Parliament, negotiations with the Management and Planning Organization were not successful in making gender justice an issue of concern in social and economic development plans. But by the end of the parliamentary term, after great efforts on the part of the faction and many women's NGOs, gender-based analysis became part of the plan approved by the whole assembly. The considerable cooperation of the Management and Planning Organization was crucial in getting the budget for Social and Economic Development passed with this added consideration. This bill, if implemented, has great promise for women's lives and offers real possibilities for improving their condition.

The Women's Faction of the Sixth Parliament took its job seriously. We worked hard to frame arguments in Islamic terminology, bring about change, and make a lasting impact on women's rights in Iran. We concentrated our efforts on two areas: the executive branch and the judicial system. In the judiciary, the Women's Faction not only worked with the parliament to depoliticize the court system but also tried to prevent the execution of certain unjust sentences rendered by the courts. We made huge efforts through debates and petitions to repeal the sentence of death by stoning, and the law of retribution. We negotiated with top clerics of the Guardian Council and the president of the Expediency Council on these and other issues relating to justice and women's position in society. The changing nature of society and the need to address these challenges appropriately were brought before top clerics by the women faction. We hoped it would be possible to capitalize on the change in the law regarding blood money (set equally for Muslims and non-Muslims) by pursuing a similar change in the law of retribution setting men's and women's blood moneys equal, but opposition remained strong and kept the unequal law of retribution intact.

Efforts to promote issues of women's equality in the executive branch were pursued with thought and care. For example, we attempted to equalize married women's and men's wages. The cabinet had passed a discriminatory regulation that made base pay unequal for men and women, obviously in violation of women's rights. After six months of debate and struggle by members of the faction, the regulation was rescinded.

We also looked to our own administration, seeking the appointment of female ministers during the formation of President Khatami's second cabinet, but resistance due to traditional and historical biases proved too strong. Although the percentage of women in managerial posts increased in the era of the reform program, their total numbers remained low.

During the Sixth Parliament, the women faction had many meetings with MPs of different countries and with journalists, to explain the realities of the Iranian society and its progress. Although there is still much to be done to improve conditions for Iranian women, we actively worked to counter the huge amount of negative propaganda against the Islamic Republic of Iran regarding women. All the female MPs presented the many and considerable achievements of Iranian women in the face of adversity, common to many Islamic and developing countries.

Those of us with ties to NGOs worked to strengthen relationships among ourselves and our organizations. This attitude of cooperation between government and civil society is a new phenomenon in Iran. In addition to our duties as members of a specialized commission of Parliament, members of the faction pursued other tasks in support of women's issues. We played influential roles in different parliamentary committees. For the first time after the revolution, a woman was elected to a leadership position in the Parliament. In the last months of the Sixth Parliament, that number grew to two, a modest but encouraging success story.

The Women's Faction in the Sixth Parliament, supported by the majority of the reformist members of the Parliament (and even, in some cases, with the assistance of the minority camp), made strides in improving conditions for Iranian women. The faction attempted to explore the capacities of the constitution, applying a progressive interpretation of Islamic thought regarding the duties and human capacities of women. We tried to demonstrate the flexibility of Islamic law, but the resistance of the conservatives and the opposition of the Council of Guardians were very strong. Clearly, change is a time-consuming struggle, and supporters of women's rights must continue these efforts in civil associations. We hope that the current Women's Faction of the Seventh Parliament will build on past successes and strengthen women's progress and their ability to participate in controlling their future.

During the seven years of reform, the percentage of women who took an active role in municipal and national elections increased considerably. Women have to maintain a pace of reform and not be intimidated by external forces or rigid obstacles. Their involvement in politics is not limited to participation in elections, but includes civil practices that require interaction with other citizens. Through such practices, women are challenging the autocratic power of the state by promoting democratic and representative institutions. Given the complex political situation, Iranian women favor slow change that builds on rights already established. They face two challenges simultaneously: conservative forces and the lack of effective civic-minded cultural and institutional infrastructure. The battle on both fronts looks increasingly difficult, but the process of reform will continue. The result will be the development in Iran of a civil society based on the rule of popular consent and a plurality of opinion, to which Iranian women have made a significant contribution.

Elaheh Koolaee is a former member of the Iranian Parliament, representing a voice for reform and democratic change in the Islamic Republic of Iran. She is also a professor of political science at Tehran University, specializing in Russia and Central Asia with emphasis on the Caspian region and oil politics. Author of twelve books and numerous articles, Koolaee is one of the progressive voices on women's rights in the Islamic Republic of Iran. Dr. Koolaee, in her capacity as a member of parliament, has been instrumental in passing some of the reformed laws on behalf of women and reform of family law in Iran.

Notes

1. Mohammad Hossein Hafezian, "Political Participation of Women and the Islamic Revolution of Iran," *Discourse: An Iranian Quarterly*, 3 (2002), p. 51.
2. Elaheh Koolaee, "Women in the Public Sphere: The Case of the Islamic Republic of Iran," World Bank Annual Meeting, Dubai, September 20, 2003.
3. His speeches and messages have been collected in Ruhollah Khomeini, *Sahifeh Noor (The Book of Light: Collection of Khomeini's Messages, Letters, and Announcements)* (Tehran: The Center for Publishing Ayatollah Khomeini's Works, 1365, 1986).
4. Elaheh Koolaee, "A Glance at Women's Faction's Activities," *Shargh* no. 223, 4.4.1383, (2004) p. 3.
5. There have been many books and articles published on this topic by conservative sources and their institutes.
6. Eight of thirteen female MPs teach in universities, and half of them have Ph.D.s in scientific fields.
7. "Increasing the Percentage of Women in Higher Education," Office for Social

Planning and Cultural Studies, Women's Studies Division, 2002.

8. "Developing Women's Participation in Higher Education," Office for Research and Cultural and Social Planning, Women's Studies Division, 2001.

9. This committee was a part of the Cultural Commission of the Majles Parliament.

10. Nayereh Tohidi, "Women's Rights in the Muslim World, the Universal-particular Interplay," *Hawwa Journal on Women in the Middle East and Islamic World* 1.2 (2003), pp. 152–188.

11. This amendment could have had great cultural, social, and economic impact on the situation of women in Iran, but since it met with resistance from the Guardian Council, it was sent to the Expediency Council, and finally, only five of the proposed parts were approved.

12. Mohammad Effatti, "Obstacles to Rural Women's Participation in Socioeconomic Activities," *Jihad* 14, 169 (Azar, 1373; 1994), pp. 17–23.

13. Nasrin Jazani, "An Approach to Gender Analysis in Iran," Shalid Beheshti University Press, Tehran (2002).

14. Elaheh Koolaee, "Women in the Era of Globalization." Paper presented at Conference on Women's Roles as Dialogue Among Civilizations, Tehran, 2001.

15. "Gender Issues in the Fourth Program for Development, Job and Social Protection," Center for Women's Studies, Tehran, June 2004.

Women and Civil Society in Iran

Mehrangiz Kar

Iranian women played a major role in the developments that led to the formation and consolidation of power by the moderates during the reform period (1997–2004). With their active presence at the polling stations, women altered their image of passivity and voted overwhelmingly for the reform programs suggested by Mohammad Khatami, who, prior to the election, promised women greater involvement and participation in the political arena. To most Iranian women, even secular ones, Khatami was a more qualified candidate than his rivals, as his platform to eliminate state violence against the citizens and to defend civil liberties and women's rights had a mass appeal.

The 1997 presidential election, which came to be known as the Second of Khordad movement, was able to enhance the political current, which had been frozen since the 1979 revolution and the suppression of opposition groups.

Women, in fact, not only took advantage of the reformist momentum but also made vast contributions to it, but they were unable to obtain major changes in their legal status. Now, eight years after the reformist election, it appears that the political and legislative moves to bring substantive change in the structure of power have come to a halt. The president failed to reform the system from within, and the unelected Council of Guardians and the theocracy in power overruled the reformists by disqualifying opposition, undermining the electoral process, and assuring the control of the conservative religious faction in both local and parliamentary elections. With the power to dismiss, reverse, or reject, the ruling religious elite has been able to limit reformists' achievements in both content and consequence. It is not surprising, therefore, that attempts to reform the structural elements of the Islamic regime have been seriously thwarted, and the right-wing specter, in its determination to reverse the social and cultural freedoms of the reformist era, has closed down most of Iran's reformist press and moved against civil-society groups that promoted the reformist agenda. The female members of the current Parliament aspire to limit the achievements of their predecessors and have moved in the opposite direction from the women deputies of the Sixth Parliament, who made history by standing up for women's rights and promoting the issues of gender justice and equality. The current women deputies opposed the bill to join the UN Convention on the Elimination of All Forms of Discrimination Against Women (CEDAW) and removed the "gender equality" clause, meant to provide equal training and employment opportunities for women from the five-year state development plan.[1] The recent crackdown on journalists, the arrests of advocates of women's rights, the filtering of the Internet, and arrest of online journalists and Web masters are all attempts to stop the trend toward liberalization and to curtail the freedoms gained during the reform era.

The hard-line clerical establishment's intransigence in defense of its interests, at the expense of society's needs and aspirations, ignores the sociopolitical developments of the past decade and denies the public's desire for freedom and civil rights—particularly women's rights. By mass disqualification of the reformist candidates in 2004, the religious establishment served notice that it is determined to keep its comfortable hegemony in the power game—although in the long run, given Iran's young population and the shift in political discourse from the language of religious duty to the language of individual rights and free expression, the enduring effect of the conservative establishment is in doubt.

I believe change and democracy, when it comes, will come from outside the religious establishment. It is possible that the critics of the theocratic state, who are at the present a majority of silent spectators, will at the opportune time challenge the foundation of theocratic power and institutional structure of the Islamic regime.

Whatever strategy prevails, the reform movement, despite its limited scope, has succeeded in altering the political discourse by challenging the state's accountability to its citizens. In the eight years since the start of the reform movement, the courageous women's rights activists and the determined political and human-rights groups, with the help of a dynamic press and against intense and sometimes violent opposition, have paved the way for a more pluralistic discourse on civil society by injecting new debate about the nature and structure of the state and by calling for more account-ability, transparency, and openness.

In order to convey the role women played in the reform period, I will discuss a number of key areas in which women's participation was impor-tant in the reform movement and continues to influence the political land-scape today.

Civil Society: The Role of Women in the Press

The emerging public sphere and the discourse on civil society (*jame'eh-yeh madani*) in opposition to religious society (*jame'eh-yeh mazhabi*) became possible as the result of the reformists' massive victory in the national and local elections of 1997 and 2000. The press played a crucial role in advanc-ing the reformist agenda by providing the platform for a debate on progres-sive ideas, civil society, human rights, and a vision for a democratic system of governance. In the press, discourse on civil society created a forum for social and political protest and a context for political interaction. It provid-ed a basis for women to voice their concerns about gender inequality and human-rights violation, to become more assertive and to assume a greater role in the debate on Islamic law, and democracy.

Young women participated quite visibly in the reformist press. This was manifested in its best form in the publication of the newspaper *Tous*, which was one of the first reform dailies to open after Khatami's election in 1997. It was aimed at students, professionals, the educated and literary set and became the most popular newspaper in Iran. Many more reformist papers followed, and despite arrests, pressure, and many ups and downs, they con-tinued in a dynamic and engaged atmosphere. Women worked with men in different press outlets, and all were determined to stay on the scene to ensure the continuity of debate, even if only one newspaper remained open and the others were shut down. When one newspaper was closed, they con-tinued their work by joining another.[2] Following a wave of attacks on the reformist press, the conservative camp reactivated the Press Court after the election of 1997 to actively undermine the reformist media. The Press Court summoned many women journalists to special tribunals and charged them with violations of laws governing the press. They were interrogated, charged, and sentenced.[3]

In response to these pressures, women formed the Society of Women Journalists in 1998. Their statements regarding respect for law, freedom of expression, women's rights, and political freedom during the most critical time in the history of the reform movement had a considerable impact on the freedom of the press in the country.[4]

Today, we can easily claim that women journalists will be the principal players in any future movement to bring about political change in Iran. They have become powerful in the realm of practice and implementation and have become both initiators and activists in their goals for emancipation. During the reform period, women's professional demands were expressed alongside the demands of their male counterparts. Women's views, especially regarding their legal status, were highly visible. By using their pens to criticize the misogynist laws of the Islamic Republic, they directly and collectively put pressure on the authorities to change the sentences imposed on women deemed guilty of some form of misconduct by the judiciary.[5]

In addition, women journalists created a network inside and outside Iran through Internet sites, which enabled them to discuss women's issues, report abuse or violations of women's rights, and draw attention to the plight of Iranian women in the context of global communication. I believe women's voices documented in this way will influence and change the process of historical writing, will reflect their journalistic sophistication and political participation, and will thus eventually end men's monopoly in the media.[6]

In spite of female journalists' efforts to open the profession to more women and to share work on equal terms in the press environment, gender still is an obstacle and the determining factor in hiring and decision making. This despite the fact that half the students in journalism schools are women.

As one woman journalist, Fariba Davoudi Mohajer, explained:

If I were given a newspaper [to write], I would use it to talk about having the right to divorce. I would write articles about women having the right to presidency. I would write about how men and women were created, have evolved equally, [and] have equal rights.

I would present the issues and thoughts of women. So the best way for them is not to give me a publishing permit, or label me a radical and take away my editorial power to choose my stories.[7]

The culture of male dominance has affected women journalists both politically and financially. The repeated closure of newspapers and the law forbidding rehiring by other papers has led to widespread unemployment. Lack of job security, long waits in obtaining permits to publish a newspaper, and repeated shutdowns of the press have affected women journalists. A comparison of the number of permits granted between 1997 and 2000 shows that of over seven hundred publication permits, only fifty-nine were issued to women publishers, and only nine journals had a female editor-in-chief.[8] But, despite the many obstacles—cultural as well as political—women journalists have kept a high profile and remain players. In the words of Lili Farhad Pour, who has been a journalist for over fifteen years and has been contributing editor to such reformist papers as *Tous*, *Jame'eh*, *Neshat*, and many others, journalism is "an access tool, [a] means of power control and activism . . . in [the] quest for equality."[9]

Civil Society and NGO Participation

The reform period was marked by a distinct opening in the social sector that allowed a great number of Iranians to take a more active role in addressing social issues. Women took advantage of this new opportunity, and by establishing nongovernmental organizations (NGOs), they took on a more active role in addressing the needs of society and women. However, women's NGOs are relatively few in number, organizationally weak, and politically ineffective.[10] There are several reasons for this. First, the main government bodies responsible for developing an agenda for women—the Bureau of Women's Participation, which is responsible for policy at the national level, and, in the Ministry of the Interior, the Office on Social Policy's Department for Women, which is responsible for the provincial levels—have failed to articulate a comprehensive policy.[11] They have focused on increasing the number of women's NGOs rather than developing their strengths as organizations addressing such issues as women's participation in the workforce, prevention of violence against women, or the problem of runaway girls and prostitution. Again, many of these NGOs are newly formed, have limited expertise and financial resources and therefore remain weak and ineffective in influencing public policy. Only a few women's NGOs have been able to tap into the financial resources available nationally and internationally. This has limited their ability to take on effective advocacy roles on behalf of women. Additionally, the government's relationship to NGOs is unclear at best, and the autonomy of individuals and associations is in doubt. A major challenge facing women's NGOs in Iran is the lack of government neutrality, which undermines the sector's development and threatens its independence.

Another reason for the NGOs' weakness and lack of development is the long and arduous licensing process. The religious authorities reject women activists' applications, especially those of secular women like me; I tried many times to establish a women's legal rights research center and was never given justification for being denied permission.[12] The exclusion of experts from this sector has limited its effectiveness. Under current law, anyone establishing an NGO must obtain a security clearance from the police and the Ministry of Information before being granted a license.[13] The current law allows the state to issue permits to or to revoke the licenses of any organization, whether political or civil, without an explanation. A case in point is the Iran's Pen Society, which—despite its international reputation—has not been allowed to operate since it was originally formed as a secular writers' association. Although lacking official existence, the secular voice has not been silenced, and its popularity is manifested in numerous books and translations in circulation and in huge demand.

Women's broader access to education and their impressive achievement in higher education have also been instruments of empowerment and social mobilization. In the 2003-2004 academic year, of the 1.8 million students who took university admission tests, the overwhelming majority were female. Currently, over 63 percent of university students are women. The new generation is more educated, politically aware, and socially involved. I believe the pressure for movement toward civil society and democracy will continue because of the needs and views of the young, educated, and mobilized population in all sectors of society. The active participation of women in NGOs will especially give younger women experience in working in a team setting, in organizing, and in developing a platform for action. So while there may be little immediate result from such activism and the women's NGOs, in the long run they may help to formulate a more solid women's movement and a shift toward an open and responsive society. As Mahboubeh Abbasgholizadeh, the editor of the women's journal *Farzaneh* and director of a women's NGO's training center, observed in her presentation at the Asia Pacific NGO Forum:

> I searched relentlessly for the voice of the young girls of my country, which I finally found in Internet chat rooms, websites, student meetings, youth NGOs and long unemployment lines. . . . They asked me to tell anyone who would listen that the ideological stereotyping, labeling and partisan games which have become a trend in Iran do not belong to our generation . . . that they want to have the right to make decisions regarding their future and their private lives, their equal civil rights with men, their right of participation in the public sphere, the right to choose their clothing, their right to love, their right to enjoy life and other natural human rights.[14]

This generation is reacting naturally. It yearns for a free and normal existence and is slowly moving toward a democratic, transparent, youth-oriented society. One generation has come to an end and with it, certain extreme positions, whether the individuals in that generation were clerics, religious nationalists, communists, or royalists. Those who participated in the revolution and were later suppressed, silenced, or forced into exile were like a bridge to the past. We have already crossed this bridge; it no longer serves any purpose. The new generation is moderate and pro-reform but unwilling to support anyone blindly. The revolutionary generation has given way to a reformist generation that favors evolution over revolution. They speak through their votes. We saw this in the public support for Khatami, and we witnessed it again with the massive boycott of the recent parliamentary election, when the youth abandoned the voting process in droves. The state's poor performance on a whole range of issues as well as continuous social pressure, contribute to the shifting ground in the country's governance that in the next few years could result in the emergence of an institutional democracy in Iran—despite the continued struggle of the factions opposed to such development.

Feminist Topics in Women's Press

Being a woman and an activist in a traditional society is problematic, especially when religious belief overpowers the legal system. Before the reformist movement, feminism was thought to be infatuated with modernity and Western permissiveness, which were bound to endanger family structure, society, culture, and ultimately Islam itself. A feminist was perceived as a rootless secular with loose sexual behavior. Whenever people wanted to accuse or discredit a woman, they would call her a feminist. Censorship laws, applied to both the press and book publishing were such that it was nearly impossible to obtain permission to publish anything that contained feminist ideas.

The reform period did not change the laws governing publications and censorship; nevertheless, during this time women writers, novelists, and storytellers published many books incorporating feminist ideology.[15] The officials at the Ministry of Culture and Islamic Guidance who were responsible for protecting revolutionary and Islamic principles in the press at the time eased their restrictions and looked at such proposals with an open mind, ultimately giving permission for the publication of feminist books written or translated by scholars and experts. These efforts led to the creation of a feminist culture and increased the overall effect of the feminist movement in Iran.

The new climate of reform facilitated the emergence of a new group of feminists with a woman-centered interpretation of Islam, who believe that by reforming religion, women can attain their legal rights. This group challenges traditional interpretations through political activism and women's journals. *Zanan*, established in 1991, is an influential women's journal that opened up the debate on women's rights in Islam by introducing a feminist interpretation of Islamic sources, inviting a pro-woman religious debate and challenging the state to live up to its promise of Islamic equality. *Zanan* also publishes debates and discussions of women's social and legal position, translations of major works by Western feminists, and criticism of judicial treatment of women.

Feminist activists during and since the reform period have passionately debated over the compatibility of Islam, with feminism, human rights, and universal women's rights. In the process, secular and Islamist feminists have come closer to recognizing their common interests. Thus, if the political environment is favorable to the advancement of women's rights in Iran, it will enable and empower feminism despite its belonging to a different category or ideology.

In the area of filmmaking, the freer atmosphere brought a breakthrough for Iranian cinema, allowing women directors to make impressive films with feminist themes. A unique feature of the Iranian cinema has been the significant role of women both behind and in front of the camera. The powerful presence of women in films plays a central role in this transition. Films in which women and love are rehabilitated such as Tahmineh Milani's *Two Women* (1998) and Rakhshan Bani Etemad's *May Lady* (1997) deal with feminist themes, questioning gender roles and love relations. They examine Iranian society through such issues as poverty, crime, divorce, single motherhood, love, and polygamy. Milani's later film, *The Hidden Half* (2001), focused on the involvement of secular and leftist groups in the 1979 revolution and resulted in her temporary arrest. Milani said in an interview, "Because *The Hidden Half* talks about the unspoken issues of a generation, it offends many. It says, 'Look what you have done to the people with your unjust and heartless judgments'; we have to go and open up this part of history and speak about the past, so the wounds that last in the society today, will be healed."[16]

One feature of these films is the demanding voice of a younger generation that wants personal freedom and questions gender restrictions and limitations imposed by the state policy.

Female MPs' Visible Role in Protests

Another trend toward reform and democratization was manifested in the parliamentary election. The number of women representatives in the Sixth Islamic Parliament was still fewer than their proportion of the population in the country. Nine women were elected to the Majles (Parliament) initially, and then midterm elections increased their numbers to thirteen. However, women representatives in the Sixth Parliament, with great courage and strength of wit, were able to amplify their political influence in the country and highlight the politics of gender.

Their most significant roles and actions are summarized as follows:

First, the amazing increased participation of women deputies in democratic discourse was reflected in the parliamentary records, which manifested the power of free speech and open discussions in Parliament, and proved the courage of the women deputies, who, despite the harassment and pressure of the hard-liner–controlled judiciary, articulated their demands with authority and conviction. Women deputies such as Elaheh Koolaee in her speeches at the parliament on issues of national security and foreign affairs, expressed their informed opinion with a greater voice.

Second, women deputies formed a bloc to push for reform, to take measures to constructively criticize the dominant political strategies of the ruling clergy, and to protest the violation of citizens' rights, the serial murders of members of the political opposition, and the oppression of students at the universities. Fatemeh Haqiqatjoo, a brave thirty-year-old MP, gave a parliamentary speech defending the rights of the students to protest. She revealed that a violent militia attack had occurred inside university dormitories during student protest in June 2003 and had resulted in deaths and serious injuries to the students. As a result of her advocacy on behalf of the students, Haqiqatjoo was sentenced to prison (the sentence was suspended on appeal). In 2004, after the Guardian Council's mass disqualification of the reformist deputies barred them from reelection, Haqiqatjoo gave a rousing speech criticizing the ruling theocracy, accusing it of undermining democratic elements of the Islamic Republic, and then resigned in protest.[17]

Third, commitment to reversing gender inequality led the women's bloc to push for reform of family law, which met with limited success. Bills allowing single women to study abroad, amending articles of the civil code to increase the minimum age of marriage to thirteen for girls, and increasing women's custody rights to age seven were among their successes. However, they were not successful in their effort to ratify the UN Convention on the Elimination of All Forms of Discrimination Against Women (CEDAW).

The women deputies of the Sixth Parliament were devout Muslims and experienced revolutionary personalities who used the parliamentary forum to courageously discuss democratic ideas in the context of human rights and gender equality. They tried to approach the issues through dialogue with religious experts. They made their way to the homes of high-ranking clergy members in Qom, discussed the idea of equality in Islam, and sought new interpretations to apply to the concept of gender equality, in an attempt to gain the approval of the religious authorities. This approach by the women representatives was unique and new. It helped bring the issue of gender equality to the public's attention and created an atmosphere in which such discussions could take place.

As part of holding the religious authority accountable to women, they asked the Guardian Council to explain Provision 115 of the constitution, which outlines the conditions of eligibility to run for presidency. It states, "The president must be elected from among distinguished religious and political *personalities* (*rejal-e siyasi-ye mazhabi*)." They asked about the definition of a religious-political personality but obtained no definitive answer. Nevertheless, some women volunteered as candidates during the 2001 presidential election, until the Guardian Council intervened to stop their activities by declaring them ineligible to run.[18]

The shortcomings of the legal system are poignantly felt by women, who, despite obstacles and rejections, have been able to articulate new roles for themselves as critics of the political status quo. After the reformist election, women were accused of expressing dissident political opinions and viewpoints, and were tried for political crimes. In April 2000, a mixed group of male and female reformists and feminists was invited to participate in an international conference in Berlin to discuss the future of Iran after the reformist elections. The hard-liners used the occasion to attack the reform movement by issuing arrest warrants for the participants. Shahla Lahiji, a writer and publisher, and I, an attorney, human-rights activist, and writer, were arrested for "threatening national security" and "conspiring against the government." We were sent to the notorious Evin prison for almost two months, first in solitary confinement, then in the same section as criminals and murderers. I was tried and sentenced to a four-year prison term but released on bail prior to the appeal hearing in November 2001.[19] The sole evidence against the conference participants were their academic presentations, which later were published in authorized book form under the title *Berlin Conference: Service or Treason*.

Being a woman and an activist in a traditional society, especially when religion is predominant in the legal system, is challenging. Nevertheless, this is a good era. The taboos are breaking one after another. There was a time when we had only male political prisoners, who said that "prison is a place for men only," twirled their mustaches proudly, and talked about their prison memories. Now women like me, with no beard or mustache to boast of, have an ocean of images stored in our hearts from just a short period of imprisonment.[20]

In another political case, known as the "videotape files," Shirin Ebadi, a lawyer and human-rights activist, was arrested and charged with videotap-ing her client's confessions, which incriminated several persons within the government, and accused of making them available nationally and interna-tionally. This incident demonstrated the equal treatment of women only in being arrested for political expression alongside men. This came about after the earlier suppression of opposition forces and increased as a reaction to the reform period.

In 2003, Shirin Ebadi received the Nobel Peace Prize. In addition to being a lawyer and human-rights activist, Ebadi served as legal advisor to the majority of the reformists in the Sixth Parliament.

The reformist parliament was a turning point in gender politics, but the movement toward equality failed to bring about democratic change and put an end to the power of religious authority. In assessing the reformist failure, one must carefully evaluate the constitution of the Islamic Republic, which I believe is the main impediment to political reform in Iran. The mecha-nisms afforded by the Islamic constitution is in opposition to liberal-demo-cratic reform. [21]

Since the election of the pro-reform president Khatami in 1997, there have been two basic approaches to evaluate the system. One is the "Islamic reformist" approach, which believes in the capacity of the constitution to lead the Islamic regime toward democracy. The other is the "secularist" approach, which remains on the fringes of the system and believes that the constitution contains profound impediments to meaningful reform.

Although some articles in the constitution allow basic rights and free-doms for the Iranian people—articles that grant people the right to elect the president, the parliament, and the local councils—there are fundamental obstructions that nullify the elected officials' efforts to bring about mean-ingful change. To begin with, the constitution has contradictory provisions regarding the elected governing body. It stipulates that Parliament is to be an independent legislative body; but the freedom to enact laws is subject to the will of the appointed Guardian Council (six jurists and six clerics), whose authority outstrips that of any elected official close to the highest office of the executive branch, the Supreme Leader (currently Khamenei), who is accountable only to God.

Bills passed by Parliament are not binding until the Guardian Council attests in the first instance that the presumptive law does not contradict the basic tenets and provisions of Islamic law and, only secondarily, that it does not contradict the constitution. For example, during the reform period, every single bill related to women and the family was rejected by the Guardian Council on the grounds of incompatibility with Islamic law.

Once a law is rejected by the Guardian Council, it is sent back to Parliament with specific comments and objections. The parliament must then revise the bill and return it for further evaluation. This process of back-and-forth can go on for quite some time with no results. To resolve disputes between the council and Parliament, yet another body (the Expediency Council) has been created; its members are also appointed by the Supreme Leader. Tension between Guardian Council and Parliament is, in other words, paralyzing Iran's legislative ability.

One might think that the election of a reformist legislature would naturally mean democratic progress. But this has not been the case in Iran, and one has to be naive to think that genuine democratization will occur under the current system. The obstacles in the constitution and the legal framework of Iran are profound and insurmountable. Moreover, although Parliament is an elected governing body, the power of the Guardian Council to purge candidates and invalidate results indicates that reform from within the system is no longer possible. The conservative elite continues to control the major power centers of the Guardian Council, the judiciary, the Revolutionary Guard, and counts on the support of the Supreme Leader.

The Legacy of Political Empowerment

Even among the most ardent supporters, disenchantment with the reformists runs deep for their failure to bring about change and their reluctance to confront the religious hierarchy. Demonstrating anger against the reformists for their inability to effect substantive change was yet another role that women took on during this period. Realizing that elected reformists were unwilling to risk their positions to push for promised reforms, women chose not to participate in the local elections in the 2001 and the 2004 parliamentary elections. The contrast with the 1998 local elections was stark. The local elections of 1998 had resulted in an unprecedented number of women on local and rural councils: 297 women to city councils and some 484 to rural councils. What is more, in fifty-six cities women topped the list of elected councilors in terms of votes received, and in another fifty-eight cities they came in second. These are signs of change in social attitudes and public perceptions of women's capabilities.

The various roles women have played since the start of the reform period in 1997 has attracted the world's attention to Iranian women's capacities in formulating a protest movement. While this protest has not yet developed into an organized movement, it has managed to attract international attention. Recognition and awards like the Nobel Peace Prize, awarded to Ms. Shirin Ebadi in 2003, demonstrate that the world is now aware of the fact that Iranian women have a real commitment, an impact on the political process, and the desire to bring about political change.

Despite the reversal of many of the reformists' actions in parliament and a renewed atmosphere of opposition to public debate on the nature and structure of the state, the determined efforts of women activists cannot be erased. With the help of a dynamic press and determined political and human-rights groups, calls have been made for greater accountability, transparency, and openness from the state. The way has been paved for a more pluralistic discourse on civil society. The new path is uncertain as entrenched ideas are challenged by calls for equality and freedom by a population that is getting younger and craves independence. As I said when I accepted the 2004 Human Rights Award, "If the last two decades of pain indicate how women will react when faced with turmoil, then we do not have to worry, for we have met strife with determined spirits."[21] How Iran navigates this shifting ground will determine the future of its people and its place in the world.

Mehrangiz Kar is an Iranian human-rights lawyer and writer who has published widely on women's issues in Iran, a former political prisoner, and former editor of the now banned literary review, *Zan* (Woman). She is at present a fellow at Radcliffe College at Harvard University and previously a visiting scholar at the American University Washington College of Law. A graduate of Tehran University Faculty of Law and Political Science, Kar is a member of the bar association in Iran. Author of several books, including *Angels of Justice and Patches of Hell*, a collection of essays which looks at the status and position of women in pre- and postrevolutionary Iran; *Women in the Iranian Labor Market;* and *Legal Structure of the Family System in Iran.* She received the 2004 Human Rights First Award as well as the Ludovic Trarieux International Human Rights Prize in 2002.

Notes

1. The concept of "gender equality," meaning equal training and employment opportunities for women, had been approved by the preceding parliament. Following the objection of the Guardian Council, the current conservative-dominated parliament deleted the phrase "gender equality" from the state development plan in order to prevent the "bullying of men," as one female deputy put it.

2. Ramim Karimian and Sha'banali Bahrampour, "Iranian Press Update," *Middle East Report* 212 (1999).

3. Journalist Fariba Davoudi Mohajer was arrested for undeclared reasons in February 2000 and released after posting bail. Shahla Sherkat, the editor of *Zanan*, was tried and fined for her participation in the 2000 Berlin conference. Several other women journalists, both secular and Islamist feminists, who worked with reformist journals were banned as a result of the crackdown. "Iran: More Journalist Arrests," Freedom Forum, March 14, 2001, http://www.freedomforum.org/templates/document.asp.documentID=13377.

4. Nazanin Shah-Rokni, "Jamileh Kadivar: I Have Not Climbed the Ladder of Fame and Power of Men in My Family," *Zanan* 63 (June 2000), pp. 7–13, http://netiran.com/fn-artd (908).

5. Shadi Sadr, a human-rights lawyer, is the editor of an online daily news site focusing on women in Iran. She and other women journalists (Lili Farhad Pour, Jila Bani Yaghoob, Fereshteh Ghazi, and many others) investigated incidents of violence against women, including street murders and honor killings and reported on many social ills, such as prostitution, addiction, runaway girls, and the condition of women prisoners and women on death row.

6. The Internet has opened a new window of opportunity for women to express their views and to reach out to the outside world. Alfred Hermida, "Web Gives a Voice to Iranian Women," BBC News, June 17, 2002, http://news.bbb.co.uk/1/hi/sci/tech/2044802.stm.

7. Fariba Davoudi Mohajer, "Women Journalists in Iran and Women in Iranian Press," Women Living Under Muslim Laws (WLUML), July 26, 2004, http://www.wluml.org/English/newsfulltxt.shtml?cmd[157]-x.157.61621.

8. Ibid.

9. Lili Farhad Pour, prepared remarks for the conference: "Women's Literary and Artistic Creativity in Contemporary Iran," University of Toronto, November 6–7, 2004.

10. The problem that women's NGOs face is a lack of expertise and the absence of

well-defined goals. Iran has some one hundred fifty women's NGOs, but they lack independence and effective advocacy powers, particularly on issues like violence against women, legal rights, and criminal justice. There has been some success in the areas of women's health and family planning, as well as traditional charity works. Humanitarian work has a long tradition in Iran, and the coordinated committee of women's NGOs were specially effective in helping the Bam earthquake victims.

11. Although the number of women's NGOs in the past seven years has increased, they are mostly involved in charity or cultural and service-oriented activities.

12. In 1999, during the reform period, I applied for a license to start an NGO for research into the legal and social rights of women and to address issues of women's rights in Iran. Despite being an activist and human-rights attorney, with many years' work defending women's rights, I was told that my application was denied for "lack of competency." My license was denied during the period of reform and the moderates' ascendancy, which indicates the distinct line—even then—separating secular individuals from Islamists.

13. An NGO is expected to be fully independent of the government, but in Iran governmental approval is required to start one. In order to obtain a permit, the applicant is required to be registered, fingerprinted, and thoroughly investigated by various police and security forces. The selection process is deeply rooted in the structure of the Islamic regime and ideology, and it is a serious impediment to the development of civil society.

14. Mahboubeh Abbasgholizadeh, "Identity, Women, and Islam: Iran's Case," Presentation at Asia Pacific NGO Forum. http:/www.wluml.org/English/newsfultext .shtm?cmd[157]=x-157-61622.

15. Mehrangiz Kar, Parinoush Saniee, Fariba Vafi, and Roya Pirzad wrote about feminists subjects and published during the early part of the reform period.

16. Tahmineh Milani, http://www.pbs.org/adventuredivas/iran/divas/milani.html.

17. Ziba Mir Hosseini, "Fatemeh Haqiqatjoo and the Sixth Majles: A Woman in Her Own Right," Middle East Report 233 (Winter 2004). http://www.merip.org/ mer/mer233/mir-hosseini.html.

18. In order to safeguard the precepts of Islam and the constitution, Articles 98 and 99 authorize creation of the Council of Guardians to supervise the election of the president, the parliament, the national and local elections and general referendum. The Council of Guardians is endowed with the responsibility for interpretation of the constitution and has veto power over the legislative body. It is composed of six clerics appointed by the Supreme Leader and six jurists selected by the judiciary and approved by the Assembly, per Article 91 of the Iranian constitution.

19. The arrest of human-rights activists and reformists who attended the academic conference in Berlin in 2000 was the beginning of a sustained crackdown on those who call for the respect of human rights and the rule of law in Iran. In Berlin, I stated that Iran's legal structure in various ways operates completely against women's human rights, that the Islamic system has violated the human rights of

the Iranian nation for the past twenty-one years, and that it is necessary to examine the state's record for these violations. This is what the people of Iran expect from the reformist current in Iran. (I was finally allowed to leave Iran for medical reasons, but my journalist husband, Siamak Pourzand, was arrested after my departure).

20. Mehrangiz Kar, "Prison's Revelations;" Payvan, http://www.payvand.com/news/01/feb/1006.html

21. In November 2004, citizens called for a national referendum to create a new constitution. I was one of the original signatories. From the declaration: "The experiences of the last twenty-six years . . . clearly demonstrate that there is but one ultimate path for ending the continuing state of crisis and freeing the suffering Iranian nation: the creation of a Democratic System of Government which is in harmony with the provisions of the Universal Declaration of Human Rights. . . . In order to achieve such an end, the drafting of a new national constitution and the choosing of a popular system of government is the first imperative step. . . . We the signatories of this appeal . . . for the staging of a national referendum with the free participation of the Iranian people, under the supervision of appropriate international institutions and observers, for drafting of a new constitution that is compatible with the Universal Declaration of Human Rights and all its associated covenants." For examples, see "Three Perspectives on an Initiative for Dialogue Between Iranians Inside and Outside Iran," Radio Free Europe and Radio Liberty, Iran Report, March 1, 2005, no. 9.

For many Muslim women in the era of globalization, particularly in rapidly modernizing and industrializing countries like Malaysia, the realities of life today have put them on a collision course with patriarchy's construction of the "ideal" Muslim woman in the name of religion.[1] They will no longer accept the idea that Islam actually promotes injustice and ill treatment of half the human race. They are challenging the values of patriarchal society, where power and authority reside exclusively with the husband, father, and brother, to whom the wife, daughter, and sister owe obedience. For too long, men have defined what it is to be a woman, dictated how to be a woman, and used religion to confine us to this socially constructed inferiority.

Times, however, are changing. We live in an era when women are educated, travel the world, and hold positions of power and responsibility in increasing numbers. Today in Malaysia, almost 70 percent of the students enrolled in public institutions of higher learning are girls. Female labor-force participation is at 47 percent and rising. It can only be expected that women, armed with increasing knowledge, education, and economic independence, will gain more confidence and courage to speak out in the face of injustice. When injustice is committed in the name of religion, today's women will go directly to the religion's source to find out for themselves whether it could indeed be so unjust to half its followers.

Rejecting religion is not an option for most Muslim women. We are believers, and as such we want to find liberation, truth, and justice within our own faith. We feel strongly that we have the right to reclaim our religion, to redefine it, to participate in it and to contribute to an understand-how Islam is codified and implemented—in ways that take into consideration the realities and experience of women's lives today.

Sisters in Islam was born of this sort of faith in Islam as a force for social equality, and of deep concerns over the injustice women suffered under the fundamentalist Islamist interpretation of the law under the *shari'a* system. As professional women and activists, we sought answers to the pressing question we and our sisters faced: What Islam and whose Islam is the right Islam? We began to study the Qur'an and the traditions of the Prophet to better understand Islam. With this knowledge and newfound conviction, we armed ourselves to stand up and fight for women's rights to equality, justice, freedom, and dignity, all within a religious framework.

This movement is cast against the background of the rise of political Islam in countries throughout the Muslim world, which has posed particular challenges to civil-society groups engaged in the push for democracy, human rights, and women's rights in Muslim societies.

Many Muslim states are in crisis today—politically, economically, socially. Many remain under the authoritarian rule of entrenched monarchs, despots, or autocratic elected leaders. Many have failed to satisfy the yearnings of their populations for freedom, economic prosperity, justice, peace, and stability. Many of these leaders are seen as lackeys or as propped up by the "omnipotent" West.

As these states and their leadership become delegitimized in the eyes of the discontented, disenfranchised, and marginalized members of society, the reactive search for an alternative governing ideology in many Muslim countries today often takes the form of religiosity. In these societies, Islamist activists have become the most vocal and effective opponents to the ruling elite as they successfully construct and package religion into an ideology for political struggle against the oppressive state and a hegemonic Western world.

The political ideals of Islamism—an Islam used as a political ideology—have had widespread appeal for disparate social groups in Muslim societies: young urbanites, upwardly mobile professionals adrift from tradition and culture, the underclass left behind by the prosperity and modernization that have benefited only a small segment of society, and socially conscious citizens who are outraged by the corruption, mismanagement, and authoritarianism of the ruling elite and who see no hope for change.

Harnessing this discontent, political Islamists whose objective is to topple the existing political order and replace it with an Islamic one have crafted and packaged religion into an appealing political ideology of protest and resistance. The complexity and depth of religion is reduced to one fixed, ideological worldview to determine and direct public behavior.[2] This worldview defines Islam as an antithesis of an ideological enemy, be it the despotic ruler, the hegemonic West, or—more likely—the despotic ruler and his alliance with the infidel West.[3]

Thus, when Islam is packaged as a political ideology, the true Muslim believes in three things: the Islamic state (no separation between religion and politics) against a secular nation-state (separation between religion and politics); divine law against human legislation; sovereignty of God's rule on earth against sovereignty of the people.

The forces of Good are on one side, battling the forces of Evil on the other.

This packaged ideology made up of clear and unambiguous messages is then presented as the one true authentic face of faith and piety with no room for doubt and uncertainty. This ideology is sold to societies undergoing massive transformations and dislocations from traditional to modern, from rural to urban, and from agricultural to industrial and reeling under the impact of globalization. It is sold to the discontented, the marginalized, the victimized. It becomes appealing either as an idiom of protest or as an authentic source of faith and tradition for people who are torn away from their own religious and cultural roots and seek refuge from modern conditions of uncertainty in absolute truths.

The Islamic resurgence that has engulfed most Muslim countries today has produced different levels of tension and competing ideologies within these societies, again prompting the question, "Whose Islam is the right Islam?" Muslim women's struggle for equality and justice must therefore be understood as taking place in societies that are undergoing change and turmoil and where Islam is increasingly shaping and redefining lives.

However, all too often, in the turn to Islam as a way of life and the solution to the ills and injustices that beset these societies, women's rights, status, role in private and public life, dress, and behavior have all become the first battleground to prove one's authenticity and piety.

It is therefore not surprising that in many Muslim countries today women's groups are at the forefront in challenging traditional religious authority within government and Islamist political activists and their use of religion to subordinate women and perpetuate discriminatory laws and practices.

The Sisters in Islam is one such group. We began in 1988 with just a few women, with the intention of exploring ways to push the boundaries of women's rights within Islam, within Malaysia. For a long time there were only eight of us, but the group has grown steadily. In 1993, we were registered as a nongovernmental organization (NGO). In 1998, we finally set up an office, hired a full-time staff, and saw our membership grow to thirty. And we have just opened our membership to men.

Our advocacy work takes many forms and is important because we are believers, and as believers we want to fight for change from within our religion. In addition, the knowledge that the Qur'an supports the universal values of equality, justice, and dignity for women is so empowering and liberating to us that it gives us the courage and conviction to stand up and argue with those who support discrimination against women in the name of religion.

Of course, there are many other Muslim women activists who have decided that it is futile to work with religion because they believe that all religions, including Islam, are inherently patriarchal and unjust to women; to work with religion will only serve the interest of the male oppressors who use religion to control women and maintain their subjugation. To such activists, the choice that groups like Sisters in Islam have made—to work within the religious framework—dooms them to failure because they are taking the contest for women's rights to the turf of patriarchal religion, and those with religious authority will always win. For every alternative interpretation that women can offer to justify equality and justice, the *ulama* (the community of the learned religious scholars) will offer a hundred others to challenge that interpretation, these feminists say. They have therefore chosen to struggle for women's rights within the framework of universal values and principles.

However, in the past ten years, more and more progressive Muslim scholars and activists have challenged the Islamic agenda of the Islamist activists and *ulama* and their intolerance and outright oppression of women. These works, which recognize equality between men and women in Islam, argue for the imperative of *ijtihad* (reinterpretation of the Qur'an in the context of changing times and circumstances), address the dynamics between what is universal for all times and what is particular to seventh century Arabia, look at the sociohistorical context of revelation, and articulate the need to differentiate between what is revelation and what is human understanding of the word of God. Such research, interpretive methodology, and conceptual frameworks, developed to deal with the challenge of Islam and modernity, have enabled more and more Muslim women activists all over the world to recognize the validity and possibility of working within the Islamic framework and to believe that we can indeed find liberation within Islam.

Our strength comes from our conviction and faith in an Islam that is just, liberating, and empowering to us as women. Groups like Sisters in Islam are reclaiming the Islam that liberated women and uplifted our status by giving us rights considered revolutionary fourteen hundred years ago: the right to own, inherit, or dispose of our own property, the right to divorce, and the right to contract agreements, all introduced by Islam in the seventh century.

This ethical vision of the Qur'an that insistently enjoins equality and justice, this liberating and revolutionary spirit of Islam today guide our quest to be treated as fellow human beings of equal worth and dignity.

How and why did women's groups like Sisters in Islam and individual Muslim scholars—women and men—many of whom have been incredibly generous with their time and scholarship in helping us activists, decide to study the Qur'an and strive to hear the voice of the divine will speaking to our concerns?

Let me just share with you the process Sisters in Islam went through. Like many other women's groups, we were mobilized by injustice, oppression and ill treatment. As professional women and as activists, we found that other women often approached us to confide their marital problems and the troubles they faced when they approached the religious authorities to seek redress for these troubles. We first got together to look into the problems women faced with the implementation of the Islamic family law.

However, increasingly, we felt that dealing with law alone was not enough. We felt powerless in the face of complaints by women who suffered in silence because Islam demands that they be obedient to their husbands, because Islam grants men the rights to beat their wives and to take second wives. We felt powerless as we heard, again and again, in religious classes, on the radio and the television, in interaction with religious departments and *shari'a* courts that men were superior to women, and had authority over them, that the evidence of two women equals that of one man; that a woman must obey her husband, that a man has a right to beat his wife, that he has a God-given right to take a second wife and therefore it is a sin for a woman to deny him that right; that a wife has no right to say no to sex with her husband; and that hell is full of women who leave their heads uncovered and were disobedient to their husbands.

Where is the justice for women in all these pronouncements? This questioning, and above all the conviction that Allah could never be unjust, eventually led us to go back to the source of our religion, the Qur'an. We felt the urgent need to read the Qur'an for ourselves and to find out if the text actually supported the oppression and ill treatment of women.

The process the Sisters of Islam went through was a most liberating and spiritually uplifting experience for all of us. We took the path of *iqra'* ("Read," the first word revealed to Prophet Muhammad), and it opened a world of Islam that we could recognize, a world for women that was filled with love and mercy and with equality and justice. We had no need to look any further to validate our struggle. Women's rights were rooted in our tradition, in our faith. We were more convinced than ever that it is not Islam that oppresses women, but interpretations of the Qur'an influenced by the cultural practices and values of a patriarchal society that regards women as inferior and subordinate to men.

For much of Islamic history, men have interpreted the Qur'an and the traditions for us. The woman's voice, the woman's experience, the woman's realities were silent and silenced in the reading and interpretation of the text. Thus, when we read the text, we discovered words, messages, and meanings that we had never been exposed to in all our traditional education on Islam.

For us, it was the beginning of a journey of discovery. It was a revelation to us that the verse on polygamy (Sura al-Nisa 4:3) concluded, "if you fear you shall not be able to deal justly with women, then marry only one." How was it that the half of the verse that says a man is allowed up to four wives became universally known and accepted as a right in Islam and codi-

fied into law, but the half verse that promotes monogamy is unheard-of . . .
until women began to read the Qur'an for ourselves?

It dawned on us that when men read the verse, they only saw "marry up
to four wives." In that phrase, they saw the word of God validating their
desire and their experience. When women read the verse, we clearly saw "if
you fear you shall not be able to deal justly with women, then marry only
one." Those were the words of Allah that spoke to our fears of injustice. We
understood that the right to polygamy was conditional, and that if a man
could not fulfill the conditions of equal and just treatment, then Allah said
to marry only one. In fact, the verse goes on, "This will be best for you to
prevent you from doing injustice." What further validation do we need to
argue that polygamy is not a right in Islam but is actually a responsibility
allowed only in particular circumstances?

We did more research on the subject and found out that our interpretation of the verse on polygamy was not new. It is certainly not the invention
of the women's movement of the twentieth century. There were many
prominent *ulama* and Islamic movements over the centuries that saw
monogamy as the ideal state of marriage in Islam. But their views were marginalized by the ruling elite or the religious establishment.

In the late nineteenth and early twentieth centuries, renowned Egyptian *ulama*, such as al-Tahtawi and Muhammad Abduh (who was Egypt's
Grand Mufti), both held the opinion that the Qur'an viewed monogamy as
the ideal form of marriage in Islam. In this century, Abdullah Yusuf Ali, the
author and interpreter of the most widely used English translation of the
Qur'an, held the same view. However, in the new edition of his translated
Qur'an, published in 1989, his commentary on the verse on polygamy, in
which he says that the ideal and original state of marriage in Islam is
monogamy, has been deleted. Maybe the publishing house's review committee felt that too many women reading his translation of the Qur'an and
were quoting his interpretation to oppose polygamy. God only knows.

Those who support polygamy very often say that they are only following the Prophet's way; but they have conveniently ignored the fact that the
Prophet married a woman fifteen years his senior and remained monoga-
mous for the twenty-five long years of his first marriage, that is, throughout
the life of Khadija, his first wife. It was only after Khadija's death that he
married other women, and except for Aisha, the other women were all wid-

ows or divorcees whom he married to cement family ties and unite warring tribes—very different reasons from those of most Muslim men taking second wives today.

Moreover, an authentic *hadith* (saying of the Prophet)—sunan Ibn Majah—that reported that the Prophet objected when his cousin Ali Ibn Abi Talib, the fourth caliph of Islam, who was married to the Prophet's daughter, Fatima, wanted to take another wife. He said Ali could take another wife only if he divorced Fatima, "because my daughter is a part of me and what saddens and hurts her, saddens and hurts me too, and any problems that befall her will befall me too."

And while from youth we knew that a Muslim man could have four wives, we did not know that the verse on polygamy actually advocated monogamy, or that key Islamic scholars had supported monogamy, or that an authentic *hadith* expressed the Prophet's displeasure that his son-in-law wanted to take a second wife. In fact, the Prophet's descendant Sakina, the granddaughter of Ali and Fatima, inserted a clause in her marriage contract forbidding her husband to marry another woman during their marriage.

Therefore the question that arose was obvious to us: *Who* decides which interpretation, which juristic opinion, which *hadith*, which traditional practice will prevail and be the source of codified law to govern our private and public lives and give reason to punish us if we fail to obey, and which would fall by the wayside? On what basis is that decision made? Whose rights are protected and whose interests are denied? It was clear to us that this was more about power and politics than about living the divine will on earth.

As feminists, believers, and activists living within a democratic constitutional framework, we decided to assert and claim our right to have our voices heard in the public sphere, to intervene in the decision-making process on matters of religion, and to force it to take into consideration the realities of our lives and the justice enjoined by the Qur'an.

We know we have an uphill task before us as we continue to study and campaign for women's rights and for the right of people like us to participate in matters of religion—people who did not go to that venerable university in Egypt for the study of Islam, al-Azhar, who cannot speak Arabic, and who are not covered up.

Through our readings, consultations, and studies with progressive Islamic scholars inside and outside the country, and through networking with other women's groups engaged in the same struggle, we claimed our right and created a public space for women like us to stand up and argue for justice and equality for Muslim women in contentious areas such as polygamy, equal rights, dress and modesty, domestic violence, *hudud* laws, freedom of expression, freedom of religion, and other fundamental liberties.

Our advocacy work takes two main forms: memoranda and letters to the government on law or policy reform; and letters to the editor on current issues to educate the public and to build a constituency that would support a more enlightened interpretation of Islam on specific issues.

Central to our advocacy work is our research into alternative interpretations of the Qur'an and alternative juristic positions in Islam that uphold the principles of equality, justice, freedom, and dignity. This work feeds into our writing and press statements on contentious issues where the conservative religious authority or the Islamic movements are pushing for laws and policies that discriminate against women or violate fundamental liberties.

As part of our effort to influence law and policy making, Sisters in Islam has submitted several memoranda and letters to the Government on issues such as the appointment of women as judges in *shari'a* courts; the right of Muslim women to equal guardianship of their children; reform of the laws on polygamy specifically; reform of the Islamic family law as a whole; the administration of justice in the *shari'a* system, and reform of the *shari'a* criminal laws.

In these memoranda, we express our concerns about provisions in the law that discriminate against women, in substance or implementation, violate fundamental liberties, or conflict with the federal constitution and with civil law; we then offer a justification for why these laws should be amended or repealed and provide specific wordings or positions to make clear the changes that we want to see take place.

Our memoranda to the government are often accompanied by letters to the editors of the major newspapers in the country. This strategy plays a crucial role in educating the public about alternative positions in Islam on a particular issue. We hope that this process will engender a more informed public discussion on issues, build a constituency that supports our advocacy, and pressure the government to take our voice into consideration. Some of our letters and memoranda are submitted jointly with other women's groups to demonstrate to the government and the public that Sisters in

Islam has not taken an isolated position on a particular issue—that in fact the women's movement is speaking with one voice.

In addition to our letter writing, we have an extensive public education program. We conduct monthly study sessions, organize a public lecture series where we invite progressive Muslim scholars from overseas to speak on topical issues in Islam from a rights perspective. In the past two years, we have embarked on a training program on women's rights in Islam that targets such opinion makers as grassroots service providers, human-rights lawyers, student leaders, and young professionals. This training is now much in demand at the international level. We have trained groups from Afghanistan, South Asia, and West Africa.

We also run a weekly legal-literacy column in the daily newspaper with the largest circulation in Malaysia, giving advice on Islamic family law matters. The overwhelming response to this column led us to open a legal clinic to handle the hundreds of telephone calls and e-mails, mostly from women, for assistance on Islamic family law matters.

In our struggle for women's rights and creating the space to speak out in public on Islam, we have encountered opposition and made some enemies. We have been attacked and condemned by conservative Islamist scholars and Islamist activists and movements—a common experience for women's groups and progressive scholars in other Muslim countries as well.

The attacks and condemnations usually take three forms:

First, they undermine our right and our legitimacy to speak on Islam by questioning our credentials. They say we have no right to speak on Islam because we are not traditionally educated in religious schools, do not have a degree in Islam from a recognized Arab university, do not speak Arabic, and do not cover our heads. They say we are Western-educated feminists from an elite stratum of society who are trying to impose Western values on Islam and the *umma*. To them, the discourse on Islam is the exclusive domain of a certain group of Muslims, the *ulama* with the right education, status, and position. Others do not have the right to express their opinions on Islam.

Second, they accuse us of having deviated from our faith. They equate our questioning and challenging of their obscurantist views on women and fundamental liberties and their interpretations of the Qur'an, with questioning the word of God. Therefore, they say, we doubt the infallibility of God and the perfection of the message. Consequently, we are accused of being against Islam. They also condemn us for using our own brains, logic, and reason (*aqal*) instead of referring to classical exegetical and jurispruden- tial texts of the early centuries of Islam. They claim that these texts by the great theologians and jurists of centuries past have perfected the under- standing of Islam and the doors of *ijtihad* should therefore remain closed.

Third, they contend that it is dangerous to offer alternative opinions and interpretations of the religion as this could confuse the *umma* and lead to disunity. There can only be one interpretation, decided on by the *ulama* and all citizens must abide by this interpretation. Views that differ from the mainstream ones are an insult to the Qur'an, inculcate hatred against *shari'a*, and degrade women.

It is ironic that many of those who challenge and question the creden- tials of women's groups to speak on Islam themselves often do not speak Arabic and have not been traditionally educated in Islam. Many of those at the vanguard of the Islamic movement calling for the establishment of an Islamic state and imposition of *shari'a* rule are professionals, engineers, doc- tors, professors, and administrators without any formal religious training. Their right to speak out, however, is not questioned. The issue, therefore, is not so much who has a right to speak on Islam, but what is being said about Islam. Thus those who echo the mainstream view on men's rights and women's inferior status in Islam, those who believe in the leadership of the mullahs, and those who advocate the establishment of an Islamic state and the imposition of Islamic laws have the right to speak on Islam, but those who challenge these views do not.

Such Islamist forces' claims—that their perspective and interpretation of Islam, its values, and its view of human rights and women's rights are the "universal" and legitimate view for all Muslims at all times—must be chal- lenged. In the face of general ignorance, fear, or indifference on the part of the public at large and the obscurantist view of the traditional *ulama* and Islamist activists on issues such as women's rights, *shari'a* law, and funda- mental liberties have dominated the Islamic agenda in much of the Muslim world.

It must be understood that while all Muslims accept the Qur'an, the human effort in interpreting it had always led to differing opinions. It is precisely because of this wealth of diversity that Islam has survived and flourished in different cultures and societies: All could accommodate the universal message of Islam. And yet in many Muslim societies today, anyone who offers alternative views faces condemnation as an infidel or an apostate by those who choose to deny or negate the complexity and diversity of our rich heritage.

There is also a denial of the historical context within which the *shari'a* itself was constructed and of the consequently historical character of its development and application within early and classical Islamic civilization. For example, in classical Islamic jurisprudential texts, gender inequality is taken for granted, a priori, as a principle.[4] Women are depicted as "sexual beings," not as "social beings," and their rights are discussed largely in the context of family law. The classical jurists' construction of women's rights reflected the world in which they lived, where inequality between women and men was the natural order of things and women had little role to play in public life.

But the conservative *ulama* that dominate the religious authorities and Islamist activists of today seem unable or unwilling to see Islamic law from a historical perspective as rules constructed to deal with the socioeconomic and political context of their time. They did not see that given a different context these laws must change, to ensure that the eternal principles of justice are served. Even though the source of the law is divine, human understanding of God's message and human effort at codifying God's message into positive law are not infallible. The knowledge produced and the legal constructs derived are both the products of human engagement with the divine text. The law can therefore be changed, criticized, refined, and redefined. Unfortunately, in the traditional Islamic education most of our *ulama* have gone through, the belief in *taqlid* (imitation) and the belief that the doors of *ijtihad* are closed are strong. This is based on the notion that the great scholars of the classical period who lived closer to the time of the Prophet were unsurpassed in their knowledge and interpretative skills.

But to adopt such an attitude is totally untenable in today's world, when we face new and different challenges: modernity, change, and the issues of human rights, democracy, and women's rights. How do we find solutions from within our faith if we do not engage in *ijtihad* and produce new knowledge and new understandings of Islam in the face of new circumstances?

This problem is compounded by the fact that most Muslims have traditionally been educated to believe that only the *ulama* have a right to talk about Islam. What are the implications to democratic governance, human rights, and gender justice, if only a small group of people has the right to interpret the Qur'an? If only the *ulama* can codify the text—and they very often do so in a manner that isolates the text from the sociohistorical context of its revelation and solidifies classical juristic opinion, especially on women's issues, even though it was based on the sociohistorical context of the lives of the founding jurists of Islam—our textual heritage becomes detached from the context of the world we live in today.

I feel very strongly that the role played by civil-society groups, such as women's-rights and human-rights activists and public intellectuals, will be key in bringing about change and establishing the terms of public engagement with Islam in many Muslim societies.

For this to happen, however, the public space for debate on Islam and Islamic issues has to open up. Unfortunately, in many Muslim societies today there is no public space to talk not only about Islam but also about other issues deemed sensitive by the power elites. Someone once said that bad secularism leads to bad religion. The problem we face today in the Muslim world is that many Muslim governments and leaders rule in less-than-exemplary ways and lead less-than-exemplary lives. Many Muslim leaders have neither the moral authority nor the credibility to talk about an Islam that represents justice, peace, and tolerance, for they lead their lives and govern other people in ways that are unjust, intolerant, hostile, and violent. Many Muslim countries are led by autocratic rulers and monarchs, and freedom of expression, assembly, and association do not exist or are very restricted. Our traditional upbringing, culture, and political system do not encourage us to engage freely in debate. Of course, when political Islam emerges as an alternative to challenge that autocratic state, it is an Islam led by those whose mindset and cultural framework are just as closed and limited.

But this cannot continue. September 11 was a wake-up call to many Muslims. Ironically, it has been positive in many ways for those of us engaged in the debate on what Islam and whose Islam is the right Islam. One important impact in a number of Muslim countries has been the opening of the public space for debate, discussion, and diversity of opinion on Islam and Islamic issues. Both Muslims and people of other faiths have been allowed to express their views in the public sphere.

In many parts of the Muslim world and within minority Muslim communities, scholars, writers, and activists are beginning to debate such issues publicly: What is the role of religion in politics? Is Islam compatible with democracy? Who has the right to interpret Islam and codify its teachings into laws and public policies? How do we deal with the conflict between modern constitutional provisions of fundamental liberties and equality with religious laws and policies that violate these provisions? Should the state legislate morality? Is it the duty of the state, in order to bring about a moral society, to turn all sins into crimes against the state? Can there be one truth and one final interpretation of Islam that must govern the life of every Muslim citizen of the country? Can the massive coercive powers of a modern nation-state be used to impose that one truth on all citizens? How do we deal with the new morality of democracy, of human rights, of women's rights, and where is the place of Islam in this ethical paradigm of the modern world?

Our position in Malaysia is that if religion is to be used to govern the public and private lives of its citizens, then everyone has a right to talk about religion and express views and concerns on the impact of laws and policies made in the name of Islam. The world is far more complex today than ever before. No one group can have a monopoly on knowledge. In a modern democratic nation-state, *ijtihad* must therefore be exercised in concert and through democratic engagement with the *umma*. The experience of others who have been traditionally excluded from the process of interpreting, defining, and implementing Islam must be included. The role of women, who constitute half of the *umma*, must be acknowledged and included in this process of dialogue, policy making, and law making.

This search for answers to important questions on the role of Islam in today's modern nation-state cannot remain the exclusive preserve of the religious authorities, be they the *ulama* in government, the opposition parties or Islamist activists pushing for an Islamic state and *shari'a* law.

Muslims and all citizens have to take responsibility for the kind of Islam that develops in our societies. The fact that Islam is increasingly shaping and redefining our lives means all of us have to engage with the religion if we do not want it to be hijacked by those who preach hatred, intolerance, bigotry, and misogyny.

If we as believers want to live according to the tenets of our faith, a simplistic call to return to an idealized "golden age" of Islam that has little bearing on the realities of today's world cannot be the answer. And yet, the answers can be found within our faith—if only we have the intellectual vigor, the moral courage, and the political will to strive for a more enlightened and progressive understanding of our faith in our search for answers to deal with our changing times and circumstances. For those of us in Sisters in Islam, this is not heretical, but an imperative—if religion is to be relevant to our lives today.

Zainah Anwar is the executive director of Sisters in Islam, a group of Muslim professional women committed to promoting the rights of women within the framework of Islam, and was a member of the Human Rights Commission of Malaysia. She is a graduate of Tuft's Fletcher School of Law and Diplomacy, Boston University, and Mara Institute of Technology, Malaysia.

Notes
1. A version of this paper was presented at the Severyns-Ravenholt Lecture Series, University of Washington, Seattle, October 14, 2004.
2. See Abdolkarim Soroush, *Reason, Freedom, and Democracy in Islam: Essential Writings of Abdolkarim* (Oxford University Press, 2000).
3. See Bassam Tibi, *The Challenge of Fundamentalism: Political Islam and the New World Disorder* (Berkeley: University of California Press, 1998).
4. Ziba Mir-Hosseini, "The Construction of Gender in Islamic Legal Thought and Strategies for Reform." Paper presented at the Sisters in Islam Regional Workshop on Islamic Family Law and Justice for Muslim Women, Kuala Lumpur, June 8–10, 2001.

Women and the Dynamics of Transnational Networks

Meena Sharify-Funk

No topic other than Islam's relation (or lack thereof) to political violence has caused more ink to be spilled than the status of women in Islamic culture. The mere existence of this literature is testimony to contemporary transnationalism: It has been composed by women in the Muslim world and women in non-Muslim countries; many of the authors claim Islamic identity or heritage while others do not; and the Muslim norms under scrutiny may be found in countries of immigration as well as in countries of origin. Regardless of their heritage, cultural background, or geographic location, scholars who write on "women and Islam" participate in a common discursive space that is thoroughly transnational, demonstrating that no cultural space can be insulated from "otherness."[1]

The literature on women and Islam incorporates many controversies and disagreements, but its principal themes testify to ongoing transformations, cultural exchanges, negotiations, and frictions. It provides evidence of hermeneutic and philosophical revolutions and counterrevolutions—of the secular revolution that gave rise to secular nationalist/socialist feminism, countertrends that celebrate "Islamic authenticity" in the face of "foreign" ideologies, and a more recent rise in "Islamic" feminism(s). Despite all of these fermenting ideas, much of the literature on women and Islam maintains a curious silence on transnational interpretive processes and instead offers a predominantly structuralist account of social change that focuses on localized impacts of global economic forces. The prevailing focus on impersonal forces results in an absence of attention to *social hermeneutics* and misses opportunities to investigate new identities and "hermeneutic fields" constituted by transnationalism.[2]

Though the literature on women and Islam raises a number of profound questions about social change in the Muslim world, a number of gaps and silences must be addressed for a fuller understanding of contemporary Muslim realities. There are many unanswered questions: How do feminist critiques of patriarchy and authoritative patriarchal hermeneutics relate to transnational attitude, dialogue, and activism? How are we to understand the origins and character of new Muslim discourses and self-critiques? Are changes in Muslim discourse on women "exogenous" and best understood through transposition of westernized labels such as "modern" or "progressive" Islam? Or are they best understood as manifestations of an emergent, transnational hermeneutic field? Is it possible to conceive of Muslim identity and intellectuality in terms that transcend the conventional labels and that do not simply transpose Western categories or posit a continuity with "Islamism"? Can we reconceive contemporary Islam as a "trans-boundary," pluralistic, negotiated exchange of sacred meaning? Are Muslim women becoming catalysts for such trans-boundary thought and action?

My goal is not to provide conclusive answers to these questions but to demonstrate their relevance and importance. By tracing tendencies of transnational attitude, dialogue, alliances, and networks—tendencies that are emergent in localities throughout the Muslim world—I offer the reader an "encounter" with voices of women activists. These voices, I will argue, testify to the emergence of a new hermeneutic field in which Islamic identity and intellectuality are being rethought, and not merely through reactionary rebuttals of "foreign" ideas or reflexive imitation of the West.[3]

Women, Islam, and the Emergence of Transnational Identity

Any serious study of women, Islam, and transnationalism should be careful not to overstate the "novelty" of transnationalism or interculturality in relation to Islam. As any knowledgeable scholar of Islam could point out, Islamic thought throughout history has been shaped by transcultural exchanges.[4] In this respect contemporary developments in transnational cultural thought and activism are qualitatively distinct from one another yet continuous with a larger historical process. Thus, a "spirit of encountering the other" across cultural, ethnic, and geographic boundaries is not foreign to Islam.

Though transnationalism is not new to the Islamic experience, the public engagement of Muslim women in transnational networking represents an apparent discontinuity with the Muslim past. In recent decades, Muslim women's activism has become increasingly transnational and ever more preoccupied with religious issues. Whereas previous generations of Muslim women activists sought (and were often able) to bypass cultures of religious interpretation through participation in powerful secular nationalist and socialist movements, the resurgence of Islamic identities and cultures brought about by the revivalist countermovement has placed women's activism in a new context. Faced with a transnational Islamic revival movement, more and more Muslim women are finding it necessary and beneficial to engage in transnational networking themselves, and in the process to enter the dialogue about Islamic identity and culture.[5]

The emerging literature on Muslim women and transnationalism implicitly views Muslim women not only as objects of transnational forces but also as agents of transnational change. This literature documents how Muslim women activists, in their search for adequate responses to the gender-polarized worldviews of Islamic traditionalists and revivalists, have sought to create their own transnational space for intellectual reflection on Islamic norms and identity. In the process, their sense of identity and agency is changing, along with their ideas about how women's rights can be reconciled with Islam.

Increasingly, these Muslim women activists are articulating a "Muslim feminist" critique of traditionalist and revivalist tendencies to monopolize the (re)construction of Islamic culture.[6] Although "Islamic feminism" does not have a uniform methodology for questioning the patriarchal monopolization of authority—whether in the public sphere (in which male Islamic jurists and political leaders dominate the interpretation of Islamic texts and the articulation of social norms) or the private sphere (in which men are designated the "providers")—Islamic feminism, in general, is resistance to the subordination of women by conservative, traditionalist men.[7] If Islamic modernism ushered in intellectual, ideational equality (modernism is often a more academic than activist enterprise) of all Muslims as individuals, it is Islamic feminism that is now calling for the construction of egalitarian communities.

As Muslim feminist activism emerges from the "pioneering" secular feminist activism found throughout the Muslim world, its world significance is increasingly recognized:

> Islamic feminism is a global phenomenon. It is not a product of East or West. Indeed, it transcends East and West. As already hinted, Islamic feminism is being produced at diverse sites around the world by women inside their own countries, whether they be from countries with Muslim majorities or from old established minority communities. Islamic feminism is also growing in Muslim diaspora and convert communities in the West . . . Islamic feminism transcends and destroys old binaries that have been constructed. These include polarities between "religious" and "secular" and between "East" and "West."[8]

For contemporary activists, the transnational has become a form of "public space" that enables women to transcend their isolation and derive inspiration for actions from their own local realities. It is beyond the boundaries of the nation (not to mention the family and the tribe) and yet it is bounded in the same sense as the Internet: It is an open network constituted by those who actively participate in it and engage in dialogue. In other words, it transcends the more limited statist national identity in order to explore, live, illustrate, and act on such an identity. Inherent in transnational identity is the wish for new frontiers and the desire to dwell in the "space between"—an interstitial space where one's identity may be local and at the same time beyond any specific locality.

As Cassandra Balchin said in an interview at the London office of Women Living Under Muslim Laws (WLUML),

> In a globalized context, the transnational is where there is a greater flow of information (i.e., strategies and ideas) across boundaries which can be national boundaries as well as other boundaries. This is very important for constructing networks: breaking boundaries so that the "trans" basis is not just "transnational" but also "trans"-a lot of other boundaries.[9]

Increasingly, women are living in social spaces that are "trans"-national, "trans"-cultural, and "trans"-local. Context-transcending and identity-transforming experiences ultimately lead to new alliances and networks, but they begin with an attitude that seeks dialogue as a means of encounter.

Tracing Tendencies of Transnational Attitude and Dialogue

To understand how contemporary Muslim women are experiencing the transnational, I conducted a series of interviews with Iranian, Pakistani, Malaysian, Egyptian, and Moroccan activists. One of the primary goals of these interviews was to derive an understanding of how contemporary activists perceive transnational engagement. What inspires Muslim women to engage one another across great distances?

In an interview at Tehran's Institute for Women's Studies and Research, Mahboubeh Abbasgholizadeh, the editor of *Farzaneh* (an Iranian women's studies and research journal), began by sharing her personal experience of "feeling alone" in Iran, as if she were "in exile" in her own homeland. It was in the space of the transnational that she felt a sense of belonging:

> The transnational is not limited to geographical or cultural contexts. I meet individuals from different parts of the world and I instantly connect with them. . . . For example, when I met with Farida Shaheed I felt I had so much in common with her and that I can communicate with her very easily.[10]

After these initial comments—which were offered immediately after the interviewee had completed her work as host of an international Muslim women's workshop, with participants from Turkey, Afghanistan, and Europe—Mahboubeh compared herself to Hans Christian Andersen's ugly duckling and stated, "The transnational is this: that all the ugly ducklings will come together from all over the world and that they will understand that they are not so ugly as everyone has said; rather, they are beautiful swans."

As these words suggest, feeling like a marginalized "Other" is common among those who seek or develop a sense of transnational identity. Similar sentiments emerged in many other interviews throughout the Muslim world. This feeling of marginalization in one's homeland can lead to a search for other "Others" who are somehow like oneself. These Others can then be encountered as sources of knowledge or as partners in dialogue. In the process, each Other is greeted as a bearer of distinctive but not necessarily contradictory truths, and dialogue becomes a basis for new discoveries.

Having encountered Others via transnational dialogue, Mahboubeh felt that there were many Muslim women like herself. These women were like her in the sense of sharing experiences that did not necessarily mean a sameness of insights or contexts. This shared attitude did not in itself constitute "sameness" among the women activists. An attitude of openness was still required for learning. In learning about each other's similarities and differences, Mahboubeh compared transnational dialogue to sharing recipes or learning a new way to prepare a traditional dish. The participants must overcome their differences, their aversion to change, and their beliefs that their own way is the best or only way to accomplish something.

> Someone tells me this or that, and then each one of us analyzes how to practice this or that in our society. Unfortunately, in the kitchen, we always have these problems [when two people are cooking together]. Farida [like other transnational participants] must be very honest and hear all of the recipe.

> Transnational dialogue is like [this]: there are roles, attitudes, morals, and emotions. . . . Through this work, you form yourself and find yourself.

As Mahboubeh's words suggest, Muslim women activists develop new understandings of their identity through dialogue: their senses of local particularism and of transnational solidarity are heightened. They experience a new context for thinking about their activism and their own place in the world.[11]

Unfortunately, as Farida Shaheed pointed out in an interview at the Shirkat Gah office in Lahore, Pakistan, enabling people to transnationally share methods can be quite difficult.

> The greatest challenge is how do you raise people's consciousness and get them to think about the different options. In the network, the most terrible thing that happens [is] when women are isolated in the context in which we live and have no access to information . . .

they no longer dream of a different world. So depriving women of the ability to dream—[to imagine] that life can be different to us— is critical and it is the attempt of the network, therefore, to help people dream. We see this as the first step to changing reality. You only change reality when you think that life can be different.

This emphasis on overcoming isolation as the beginning of transnational network formation was reiterated by a colleague of Farida's, Cassandra Balchin of WLUML, who also emphasized Mahboubeh's point about the need to work through the differences that emerge:

> The first step [in forming a network] was to know there are other ways of being in Muslim contexts. Before Muslim women were told there is only one way of being. This was important to identify other contexts that signified difference. So, the very first step was to establish this diversity and break the myth of homogeneity. . . .
>
> WLUML has been around for twenty years. Our central purpose has been to strengthen women's purposes in Muslim communities. However, our strategies have changed in these twenty years. Initially, WLUML was to link people and have people feel less alone and break the isolation which was an immediate physical, geographical barrier. Now isolation can mean not only physical but political and ideological. . . .
>
> The early work of WLUML was dialogue: a lot of exchange and people talking to each other. This act of talking to each other was a reaching out and discussing things. We [WLUML's core group of activists] no longer do this so much because we have been swept away with activities and responsibilities. However, this dialogue is very important and rich because that is when you get to form analysis. The annual meetings of WLUML are very important because it is when we have the opportunity to sit down and reflect together, face to face.
>
> However, in forming a network, there is paradox . . . on the one hand you have to take a position which constitutes a common con-

vergence and yet, on the other hand, a network is deliberately setting itself up to have diversity in opinion, wherein sometimes there is not one position to be taken. People in the network can agree to disagree.

Dialogue [in addition to being an exchange] depends on how open people are to change. . . . I was involved in a case wherein a woman was given a fatwa against her and then the man changed and apologized to her. Is this dialogue?

According to Farida, successful transnational networking requires being open to differences—being willing to reconceptualize areas of cultural divergence, in order to impose limits on conflicts and enhance the ability of Muslim women to respond constructively to adversaries.

Therefore, for Shirkat Gah and the WLUML network, our objective is to try and inform women about the differences that exist which all may be called "Muslim." In the network, the first collective work that we did was an exchange program which we would define as a success since it opened the minds of the participants to difference. . . . We deliberately had two plans of action: 1) we brought together very diverse resource persons (persons who spoke from within the framework of interpretations and theology as well as people from the opposite genre who were absolutely secular (there is no salvation in religion). We did this so that women could experience that all of these women are from the Muslim world and they could see the different strategies that are found in the Muslim world. Then from the exchange, these women could choose their own. . . . 2) We sent Muslim women from one Muslim context to live in a very different context: so we took women from Southeast Asia and South Asia and sent them to the Middle East. We took women from the Middle East and sent them to the Far East.[12]

For Farida and Cassandra, when diverse groups respond to provocations with unprocessed emotion and local cultural ideologies, they allow a narrow contradiction to define an entire relationship. To avoid such an outcome, both words and deeds must communicate cooperative and constructive intent to deal with shared problems on the basis of common standards. Where ethnocentrism and ideological inflexibility imply a closing off of the ability to listen to the Other, the aspiration toward a larger framework of cultural encounter and shared values can open up the space for contextual understanding.

These thoughts were echoed by Zainah Anwar, the executive director of Sisters in Islam (SIS) and a colleague of Mahboubeh, Cassandra, and Farida. According to Anwar, "there is not a synthesis happening, rather there are like-minded individuals coming together." In an interview, Anwar pointed out that it was only in spring 2004 that she and Asma Khader (the general coordinator for the Arab Resource Center on Violence Against Women in Amman, Jordan) for the first time brought Southeast Asian women together with Middle Eastern women.[13] She added that although SIS is a localized organization that focuses its activism primarily on the transformation of Malaysian Islamic society, it has gained transnational support and recognition. Evidence of this support may be found in the list of eminent transnational scholars and activists who have helped shape and support the organization's growth and development (for example, Amina Wadud, Fathi Osman, Farid Esack, and Shahla Sherkat).[14] Through transnational dialogues, SIS has been able to share and learn diverse strategies for challenging traditional authority (for example, by using publications, the Internet, and broadcast media).

From 2002 to 2004, several U.S. advocacy institutions, such as the National Endowment for Democracy (NED), the United States Institute for Peace (USIP), and the Center for the Study of Islam and Democracy (CSID), recognized SIS as an exemplary organization for the promotion of "women, political participation and democracy in the Muslim World."[15] This popularity has enabled SIS to participate in, as well as be supported by, transnational Muslim women's networks, activism, and alliances. For instance, due to critical reformists' local successes in raising public awareness, many of these activists, scholars and organizations have established reciprocal working relationships and joint advocacy.[16]

From these formal engagements, conversation and dialogue emerge and a "language of familiarity" is established. Anwar adds that "a sharing of different strategies" becomes the process for initiating a transnational discourse that if nurtured, eventually supports transnational alliances.

While interviewing Anwar at a conference in Egypt, I was fortunate to also interview Heba Rauf Ezzat, a professor of political science at Cairo University and a cofounder of Islam On-line (one of the largest cyberspace Muslim networks), and witness a conversation between Rauf Ezzat and Anwar. Rauf Ezzat and Anwar knew of each other, but this was the first time they had met. In the conversation, Rauf Ezzat would add to Anwar's insight that, on the one hand, the transnational is a coming together of "like-minded individuals," but that, on the other, it is also a coming together of diverse personalities. She said, "Transnational discourses are emerging out of the need for them. For instance, the coming together of secularist and Islamist discourses is an emerging new Islamic discourse. This transnational dialogue is on the horizon. . . . It will depend on future generations to take these debates to the next level."

For Rauf Ezzat and Anwar, before the resurgence of Islamic social movements, several generations of Muslim women intellectuals were trained in the framework provided by a secular revolution, in which epistemology was separated from traditional religious ontologies. With the emergence of postmodern thought as well as new popular ideologies, more Muslim women intellectuals have felt inclined to reclaim Islamic identities and ontologies. They have sought to reform premodern religious epistemology through reflection on modern critical epistemologies. In the process, they are beginning to think that which was unthinkable—or not permissible—for previous generations, which sought to avoid asking questions about Islam through a "secular bypass" of religious reasoning or a traditionalist aloofness to modernity.

Transnational Alliances and Networks: Some Illustrations

While it nurtures new relations with "opposing" interpretive communities (that is, reformist versus traditionalist, secularist versus Islamist) and intensifies dialogue with like-minded activists, transnational interaction also produces networks of local and global support for religious as well as cultural transformation. By sharing experiences, local organizations provide models for other local and transnational organizations in the Muslim world. These interactions create transnational alliances and support networks.

Many informal alliances start in local contexts and, after gaining recognition, become capable of producing transnational associations. A good example of informal alliances may be seen in the activism of the University of Tehran's Center for Women's Studies, directed by Jaleh Shaditalab.[17] Like SIS, which sought an alliance between Southeast Asian and Middle Eastern women, the Center for Women's Studies is working to create alliances among Iranian, Central Asian and South Asian Muslims. In an interview, Shaditalab strongly affirmed the value of transnational activism:

> Transnationalism is the work of networking: transaction and transfer of knowledge brings about more understanding. Transnationalism, ultimately, is a network of understanding. We can learn from each other, rather than "reinventing the wheel."

> Exchange through transnationalism is the most important part of transnationalism. Through transnationalism we also keep our culture; it is not invasion, like globalization. It is acculturation that happens. We exchange cultures and information, rather than ideologies.

> Ultimately, transnationalism is like islands of lights that are forming an archipelago. It shows that we are all interconnected.

Another example of informal transnational alliances may be found in Morocco, where women activists have created an annual event called the Caravane Civique. Although it is now an independent project that draws participants from throughout Morocco as well as Europe, many interviewees regarded the Caravane is closely allied with Fatema Mernissi's civic Islamic empowerment project.[18]

Interviews with participants yielded a number of strong statements underscoring the utility of dialogue. One participant called the project a "transnational bandwagon"; another simply stated, "There is need for information to be shared across borders . . . [as a basis for] success in alliances." A European participant stressed the importance of the project as being an "intra-Moroccan" discourse with a transnational dimension that was there only for "outside support." However, most of the participants stressed the growing importance of digital or virtual empowerment (that is, cyberspace partnerships and support networks).[19]

In addition to informal women's transnational alliances, many other types of transnational networks provide "virtual" support to groups that advocate gender equality. These networks include an informal network of scholars; ProgressiveMuslims.com; the Wisdom Circle for Thinkers and Researchers, based in Morocco; human-rights groups; and democracy groups.[20] Some observers perceive these transnational organizations, alliances and virtual communities as a "Muslim global civil society" in the making—a virtual space where diverse individuals and organizations come to negotiate the differences in Muslim identities.[21]

The most well-known formal network of transnational activism for women in the Muslim world is Women Living Under Muslim Laws. Cassandra Balchin placed particular emphasis on the virtues of forming active transnational networks:

> As a network, it constantly faces challenges of its structure and defining who does what. . . . The theory of the network for WLUML is that all of the groups that are linked are autonomous (in terms of policy, strategy, financing); however, they link with us in that they find the network interesting. This interest depends on what we are doing. Therefore, we cannot force anyone to link with us or force anyone to not link with us. Instead of organization, where you "sign up," a network is about writing to us and staying in touch so you engage in two-way flows. You send information, we send information . . . and a variety of relations emerge: those individuals/groups who engage actively with us (which we call "active networkers"), those individuals/groups who occasionally check in (an undefinable group), smaller group that gets involved in two-way activities (working on specific activities). The network, ultimately, requires a commitment to international solidarity and reaching out. In our work, we have noticed a shift: women were not so willing to engage internationally or engage beyond their immediate boundaries; however, now they are recognizing the value in reaching out to other women in transnational network. We have a smaller group of program implementation council (core group) which chooses the collective projects (overriding published documents, that is, Qur'anic interpretation, building civil societies) [rather than representatives in different regions]. We do not pursue this idea of having representation.

Women involved in the local situation know what is the best solution. We do not enforce/suggest any outside solution. This is where we different from an international organization (like Amnesty International). First level, is giving priority to the person who is at risk and the second level is giving priority to the strategy of the local group. This is the network principle: local people know the most appropriate local strategies. This recognizes that your strategy is not necessarily my strategy; however, we are interlinked: what happens in your locality does connect to my locality. Network then connotes both "insider and outsider" perspectives all at the same time.

Another WLUML woman activist, Anissa Hélie, expanded on these points:

I would add that within the networks, we also conceptualize transnational links by taking into account two-way relationship: Breaking barriers of class, communities, nations in order to work together on a common project or common good. Making sure the people involved gain from each other's interaction . . . I think also it is not just between different ethnicities or religious or national identities but also ideological estrangements. Because we work with secular and religious [groups and individuals].

Muslim women like those involved in WLUML are using networks to share information, create exchanges, pursue common projects, and develop solidarity. Their example has provided inspiration for other experiments that link local groups, and use transnational contact as a form of bridge building.

One specific example of transnational networking and bridge building is Sisters in Islam's relationship with WLUML. Historically, WLUML has been recognized as a more secular, Western-oriented network that emphasizes human rights without specific reference to Islamic knowledge claims or methodologies. Anwar commented that at first WLUML had a hard time accepting SIS's methodological framework of participatory Islamic hermeneutics. As a result, SIS saw WLUML's tactics as more concerned with the abolition of discriminatory laws and the abandonment of Muslim ways, whereas SIS was not concerned with imitating the secular interpretive practices of Western feminists. Instead it sought to develop interpretive practices that reflected its members' own cultural realities and local needs. However, due to SIS's successes in Malaysia, WLUML has come to recognize that SIS's "reconciliatory" approach is dynamic, appropriate, and contextually relevant. This shift toward greater solidarity among activists with different philosophical outlooks is reflected in speech by the founder of WLUML, Marie-Aimée Hélie-Lucas:

> We must create such solidarity so that we will be able to retain control over our protest . . . women and women's groups from seventeen countries or communities now communicate with each other through the Network, ask for documentation, compare so-called Muslim laws in different countries, send appeals for solidarity, inform each other about their strategies in very practical terms . . . internationalism must prevail over nationalism.[22]

Unfortunately, as Anwar pointed out, progressive Muslim voices in the West compete with one another to establish names for themselves. Instead of coming together on issues, Muslim reformist intellectuals are more likely to emphasize their differences (for example, Western-oriented, secularist Muslims versus critical, reformist Muslims). In the final analysis, this competitive attitude has not served the causes these reformists support or advanced the issues that need to be addressed.

Conclusion: Opening New Horizons

> *The women I network with, they inspire me. The people*
> *I have daily encounters with, they inspire me. You meet new people and*
> *find different inspiration from people.*
> —Cassandra Balchin

As the voices of these women testify, transnational dialogue and networking is providing inspiration for activism as well as a new framework for thinking about identity. When women from diverse contexts are able to make contact with one another, they feel empowered to approach their local work with greater confidence and creativity. Simultaneously, they become cocreators of an emergent, transnational discourse that projects a pluralistic attitude toward Islamic identity politics. This discourse respects local and national identities that are not specifically Islamic while also embracing wider Islamic and humanistic identities, which it seeks to integrate on the basis of a new intertextuality—new, dialogical approaches to Islamic hermeneutics. Dialogue becomes a norm that embodies what these women are working for: more horizontal and mutualistic social and gender relations.

As women enter dialogue with one another as well as with their diverse cultural contexts and the schools of thought that shape them, they begin to see themselves not as isolated Muslim women activists but as voluntary participants in a new interpretive project predicated on dialogical relations between Self and Other. Self-consciousness about being involved in transnational dialogue changes their sense of identity as well as their sense of possibility, opening new horizons for creativity. Activists begin to see themselves as interpreters—a role that was previously reserved for others—capable of engaging their cultural contexts on the basis of new "interpretive identities," or "identities as interpreters." Transnationalism becomes not only a means of empowerment but also a doorway to a redefinition of self-identity and of roles within the Islamic community.

Meena Sharify-Funk is currently an adjunct lecturer on Islam at the University of Waterloo in Ontario, Canada. She is currently studying at American University's School of International Service (Washington, DC), where her areas of specialization are International Peace and Conflict Resolution and Islamic Studies with a particular focus on the status of women in the Islamic world. She has written and presented a number of articles and papers on women, Islam, and the politics of interpretation; Islamic conceptions of peace and conflict resolution; and the role of cultural and religious factors in peacemaking. She has edited *Cultural Diversity and Islam* (2003) and *Whose Islam? Toward a New Synthesis in Contemporary Islam* (forthcoming).

Notes:

1. When studying the subject of women and Islam, one encounters the intersections of many hermeneutical circles, based on the discipline (scholars of women and Islam specialize in a variety of different disciplines (such as religious studies, philos-

ophy, sociology, anthropology, literature, ɛ
epistemological positioning (such as traditi
ernist, and postcolonial). Therefore, the su
multi/interdisciplinary in nature.

2. In a traditional theoretical sense, hermeneutics ɩ
   abstract philosophies of textual understandinɡ
   hermeneutics is a highly participatory endeavor. A
   texts are themselves authors of new understandings
   indeed for—contexts of political contestation. The
   comprehension of social texts in ways that are compr   ᷳmpo-
   raries and that answer fundamental questions of indiv.   ᷳᴗective identity
   and purpose: Who am I? Who are we? What do I belie__ ᷳᶜ What do we stand for?
   What is my or our relationship with *them*, with the Other? How do I or we read
   their intentions? What is distinctive about the actions of human beings in particular settings? How does context change? How do agents seek social change by drawing on cultural values and symbols as resources and guidelines for action?

3. See Muhammad Arkoun, *The Unthought in Contemporary Islamic Thought* (London: Saqi, 2002); Armando Salvatore, *Islam and the Political Discourse of Modernity*
   (Reading: Ithaca Press 1997); Peter Mandaville, *Transnational Muslim Politics:
   Reimagining the Umma* (London: Routledge 2001); and Recep Senturk, "Toward
   an Open Science and Society: Multiplex Relations in Language, Religion, and
   Society; Revisiting Ottoman Cultures," *Islam Arastirmalari Dergisi* (Turkish Journal of Islamic Studies), Sayi 6, 2001.

4. After the death of the Prophet Muhammad (632 A.D.) and the Four Righteous
   Caliphs (the Rashidun, 661 A.D.), Islam expanded from a small group of believers
   in the Arabian peninsula to vast political empires known to rule over more territory than the Roman Empire. Islam became a multicultural civilization stretching
   east to Iran and China and west through Africa to Andalusia. This expansion soon
   turned into an open exchange and coalescence of ideas, beliefs, goods, and customs—a veritable kaleidoscope of cultures ushering in an age of intercontextual
   knowledge. Exposure to diverse communities led to the construction of new system of thought, new positioned identities, and pluralistic realities. Consequently,
   between the eighth and eleventh centuries Islamic cities began to emerge as centers
   for political power, as well as intellectual curiosity and artistic grandeur. Famous
   cities such as Mecca, Damascus, Baghdad, Cordoba, Fez, Cairo, Esfahan, Ajmer,
   and Samarkand all hosted communities of scholars (such as Marshall, G. S. Hodg-
   son, and Ira M. Lapidus) who honored the Muslim tradition of seeking knowledge. As many scholars of Islam have stated, one would find in such cities a renais-
   sance of questioning, engaging, deciphering, and elucidating meaning from conversations with the "Other" (represented by the multiple knowledge systems
   encountered: Arab, Hellenic, Biblicist, European, Zoroastrian, Indian and so on).
   Such interdisciplinary knowledge would transfer from one Islamic city to another
   through a variety of means: through wandering Muslim scholars who, having mas-

of disciplines, and who ultimately sought the company of other wis-
... ers (be they Muslim, Jewish, Christian, Hindu, or Buddhist), through the
... whereby Muslims converged in Mecca once a year and then dispersed with
the knowledge they had gained; and through trade and merchants. As a result, the
world benefited greatly from this Muslim spirit of travel with, encounter of, and
relation to the Other (whoever the Other may be—Muslim or non-Muslim).

5. See works by Nayereh Tohidi, Valentine Moghadam, Margot Badran, and Miriam
    Cooke. All of these authors have mentioned or hinted to the impact of transna-
    tional or global feminism. In particular, see Nayereh Tohidi, "The Global-Local
    Intersection of Feminism in Muslim Societies: The Cases of Iran and Azerbaijan,"
    Social Research 69.693 (2002); Val Moghadam, "Islamic Feminism and Its Discon-
    tents: Notes on a Debate," in *Iran Bulletin*, April 2000, http://www.iran-bul-
    lentin.org/women/Islamic_feminism_IB.html; Margot Badran, "Islamic Femi-
    nism: What's in a Name?" in *Al-Ahram Weekly On-Line*, no. 569 (January 17-23,
    2002), http://www.weekly.ahram.org.eg/2002/569/cu1.htm; and Miriam Cooke,
    Women Claim Islam: Creating Islamic Feminism Through Islamic Literature (New
    York: Routledge 2001).

6. Various scholars of women and Islam have pointed out there are many differences
    between Muslim feminism(s) and Western feminism(s); this was reflected in the
    multifaceted contextual influences of the twentieth century which had residual
    effects, in the twenty-first century, on Muslim societies (for example, in the areas of
    colonialism, nationalism, revivalism, Islamism, secularism, imperialism, and cul-
    tural triumphalism). However, there are also many commonalities among these
    feminisms as can be seen in the protection of rights (divorce, inheritance, civic par-
    ticipation), the process of sociohistorical contextualization, and the reform of legal
    structures and cultural norms. For more on the relationship between Muslim and
    Western feminisms, see Mai Yamani, *Feminism and Islam: Legal and Literary Per-
    spectives* (New York: New York University Press 1996); Elizabeth Warnock Fernea,
    In Search of Islamic Feminism: One Woman's Global Journey (New York: Doubleday
    1998); Haideh Moghissi, *Feminism and Islamic Fundamentalism: The Limits of
    Postmodern Analysis* (New York: Zed 1999); and Badran, "Islamic Feminism."

7. Although the concept of Islamic feminism has been used and defined by many
    scholars of women and Islam, most authors would agree with this point.

8. Badran, "Islamic Feminism." p. 4.

9. WLUML was founded in 1984 as a transnational network calling for women
    and women's groups within the Muslim world to link together in solidarity to sup-
    port women were being subjected to unfair Muslim laws. For more information
    about WLUML's historical development, see Farida Shaheed, "Controlled or
    Autonomous: Identity and the Experience of the Network Women Living Under
    Muslim Laws," in *Signs* 19, 4 (1994); for more about WLUML advocacy see
    www.wluml.org. Since 1991, Cassandra Balchin has been working for Shirkat
    Gah, Pakistani women's organization which is the Asia Regional Coordination
    Office of WLUML network. Her first meeting for WLUML was in 1993. Ever

since 2000, she has been working to help coordinate the WLUML network and establish its international coordination office in London. I interviewed Balchin and her colleague, Anissa Hélie, on July 8, 2004, at the WLUML's London Office.

10. Farida Shaheed interviewed by the author, May 24, 2004, at Shirkat Gah Office, Lahore, Pakistan. Farida currently helps direct Shirkat Gah and WLUML. For more information about Shirkat Gah see: http://www.net-ngo.com/detailpage .cfm?ngoid=94.

11. Since interviewing Mahboubeh, her continued activisim has involved numerous hardships. Most notably, upon her return from a conference for women in Beijing in July 2004, she was arrested, interrogated, and imprisoned. The mere act of engaging in transnational civic activism was enough to bring her several months of confinement. For more information on Mahboubeh, see http://ngotc.org/ ennews.asp.

12. Farida Shaheed, interview by author, May 24, 2004, at the Shirkat Gah office, Lahore, Pakistan.

13. I interviewed Zainah Anwar on October 6, 2003, at the Marriott Hotel in Cairo, Egypt. She was attending a conference I had coordinated at the Library of Alexandria, "Contemporary Islamic Synthesis." Asma Khader is recognized as a minister of state and government spokesperson for Jordan. She also is the former general coordinator of the Jordan Office of the Sisterhood is Global Institute, a nonprofit women's rights organization, and the founder of the Jordanian National Network for Poverty Alleviation. For the Arab Resource Center on Violence Against Women, see www.amanjordan.org.

14. Amina Wadud, a professor of religious studies at the Virginia Commonwealth University, is the author of *Qur'an and Woman: Rereading the Sacred Text from a Woman's Perspective* (New York: Oxford University Press, 1999). Fathi Osman, a scholar of Muslim intellectual development and the contemporary Muslim world, has taught at prominent universities in the Middle East, Asia, and the West. He is currently a scholar in residence at the Institute for the Study of the Role of Islam in the Contemporary World of the Omar Ibn al-Khattab Foundation in Los Angeles. Farid Esack occupies the Besl Family Chair for Ethics, Religion and Society at Xavier University and is the author of many books, including *Qur'an, Liberation and Pluralism: An Islamic Perspective of Interreligious Solidarity Against Oppression* (Oxford: Oneworld Publications, 1997). Shahla Sherkat is the license holder and editorial director of *Zanan*, a Persian journal that discusses women's issues. All of these scholars and activists have influenced the formation of SIS in one way or another (for example, by suggesting strategies for reinterpreting the Qur'an).

15. NED event, June 26, 2002.

16. SIS in Malaysia, Mernissi's civil society project in Morocco, Sisterhood is Global Institute/Jordan's microfinance project. It has developed relationships with organizations including Sisters in Islam, Women's Learning Partnership, BAOBAB for Women's Human Rights, Sisterhood is Global Institute, Women Living Under Muslim Laws, National Council of Women's Organizations, All Women's Action

Society, Association of Women Lawyers, Amnesty International Malaysia, Women's Development Collective, Wijadi Labor Resource Center, and Movement Opposing the Unethical Suppression of Expression (SIS letters, February 25, 2002, and May 9, 2002). For more information, see www.sistersinislam.org.

17. See the Center for Women's Studies web site: http://cws.ut.ac.ir

18. The Caravane Civique was initially created to build a "forum for community and civic activity and break down barriers between rich and poor, artists and professionals, in Morocco." The idea came out of a conversation between Jamila Hassoune, a traveling bookseller, and Fatema Mernissi, a professor of sociology at the University of Mohamed V in Rabat, Morocco. For more about Jamila and the Caravane's history, see http://www.mernissi.net/civil_society/caravane_civique/index.html.

19. I interviewed several participants of the Caravan Civique at their annual conference which was hosted from April 9–11, 2004, at the Hotel Idou Anfa in Casablanca, Morocco.

20. BAOBAB for Women's Human Rights in Nigeria, Women's Alliance for Peace and Human Rights in Afghanistan.

21. Abdullahi An-Na'im, "Religion and Global Civil Society: Inherent Incompatibility or Synergy and Interdependence?" in Helmut Auheier, Marlies Glasius, and Mary Kaldor (eds.), *Global Civil Society 2002* (Oxford: Oxford University Press, 2002), p. 66.

22. Marie-Aimée Hélie-Lucas, quoted in Cooke, *Women Claim Islam*, p. 115.

Shirin Ebadi: A Perspective on Women's Rights in the Context of Human Rights

Fereshteh Nouraie-Simone

Meeting with Shirin Ebadi highlights the complexities of being the first Muslim woman, and the first Iranian, to receive the Nobel Peace Prize. Well before winning the prize, she had been in demand as one of the country's most vocal human-rights lawyers and activists for women and children. In a country run by men, she is a woman with a voice. She has devoted her life to tirelessly campaigning for democracy and individual freedom, taking on sensitive political cases, and standing up for the underdog and the weak. Now attention is focused on Ebadi's commitment to the peaceful struggle for democracy and human rights and to reforming Iran from within.

While the prize calls attention to the human-rights issues and democratic reforms Ebadi has championed, it also carries great responsibilities. In addition to overwhelming demands on her time, Ebadi must navigate increased scrutiny in a political environment that has dealt harshly with free-speaking individuals and political opposition. She has referred to herself as a "tightrope walker" who constantly must keep her balance.

Ebadi's greatest impact has been through her activism as a human-rights lawyer. In 1998, she defended a number of victims of human-rights violations. She represented families of dissident writers and intellectuals who had been assassinated by elements within the government and security forces. In addition to her outspoken defense of human rights, she has tirelessly worked on behalf of women and children in cases of child custody, rape, and murder, and has pressed for family-law reform. Her work places her at great and constant risk from threats posed both outside and inside the government.

The "tightrope walker" lost her balance and her license to practice in

June 2000, when she was arrested and detained in solitary confinement for twenty-five days in connection with a video-taped confession by a member of vigilante group that attacked student dissidents. The group's ties to the government were revealed on the tape. "Angrily, I am trying to write on the cement wall with the bottom of my spoon that we are born to suffer because we are born in the third world," she wrote during her confinement.[1]

I met with Ebadi in Tehran in November 2003, only a few days before she left for Oslo to receive the Nobel Peace Prize. Her modest office, in the basement of her house in Tehran, was abuzz with activity. There were constant telephone calls, requests for interviews, and clients who waited patiently to see her.

"Shirin" means "sweet" in Farsi. Shirin Ebadi is a friendly, modest woman, but also a direct, no-nonsense, pragmatic lawyer who is deeply committed to the cause of civil liberty and justice. During our meeting, she talked about the compatibility of Islam and democracy, the veil, and human rights as a central issue in the process of reforming family law and strengthening gender equality. She is outspoken yet methodical and meticulous in her approach to reform: She tries to find solutions within the framework of law. Her manner can seem guarded, as if she were practicing self-censorship, and it is not clear whether this is a professional habit she adopted as an attorney or the necessary caution learned by those who call for reform. Ebadi has taken on the fight for justice and human rights in Iran at great personal cost: She has been threatened, jailed, and banned from practicing law various times and, even after becoming a Nobel laureate, she received several threats to her safety.

I congratulated her on her award, commenting on the honor it brings to Muslim women. "This award sends out various messages," she replied, "that Islam is not a religion of terror and violence, and that the world community supports the struggle of Muslim women for freedom and justice. Personally, I feel it belongs to the Iranian people and those who work for human rights and democracy." In her Nobel Lecture delivered on December 10, 2003, she said that the award "inspires me and millions of other women in Iran and the Muslim world with the hope that our efforts, endeavors and struggles towards the realization of human rights and the establishment of democracy in our respective countries enjoy the support and solidarity of the international community."[2]

The Nobel Committee chose a passionate and courageous spokesperson for human rights, one with experience both in defending of specific individuals and in taking a systemic approach, emphasizing the changes needed to whole institutions. The committee's announcement said, "At a time when Islam is being demonized in many quarters of the Western world, it was the Norwegian Nobel Committee's wish to underscore how valuable it is to foster dialogue between peoples and civilizations."[3]

Ebadi supports progressive Islam in harmony with human rights and individual freedom. She is part of the reformist voice that emerged after the 1997 Iranian presidential election that emphasized the compatibility of Islam with democracy and human rights.

A graduate of Tehran University Law School, Ebadi was one of the first female judges in Iran and the first woman president of the city court of Tehran. After the 1979 revolution, she was forced to resign, along with more than forty other women judges, when the Islamization of government institutions was launched. She had to wait eight years to regain her license to practice law. She subsequently emerged as an important defender of human rights.

Her message to Muslim women is "Keep on fighting. Don't believe that you are condemned to inferior status. Look carefully in the Qur'an so that the oppressors will not succeed in misleading you with their commentary and their selective quotes. Do not believe you are meant to occupy a lower position in society. Get yourself an education, and invest your best efforts in competing in all areas of life. God created us as equal, and when we struggle for equality, we are doing what God wants us to do."[4]

She told me, "My problem is not with Islam, but with the culture of patriarchy and the misogynist interpretations that use biological differences as justification for oppression." At one point during our conversation, she said, pointing at her maroon headscarf, "Instead of telling women to cover their heads, we should tell them to use their heads."

Ebadi believes that when and where to wear the veil should be a matter of choice for a woman, "but since covering one's hair is mandatory under the Islamic state for all women, regardless of custom or religion, as a lawyer I understand the rules and abide by them." But Iran's laws do not apply in other countries, "and I follow their rules and customs while I am there."

In an appearance at the Amir Kabir University in Tehran, just a few days before, her public handshake with two male acquaintances had caused an uproar—not because of the politics of the parties involved, but because of the public contact between a man and a woman. The critics voiced their disapproval by draping part of the university in black as a sign of mourning. A group of students turned to Qom, the major center of Shi'a learning, to ask the reformist Grand Ayatolla Montazeri (who is out of favor with conservative clerics) about the basis of such a ban on male-female handshakes and eye contact. "Should a practicing Muslim woman who was brought up in a cultural environment where unintended eye contact and handshakes were not considered sinful be barred from eye contact or a handshake or be forced to wear the veil?" They asked. Ebadi gave me a copy of the Ayatollah's letter stating that "such restrictions were in place for women as a sign of respect and protection; however, a handshake or eye contact which was not intended as flirtation or provocation was permissible. Overall, the point of reference should be common law and custom."

This is an example of the sort of quiet victory Ebadi works for: the incremental recognition of the rights of the individual, consistent with and within the framework of interpretation of Islamic law. Ebadi underscores this point by bringing up her own example. "Before the revolution, I was a judge. However, after 1979 and the establishment of the Islamic state, based on certain interpretations, it was decreed women were not fit to be judges because they are 'too emotional'—some even said 'defective in intellect.' But we were ready to fight back by studying and working hard to show that there were no intellectual differences between male and female students in the law school. The problem lies in the religious interpretation, the politics of sexual differentiation, and the patriarchal culture that gives privilege to a man over a woman." In 1992, based on a different interpretation, the rule was again changed, this time to allow women to serve as judges and now there are two women sitting as "advisers" on the bench in the Court of Appeals.

Shirin Ebadi believes that separating Islam from despotism and Islamic law from patriarchy makes it possible to create an Islamic discourse that is democratic and respectful of human rights. "When I talk about victory, I do not mean that our problems with human rights have been resolved, but we are able to remove Islam as a justification for oppression." She continues, "We can be Muslim and faithful to Islamic tenets while striving for better laws and a commitment to human rights. My point is we need to change the culture of patriarchy, the misogynist interpretations, the mindset that says, 'women are second-class citizens,' and, 'the place of a woman is in the home, and her duty is limited to breeding male children.'"

Ebadi also has something to say about how to make the needed changes.

> Education is the key to fighting discrimination and bringing about change. We need to educate our men and women from elementary school on to make them aware of their rights and teach them to respect the rights of others. Since the revolution, we have witnessed women's mass participation in politics and education. Today, 63 percent of university students are girls. Before the revolution, traditional families with strong religious beliefs were unable or unwilling to send their daughters to university or to work. Now, fewer women are isolated from the outside world, and their exposure changes not only them but the society as a whole. I read somewhere that modernity is born in the street. Women's invasion of the public domain is a liberating factor that empowers both men and women.[5]

She sees women's rights in the greater context of human rights, believing that the way a society treats its women is an indicator of how human-rights are viewed generally by that society. Progress in women's rights is therefore not strictly a woman's or "feminist" issue but is fundamentally about social justice and serves to protect and improve conditions for the rights of all, regardless of gender.

Her work on behalf of women's rights has made her acutely aware of the practical implications of patriarchal interpretations of the law. Discussing family law and the comprehensive changes that must be put in place to create a true, working civil society, she told me,

> We need to change laws that are out of touch with women's aspirations—the realities of their lives and their sense of justice. We need to evaluate our laws, to improve and change them if necessary, so they are compatible with international human-rights law, which the Iranian Government accepted [the Universal Declaration of Human Rights], but this must also come with the promise to implement political, social, and economic changes.

In order to implement the changes, we need the infrastructure and delivery mechanisms to support the law. Knowledge of the law is not enough by itself. For example, a woman without work, insurance, or income, who has an abusive husband, may be aware of her right to divorce, but she is powerless without a support system. What choices does she have? To get a divorce, become hungry and homeless? So she can obtain a divorce from the court, but without a welfare system to back her up, without a system to secure homes for battered wives, the divorce right is meaningless—unless the right mechanism is in place to make divorce law effective.

Ebadi never strays far from her message that reform, and democratic institutions, must arise naturally from existing society—they cannot be imported or imposed by force, and change does not happen overnight. "The Islamic government is in need of reform from within, an understanding and recognition of social realities compatible with the egalitarian spirit of Islam."

The Nobel Committee emphasized this message by stating, "Ebadi is a conscious Muslim who sees no conflict between Islam and fundamental human rights. Islam is a diverse religion. How the message of justice is to be realized in practice and how human integrity is to be preserved is an essential issue for Muslims of today."[6]

Our time was up. Shirin Ebadi wanted to extend her visit with me, but the world was pressing in. As a farewell, she wished to give me a copy of her book *Women's Rights in the Laws of the Islamic Republic.* "There must be a copy here," she said, going to the bookcase. She searched in vain. Shaking her head, she bustled to the door and opening it, called out to her assistant: "Will you please go upstairs and get *Women's Rights* for me? I know my mom has a copy."

As I left, the faces of those waiting turned up to look at me. Behind me, someone else was ushered in to meet with the Nobel laureate. The waiting faces looked expectant, but patient. They knew Shirin Ebadi would see each of them, in his or her turn, in time, and in order.

In her book Women's Rights in the Laws of the Islamic Republic of Iran *(Tehran: Ketabkhaneh Ganj-e Danesh, 2002), Shirin Ebadi shows the dis-*

criminatory aspects of the laws of the Islamic regime concerning women by framing her argument in the context of human rights.

The law has always been Shirin Ebadi's strongest tool to fight for women's rights. Her work is based on the idea that the principle of human rights forms the foundation from which women's rights derive and that these rights are not in contradiction with the Islamic principles. While the political environment in Iran highlights the contradiction between reformists and hard-line conservatives, Ebadi has managed to stay out of the political fray by insisting that human rights are compatible with Islam and should not depend on who is in power or who controls the military or security forces. In a speech at Syracuse University in May 2004, she stated: "One urgent task facing us is to learn about the dynamic spirit of Islam and its nature of inclusiveness, to realize we can accept modernity without the risk of losing our faith. We should realize that Islamic governments do not have the key to paradise."[7]

In Women's Rights in the Laws of Islamic Republic of Iran, *Shirin Ebadi frames her arguments in legal terms. She is not solely critical; in looking at Iran's Islamic constitution, she finds some positive aspects, such as statements regarding the individual's equality before law, or the expansion of educational opportunities for women. At the same time, she wants to hold the government accountable and require it to abide by the international human-rights and social-justice covenants that Iran approved and signed. Shirin Ebadi's approach is legalistic and cautious, as she aims for fairness in assessing the laws concerning women adopted by the Islamic Republic, but indirectly she criticizes the discriminatory laws, simply by listing them. She uses international human-rights standards to analyze Iranian domestic laws, and finds them lacking, by inference.*

She points out that the government has entered into several international agreements, including the Covenant of Civil and Political Rights, the Covenant of Economic and Social Rights and, of course, the Universal Declaration of Human Rights. Yet by showing the contradictions inherent in Iranian laws, such as discriminatory codes based on gender, Shirin Ebadi implicitly points out the Islamic government's inconsistency. Her underlying argument is that since Iran committed to these international covenants, it must adhere to them and bring its laws in line with international standards of human rights—which will do much toward correcting sanctioned misogyny in the law and ultimately, the culture.

Excerpts from *Women's Rights in the Islamic Republic of Iran*

Chapter Thirteen: Women and the Iranian Government's Commitment to International Conventions

Introduction Women's rights are one of the most important and integral parts of human rights. According to many legal experts, "women's rights are human rights." This means that women's rights are not distinguishable from human rights and a criterion for studying the conditions of human rights in a given country is the rights of women in that country. The more respectful of the citizens' rights a given country is, the more it is committed to respecting and safeguarding the rights of its women. Therefore, if we study women's rights from the perspective of human rights, we have no need to rely on a discourse on feminism to discuss the rights of women. From this point of view, "woman" is the subject of study as a human being, and her legal status is studied with an emphasis on the rejection of any form of discrimination based on gender. From this perspective, international conventions and documents in the area of human rights are generally applicable to women's rights, including the U.N. Covenant on Civil and Political Rights, of which the government of Iran is a signatory. This convention talks about the fundamental rights of human beings and considers the civil and political rights of people regardless of gender, color, race, religion, and socioeconomic status. Although this convention does not specifically address women, women are clearly included in its concepts. The same is true of other international documents in relation to refugees, against discrimination in education, against genocide. . . . However, there are cases in which the U.N. has approved conventions and contracts that exclusively deal with women's conditions. The reason for such exclusive interest is found in the poor condition of women in different societies. In fact, the U.N. wants to direct the world's attention to women's issues and to create an awareness of the inequalities and oppression women suffer. The government of Iran has joined some of the international agreements about women's issues. . . . It has accepted the Declaration on the Elimination of Discrimination Against Women. However, as a declaration, this does not require a signature and perhaps does not have the enforcement mechanism of a convention.[8] Iran has not yet joined the Convention on the Elimination of All Forms of Discrimination against Women, known as CEDAW, which is one of the U.N.'s most important documents regarding improving the condition of women. The government of Iran believes that some of the articles of CEDAW are contrary to Islamic principles.[9]

Chapter Two: The Constitution of the Islamic Republic of Iran and Its View on Women

After the victory of the Islamic Revolution, Imam Khomeini ordered the committee be created known as "The Committee of Experts of the Constitution," which wrote the constitution of the Islamic Republic of Iran, in twelve chapters. In this committee only one woman, by the name of Monireh Gorji, had membership. After the constitution was written and approved by Imam Khomeini, it was put to vote, in December 1979, and received the approval of the overwhelming majority of the Iranian people.

The constitution of the Islamic Republic of Iran was revised according to the referendum of 1989. The revision included changes to some amendments and the addition of two chapters. Today the constitution comprises an introduction, fourteen chapters and one hundred seventy-seven articles. The general view of the constitution, including its view on women, is based on Islamic principles.

The Constitution's View on Women: The constitution's view on women is based on the traditional role of women in society, which basically amounts to women's participation in the family structure. In other words, women are considered wives and mothers. In the introduction of the constitution, in a section called "Women in the Constitution" we read the following:

> In establishing the Islamic social foundations, human forces that until now were in the absolute service of foreign exploitation regain their true identity and human rights. Naturally, since women endured more oppression under the old regime, more attention will be given to vindicating their rights. Family is the foundation of every society and the primary place for the growth and development of human beings. Therefore, the concord of ideas and ideals in establishing a family is the primary source for the evolution and growth of humans and providing the possibilities for attaining such an aim is one of the duties of the Islamic government. In this interpretation of family, women who were previously treated as

"objects" and "instruments" in the service of exploitation and con-
sumerism have regained their important and valuable responsibilities as mothers assume their leading role in raising religious children, and continue their struggle in active arenas of life alongside
men. Thus, women will assume a more important responsibility
and in the eyes of Islam will acquire a more valuable status.

The above interpretation is also recognized by the twenty-first amendment of the constitution, which says:

The government is responsible for recognizing and implementing
women's rights according to Islamic standards in all aspects and for
pursuing the following directions:
1) To establish favorable conditions for the development of woman's
   identity and the vindication of her material and spiritual rights.
2) To support mothers, especially during the period of pregnancy
   and guardianship of children, and to support orphans.
3) To establish courts for maintaining the foundation and the continuation of the family.
4) To establish [special] insurance for widows, old women, and
   women with no means of support.
5) To bestow the guardianship of children to deserving mothers in
   cases of the absence of a legal guardian.

Of the five resolutions given above, four relate to women's rights in the
family and their duties as wives and mothers, and in the first resolution,
contrary to the others, the wording of the law is so general and vague that it
is not at all clear how one should go about implementing it.

The twentieth article of the constitution says: "All people regardless of
their gender are protected by the law and enjoy all rights according to the
Islamic criteria. These rights include human rights, political rights, economic rights, social rights and cultural rights."

The statement that "all people regardless of their gender, are protected
by the law" does not necessarily mean that men and women are equal,
because some clergy and specialists of Islamic law believe that Muslim men
and Muslim women do not have equal rights. Therefore, one can say that

the writers of the constitution do not believe in equal rights for men and women but rather (as they have demonstrated in many of their writings) believe in "the balance of rights" between men and women. In other words, they believe that it is not necessary for a woman to have exactly every right that a man enjoys, but it is enough to have a comparable right. For instance, it is a man's right to demand sex from his wife at any time, and the wife has no right to refuse him. But a comparable right for a woman is to demand alimony from her husband, presuming these two rights balance each other out and create equality.

Below are excerpts from a roundtable discussion hosted by the Zanan *journal that Shirin Ebadi participated in as a legal expert in May, 1997.*[10] *She and two other specialists—a male journalist and a female sociologist—were invited to discuss the important issues facing women in Iran. The following questions were posed: What is the most urgent problem for Iranian women today? If there is a list of problems, which one, in your view, is of the utmost importance, and why? Are these issues of concern to women only, or do they present impediments to the whole society? If these problems are unique to women, to what extent are they of a national nature or applicable to women in general? What is the root of our women's problems?*

Ebadi is less guarded in this interview, which was conducted several years before she won the Nobel Peace Prize. Her perspective on these issues in partic-ular and feminism in general are expressed in a more direct and open manner than her public remarks after receiving the prize. Her answers do take on a legalistic quality, and her main argument is with the penal code of the Islamic regime and its effect on young females—but this has always been her approach to women's rights within the context of human rights. Her main criticisms focus on a legal system, which blatantly discriminates against women, for example, the "blood money" paid by a murderer to the victim's family is half as much for a woman as for a man. All these arguments serve to point out simple unfairness in the law, an approach that Ebadi believes is more powerful and has a better chance of being heard than obviously "feminist" arguments. She believes in the social power of the law and in the power of reason and justice to influence the law. This is exemplified by the final line quoted here: "Whenever opinions change the laws also change, and cultures follow these changes."

I am a lawyer, and naturally I look at women's issues from the legal perspective. I think that the most important issue for women in this country is the dominance of the misogynist ideology in the legal system. We all know that laws are the language of governments. Our laws are gender-biased to the point that the right to life, which is the foundation of human rights, is not equally applicable to men and women. If a man kills a woman the family of the victim must even pay a few million Tomans [Iranian currency equivalent to a few thousand dollars] as retribution in order for the judicial system to punish the murderer. . . . Article 300 of the Islamic penal code says that the retribution for killing a Muslim woman—whether premeditated or not—is half that for a Muslim man. This in fact means that woman's life is half of man's life. But the story doesn't end here; a woman's life can even be less than that. Article 457 says destroying vision in both eyes deserves a complete retribution and destroying the vision of one eye deserves one-half of a complete retribution. Note that in the above law there is no difference made between correct vision, squint vision, blurred vision, or any other kind. Therefore, if we compare these two articles, do you know what is the worth of a woman's life, with all her knowledge, her piety, her social value? It is equal to one of a man's eyes.

This is exactly where the problem lies. First, I must enjoy the right to life; I have to be recognized as a complete human being before the law, before I can expect to become a president, for instance. Some might say that these laws are religious laws and originate in Islam, but I strongly object and say that they are not Islamic because Islam has a unified and coherent spirit. I'll offer another example: it is said that the age of complete physical and mental maturity for a girl is nine years, and at this age the girl can marry [it has since been raised to age thirteen]. But at the time of the presidential election, they said, 'You're not mature enough to vote, and you must wait until you're sixteen years old.' How is it that a girl who is mature enough at nine years old to choose a husband for herself for an entire lifetime cannot choose a president for four years?

Another example: a nine-year-old girl is considered legally accountable. An eight-and-a-half-year-old girl goes to a store and steals a box of Kleenex or an eraser. According to the law, she is tried and put in jail. Legally this child is treated as a fifty-year-old man. Under these circumstances they do not call her father to ask "Where were you when your daughter was committing a crime?" But the same girl, whose crime at the age of nine had nothing to do with her father, if she wins an educational scholarship and wants to leave the country, needs to obtain permission from her father. So a nine-year-old girl can get married. She can have a child when she is thirteen years old. Suppose her husband dies or divorces her. She would want to work in order to feed herself and her child. Here the labor law intervenes and forbids the employment of children under fifteen years of age. Therefore in a very simple issue like puberty, the end of childhood for girls, so many contradictory laws exist. If we really wrote our laws according to the religious laws, would we have all these contradictions? I strongly say no. . . .

I have something to say [to those who say] the traditional system is a system that goes back thirteen or fourteen centuries: since then, something else has also happened in this country—the Constitutional Revolution [of 1906]. After the Constitution was written, many of the laws that are said to originate in tradition went through a logical change, according to an appropriate interpretation of Islam and social changes. In 1925 the general penal code was ratified. At the time, the venerable Moddaress, a prominent cleric and a true believer in the constitution, was in the parliament, and he was assigned the job of adapting the ratified code to the Islamic Shari'a. The signature of the martyred Moddaress, the distinguished *mojtahed* [an authoritative scholar of religious law], is on the penal code of 1925. He wrote the law that says that if a child of less than eighteen years of age is convicted of a crime, the maximum sentence the court can give him or her is five years in prison. Because the view of Moddaress as a *mojtahed* was that even a seventeen-year-old boy or girl is not mature enough to take full responsibility for his or her deeds, and a boy or girl under twelve years old has no punishment whatsoever. This was the law that we had in 1925 and that more or less worked in our society. But in 1991 they came and ratified a new penal code and said that the age of criminal responsibility for a girl is nine years, and if she commits crime, legally she is held responsible to the extent that she can even suffer capital punishment. What tradition is this? We had a penal code based on tradition in 1925, what happened to that? If we look at social changes we cannot disregard an important event like the Constitutional Revolution, and thus disregard sixty, seventy years of law making. This is not right. . . .

Not only does Islam have a unified spirit, it also conforms to the conditions of time and place. Many of the laws were changed with time and place, such as secondary rulings based on *ejtehad* [process of arriving at judgment on points of religious law]. But how is it that these secondary rulings are never concerned with women? How is it that we do not have even one secondary ruling concerning women's status? Obviously it is because of the misogynist interpretation and attitude of the writers of the law. So, in my view the most important issue is changing the attitude of the people who are writing the laws. It doesn't matter if they are men or women. Unfortunately, I have seen some women who espouse such views. Therefore, the fundamental problem is not women's rights in the family but rather women's general status and worth in the law, and a recognition of women's rights as human rights.

As I said before, I am a lawyer. I view everything from a legal perspective. In my view the law symbolizes the attitude of the government and reflects misinterpretations of Islam. But obviously such laws also lead to issues of culture and gender. For instance in 1967, after the family law was ratified, polygamy was limited by law, and this legal limitation influenced the culture and social norms to the extent that if a man had two wives he would be embarrassed to announce it, because of society's disapproval—even though before this law was introduced having three or four wives was a sign of wealth and power and was something a man could brag about and be proud of. Therefore, we can say that the law influenced the culture. And now that polygamy has become once again legal, it has again become more socially acceptable.   Another generation and it will become very normal for our sons to have two or three wives. So the laws influence culture, and if these laws are allowed to remain for some time, then our society will also regress. . . .

I completely oppose the view that seeks to divide the world by such labels as Western feminism or Eastern feminism. I do not accept such a division. Feminism is feminism; it means believing in human equality. Believing in human equality, like any other thought, has its history and its development. The most recent achievement of the discourse of human equality based on gender is that human equality is defined according to the social conditions of the people who live in a given society. Naturally, with this view, a woman who lives in Saudi Arabia cannot have the same exact rights that a Swedish woman has, because the cultural backgrounds of the two are completely different. . . .

[Some people say] feminism could create social disturbance by creating unrealistic expectations in women or by creating fear and terror among members of the society. Here is my question: Does it create disturbance to say that God created man and woman as equals? To spread and sponsor this attitude that God has said that the foundation rests on piety, does this create disturbance? We must all, together, declare that human equality is good and discrimination against people based on their gender, social status, language, race, or religion is unacceptable.

I believe that gender-biased laws affect not only women's rights but also many other rights and freedoms. Thus the sexist view transforms into the patriarchal view. These are not issues exclusively related to women. These laws affect women but also have a negative effect on men. I am against dividing men and women saying that these laws only hurt women. No, these laws hurt the entire society, they hurt justice, and they oppose the human dignity of the individuals living in the society.

What I say is not based on feminism; it is based on demanding social justice. What justice is it that under the law of retribution if I am killed my family has to pay money to the murderer's family before the punishment is carried out? What justice is it that I have to watch my father-in-law come and kill my child in front of my eyes and I would have no right to ask for his punishment? I have nothing to do with feminism; I am concerned with social and legal justice. And I emphasize once again that the problem is not in Islam; the problem is in the sexist, patriarchal attitudes of the legislatures.

Some people behind closed doors sit around a table and write their opinions as if God dictates them. This is what happens in relation to many of our laws. The roots of the problem are here. Whenever opinions change the laws also change, and cultures follow these changes.

Notes

1. Amitabh Pal, "Prize Fighter," *The Progressive,* September 2, 2004 http://alternet.org/ rights/1975.
2. Shirin Ebadi, Nobel Lecture, December 10, 2003. http://nobelprize.org/peace/laureates/2003/ebadi-lecture-e.html.
3. Ole Danbolt Mjøs, Nobel Prize Address, Chairman of the Norwegian Nobel Committee, Oslo, December 10, 2003, http://www.nobelprize.org/peace/laureates/2003/presentation-speech.html.

4. Interview with Shirin Ebadi, *Al-Sharq Al-Awsat* (London), October 19, 2003.
5. Interview with Shirin Ebadi, *Zanan* (Tehran), no. 105 (December 2003).
6. Ole Danbolt Mjøs, Nobel Peace Prize Address.
7. Shirin Ebadi, "Islam, Democracy and Human Rights." Speech given at Syracuse University College of Law, May 10, 2004.
8. Adopted and opened for signature, ratification, and accession by General Assembly resolution 34/180 of December 18, 1979.
9. CEDAW was proclaimed by General Assembly Resolution 2263(XXII) of November 7, 1967.
10. *Zanan*, 34. 1376 (May 1997), pp.12–19. Translation by Safoura Nourbakhsh.